SOUTHERN PLAINSMEN

Southern Plainsmen

CARL COKE RISTER

UNIVERSITY OF OKLAHOMA PRESS
NORMAN, 1938

First Edition, 1938

TO THE MEMORY OF HIS PARENTS
REVEREND C. RISTER AND SARAH PARKER RISTER
WHO WERE AMONG THE FIRST PIONEERS
TO COME TO WESTERN TEXAS
AND WHO ENCOUNTERED ALL THE HARDSHIPS
AND PROBLEMS OF A REMOTE
FRONTIER RELATED HEREIN, THE WRITER
AFFECTIONATELY DEDICATES
THIS BOOK

ACKNOWLEDGMENTS

IN the preparation of this work the writer's obligations to his friends are many. To the staffs of the libraries of the University of Texas and the University of Oklahoma, he wishes to express his appreciation for their many courtesies and services. To the Superintendent of the Library of Congress and his helpers he owes a large debt of gratitude for a study room, for the right to photostat materials, and for expert aid in locating source materials. Many of these advantages were made possible by a grant-in-aid of the Social Science Research Council in the summer of 1932.

In form and style the study has gained considerably from the critical reading and suggestions of Dr. B. A. Botkin of the Department of English, the University of Oklahoma, editor of *Folk-Say, a Regional Miscellany*. Dr. Roy Gittinger of the Department of History and Dr. Royden J. Dangerfield of the Department of Government, the University of Oklahoma, and Dr. R. N. Richardson of the Department of History, Hardin-Simmons University, also advised the writer in matters of content and early sources, and read parts of the manuscript. The author's wife, Mattie May Rister, has been a constant source of aid and encouragement, in indexing and copying materials and other details. For all these services the writer feels humbly grateful.

CARL COKE RISTER

Norman, Oklahoma
August, 1938

TABLE OF CONTENTS

SOUTHERN PLAINSMEN

ILLUSTRATIONS

INTRODUCTION

THE southern plains, with which this book is concerned, has no very definite boundaries. It is the southern half of the Great Plains, generally treeless, and in the shape of an irregular oblong from two hundred to three hundred miles wide and from eight hundred to a thousand miles long. Its total area is more than three hundred thousand square miles, exceeding that of the New England and the Middle Atlantic states combined. It is bounded approximately by the ninety-eighth meridian on the east, the Rocky Mountains on the west, the South Platte on the north, and the Rio Grande on the south. It embraces what is now western Kansas, eastern Colorado, western Oklahoma, western Texas, and eastern New Mexico.

Although the general appearance of the northern plains is much like that of the southern plains, certain climatic differences tend to make it dissimilar. The average summer temperature of the extreme south of the former is about sixty-five degrees; while that in the extreme south of the latter is approximately eighty degrees. Consequently the average evaporation on the northern plains is much less than on the southern plains. Moreover, the first killing frost on the northern plains comes about September 10, while on the southern plains it is two months later, thus providing for the latter a longer growing season. The average annual snowfall ranges from about thirty inches in the Dakotas to five inches in Oklahoma. Thus, since the climate of the southern plains is more salubrious, it not only was a favored resort for wild game, but it also first attracted Anglo-American settlers, and plains culture passed through its early stages in this area.

Obviously climatic conditions influenced markedly the culture of the southern plains. The early press of the nation had much to say about the extraordinary temperature changes; and, as a consequence, the sand-storm, tornado, hail-storm, norther, and blizzard were much dreaded by travelers and prospective settlers. More particularly did they have an aversion to winter travel. So considerable were barometric changes during this season that drops of from forty to fifty degrees within the space of a few hours would frequently be registered, and in a fearful blizzard in the latter part of December, 1866, a fall of a little over ninety degrees in a period of forty-eight hours was recorded.

In many respects the land presented amazing extremes. Early explorers and travelers wrote of it as "the Great American Desert." Its broad, sinuous sand-choked streams were seldom filled with water: and when the fiery sun and hot winds of August scorched its vegetation, and dried up its numerous small creeks and ponds, the brown-baked earth seemed to radiate back to the air its breath of hate. During such periods it was quite difficult for wayfarers to cross its wind-swept wastes. More than once the bones of travelers and their horses were left to bleach beside the way as grim reminders of the fate which would await all those who dared to cross its forbidden stretches. Yet, during favorable spring seasons, no region could be more attractive. The trees which grew along the larger streams were like giant dark-green hedges, inclosing great meadows of billowing and waving multi-colored flowers. Mile on mile of flower-splashed landscape spread out before the prairie traveler. The delicate shades of the beautiful cacti, evening primroses, goldenrods, wild daisies, Indian paint brush, tall waving sunflowers, Mexican poppies, scarlet malvas, bluebells, violets, and other wild flowers, all blended their entrancing shades and colors in a panorama of indescribable loveliness.

The region generally abounded in animal life. In the trees— pecan, walnut, mesquite, hackberry, and others—which grew along the streams, and on the broad prairies, were the hummingbird, sparrow, thrush, scissortail, cowbird, red-headed woodpecker, dove, partridge, blue quail, plover, curlew, prairie chicken, turkey, raven, hawk, and eagle. Hundreds of thousands of buffalo, the Indians' chief food supply, grazed the vast plains, together with herds of elk, deer, and antelope. Here, too, was the home of the bear, white wolf, lobo, coyote, silver-gray fox, prairie fox, prairie dog, ground squirrel, squirrel, panther, catamount, hare, and mule-eared rabbit, not to mention the snakes such as the dreaded rattlesnake, adder, moccasin, prairie-runner, bull snake, and chicken snake. From this multiplicity of wild life the nomadic Indian derived his clothing, his food, his shelter, and many other articles of general use.

It is not surprising that the first inhabitants of the southern plains were nomadic hunters. They were Indians who, when first encountered by the *conquistadores*, moved on foot from one camp site to another and who depended on squaws and dogs to haul their camp equipment. But when the Anglo-Americans first met them, they were the proud sovereigns of the plains. Now astride their wild ponies, moving about with the speed of an express train, they were formidable foes to all invaders. Where they had formerly been narrowly circumscribed in their activities, they now ranged hundreds of miles from their favorite camping grounds in quest of food and plunder; and even the swift-running antelope found it difficult to keep out of their way. In one day's hunt the warrior was now able to procure enough meat and skins to supply his lodge for a winter's season. As a result, he had more time for leisure, social intercourse, war, and adventure. He became a lover of sports, and the youth of both sexes engaged in competitive games which better fitted them for the strenuous obligations of later years. So in this land of plenty the red man found himself in his element. Freed from the worries of the struggle for existence, clothed in skins, and making his home wherever the wandering bison led him, he had little more to desire.

The four major tribes occupying the southern plains preceded the Anglo-Americans by little more than one hundred years. Shortly after the first quarter of the nineteenth century, the Arapahoes and Cheyennes, closely allied members of the Algonquin family, inhabited the country embracing the headwaters of the Platte and the Arkansas rivers. Both tribes had formerly lived near the sources of the Mississippi River, but intertribal troubles, as well as pressure from the white settlers on the east, had driven them from one part of the plains to another. When Bent's Fort was built on the Arkansas River in 1832, some of them moved southward to trade at the new post, and were henceforth known as the Southern Arapahoes and Southern Cheyennes. This separation was made permanent by the treaty of Fort Laramie in 1851. By the treaty of Medicine Lodge, Kansas, in 1867, these tribes were confederated. At this time their numbers had been so depleted by war and plague that they scarcely totaled fifteen hundred or two thousand. In their migrations southward, they were generally engaged in bitter struggles with those tribes upon whose lands they encroached, as well as neighboring tribes. Until they were moved to Darlington, they were usually hostile towards the Utes, Shoshones, and Pawnees. This active life of warfare and adventure forced them to abandon their old customs of living in fixed abodes, tilling the soil, and engaging in sedentary pursuits, and to substitute many of the customs of the wild tribes all about them. Yet, in all this period of transition, the Arapahoes and Cheyennes were constant allies. Writing in 1885, Richard Irving Dodge observed that for sixty years they had been "the firmest of friends, occupying the same country, living in the same camps, making peace or war with the same enemies at the same time, and conducting themselves in everything (except intermarriages` as if they were one and the same tribe." Still, they maintained their tribal identities; the children of the two groups played, fought, hunted, and constantly associated together, "yet not one in ten of the men, women, or children of either tribe can hold even the most ordinary conversation in the language of the other."

South of the Arkansas River were two other confederated tribes— the Kiowa and the Comanche. During the early part of the nineteenth century their combined population was estimated at around twenty thousand. The Comanches, a Shoshoni tribe, were the first to come to the southern plains; they had migrated from an area far to the northwest. In 1724 Bourgmont located them between the Platte and the Kansas rivers, but by the close of the century they were roaming the plains as far south as the Colorado River of Texas, and frequently made forays on Mexican settlements south of the Rio Grande. The Kiowas, whose tribal affiliations are still a matter of doubt, had also migrated from the north, following the Comanches. Just when they encroached on the new range of the latter is problematic, but it is certain that a period of almost constant warfare preceded the peace of about 1790.

In addition to these major tribes of the southern plains, there were several smaller tribes closely identified with them in their nomadic habits. Some of these—the Wichitas, Wacoes, Kechias, and Quapaws—were located by a federal officer in 1852 in the vicinity of the Wichita Mountains, in the western part of what is now Oklahoma. In justice to them, however, it should be stated that

INTRODUCTION

their culture was midway between the nomadic life of the larger tribes and the civilization of the white man. Some of them dwelt in grass-thatched houses and cultivated small patches of corn and melons. Living on the San Saba River in Texas, and hunting over the region as far north as the Colorado, were small bands of Lipans and Kickapoos, whose manners and customs were much like those of the Comanches and Kiowas. Also on the Brazos River and its tributaries were small bands of Caddoes, Tawakonies, Tonkawas, and Wacoes, all of whom, except the Tonkawas, were much like the tribes of the Wichita Mountains area. Although the Tonkawas were reputed to be friendly with the whites, and often served the army as scouts, when campaigns were carried out against hostile tribes, they were shiftless, and thieving wanderers. The Comanches charged them with cannibalism, and early visitors to their country affirmed the charge.

Although Philip Nolan invaded the range of the Comanches during the last years of the eighteenth century, the real vanguard of the Anglo-Americans did not appear until the beginning of the next. Then Zebulon Montgomery Pike, Stephen H. Long, Henry Dodge, and others led expeditions to the southern plains with a view of permanent occupation. And at the same time there were many traders, trappers, and squatters who came on their own account.

The arrival of the white intruders signalized the beginning of a terrific struggle between the red and white man for occupation. The Indian realized that he was fighting to save his princely domain and to preserve his culture. If he were vanquished he must learn "to walk on the white man's road" and be content with government subsistence. But if he were successful he would not only keep those things dear to him but he would succeed in maintaining a hostile wedge between the occupied areas of his foe on either side of him. The white man realized this also and fought desperately to remove the unfriendly obstruction. Neither of the contestants spared his blows; the conflict was inhuman and long-drawn-out. In the end the red man was defeated. The Cheyennes and Arapahoes were placed on a small reserve in the northwestern part of the present state of Oklahoma, and the Comanches and Kiowas on another directly south of them. Also the other bands were moved to smaller assignments north of the Red River. Yet for many years they continued to depredate the exposed settlements before they finally became content with their lot. During this long period of conflict, within the twilight zone of the overlapping cultures emerged a new unit for the plains folk-pattern which influenced to a large degree both races. More than one frontiersman became "Indianized," and it is a matter of common knowledge that many sons and daughters of the Indian warriors fused their own blood with that of the conquerers and accepted their culture. But there were other units yet to come.

Within the tradition-warp of the settlers the Great Creator wove his uniquely colored woof-threads to produce a distinctive southern plains pattern. Climatic influence, unique flora and fauna, novel social adaptations, border trials, economic innovations, and social democracy—all contributed to the making of an extraordinary composite whole, as will be shown in this narrative. The land gave to the nation the southern plainsman, not the embodiment of a culture superior to that found in another folk-area of the United States, but certainly an outstanding one.

SOUTHERN PLAINSMEN

1

THE HUNTER'S PARADISE

I

THE primeval conditions existing on the southern plains until the close of the third quarter of the nineteenth century gave little promise of the marvelous transformation to come. Yet, even in their wild state, the plains were not uninhabited; they were the range of multitudinous game. As such they were a prolific hunting ground, well known by sportsmen in all the civilized nations of the old world as well as in the eastern part of the United States. The press carried interesting accounts of the exploits of hunters on the prairies of "the Great West"; and impressionable youths, filled with a desire for adventure, dreamed of the day when they, too, could engage in the romantic experience of a buffalo hunt, of cooking a venison steak over a glowing camp fire made of "buffalo-chips," or of catching a fleet-footed mustang pony. Hunting parties, both large and small, were organized for extensive hunts on the prairies, and preparations were often elaborate. A Kansan tells of such an expedition which came from England, consisting of several noblemen attended by servants accompanied by huge trunks and boxes of clothing and equipment. Even a Grand Duke of Russia was entertained by General Phil Sheridan in a buffalo hunt on the plains of western Kansas.[1] In the

1. When Grand Duke Alexis visited the United States in 1871-72, he asked for the privilege of a buffalo hunt on the Great Plains. This request created considerable excitement in army circles, as is evidenced by records now found in the Old Records Division, Adjutant General's Office, War Department, and in the Sheridan Letters, on file in the Division of Manuscripts, Library of Congress, Washington, D.C. In the latter collection alone are no less than thirty-five letters and telegrams relative to the hunt. On January 14, 1872, General P. H. Sheridan, assisted by Colonel George A. Forsyth and other illustrious officers and scouts, conducted the Grand Duke on a hunt south of Fort McPherson, Nebraska. Even Spotted Tail and his warlike band of Sioux helped to make the occasion enjoyable and interesting. For some of the more interesting letters and telegrams in the Sheridan Letters, see W. T. Sherman to P. H. Sheridan, November 1, 1871; Sheridan to John Pope, November 8, 1871; Sheridan to E. D. Townsend, November 22, 1871; Sheridan to William O. Stoddard (Secretary of the Presentation Committee), November 25, 1871; Sheridan to Townsend, December 14, 1871; Sheridan to George A. Custer, January 2,

light of the unusual reputation enjoyed by this area in the first half of the nineteenth century as a "hunter's paradise," it is not amiss to turn aside from the folkways of its later inhabitants to consider its early game life.

The climate of this region made it a paradise for game. Here the buffalo, elk, deer, and antelope (pronghorn) found a winter range on the prairie grass lands, and migratory birds a refuge on the many clear-running streams. The southern part of the area was a land of sunshine; and when icy fingers of the dread blizzard occasionally reached across its hills and valleys, it was only for two or three days at a time, and often for only a few hours. Small perennial streams feeding the main rivers—the Rio Grande, Colorado, Brazos, Red, Canadian, and Arkansas—afforded an abundant supply of water to both man and beast. Herbivorous animals grew fat on luxuriant mesquite, bluestem, buffalo, and grama grasses, and other edible plants. The bear, the opossum, and other carnivorous species could vary their diet with the luscious grapes and black haws found in great abundance along many of the streams. More than one river was named *Rio de las Nueces*, or River of Nuts, by the *conquistadores;* and abundant pecan and walnut trees were another source of food for the Indians as well as some animals.

II

The largest beast found on the southern plains by early Anglo-American explorers was the bison, more commonly known as the buffalo. During the colonization of the eastern seaboard, buffaloes ranged in considerable numbers east of the Mississippi and west of the Rocky Mountains; but by 1825, they were largely confined to the area of the Great Plains. Still later, by 1850, they were divided into the northern and southern herds by the great westward migration of gold-seekers over the Platte trail. Captain Stansbury, who passed over this route in 1849, wrote:

> Today the hunters killed their first buffalo, but in order to obtain it, had to diverge some four or five miles from the road and pass back of the bluffs, the instinct or experience of these

1872; Sheridan to a "Mr. Bodisco?," January 5, 1872; Sheridan to George A. Forsyth, January 7, 1872; Sheridan to W. W. Belknap (Secretary of War), January 14, 1872; and *ibid.*, January 16, 1872.

sagacious animals having rendered them shy of approaching the line of travel. This has not always been the case, for it is a well-attested fact that when the emigration first commenced, travelling trains were frequently detained for hours by immense herds crossing their track, and in such numbers that it was impossible to drive through them.[2]

Only approximate figures can be given for the number of bison which roamed the treeless plains of the West. Conservative estimates of the southern herd alone generally run from 3,000,000 to 5,000,000, and higher. Although the animals usually grazed in small herds of from fifty to two hundred, these were generally in such close proximity as to form a large herd. On one occasion in western Kansas Colonel Richard I. Dodge rode for over one hundred and twenty miles through such a continuous herd of "hundreds of thousands." Shortly after the southern herd had been formed, a hunting party accompanying the Doniphan expedition encountered it in the same area. From the top of Pawnee Rock, the hunters were awed by the sight of mile on mile of landscape, covered with buffaloes. All the hunters of the party had spent long years on the plains, and were accustomed to seeing large herds, but never before had they seen one of this size. Thomas Forsythe, the leader of the party, estimated the number at 200,000; and another hunter approximated it at 800,000 with the estimates of the rest ranging between these two. During the late sixties, De B. Randolph Keim, impressed by the great herd, wrote: "I have seen herd after herd stretching in one solid mass of peacefully grazing animals; over a distance of eighty miles, all tending in the same direction."[3]

A stampeding herd of buffalo was an awe-inspiring sight. Some travelers who witnessed such a scene stated that the noise was deafening, and the beasts' mighty tread made the ground tremble. One such visitor to this area in the late sixties said: "The noise of their tread and the low moaning sound of their breathing, and perhaps bellowing—though I could not satisfy myself as to the latter—sounded like distant thunder;" and still another declared

2. Howard Stansbury, "Exploration and Survey of the Valley of the Great Salt Lake of Utah," in *Senate Executive Documents*, Thirty-second Congress, special session, March, 1851, No. 3, p. 246 (Entry of Wednesday, June 27).

3. De B. Randolph Keim, *Sheridan's Troopers on the Border: A Winter Campaign on the Plains*, p. 68.

that " a vast moving mass could be seen, making the earth tremble with their tramping and bellowing."[4]

The buffalo was indispensable to the nomadic Indians. Its flesh furnished him with food; he drank its blood and, for medicinal purposes, the juices of the stomach; from its horns he made glue, cups, spoons, and other useful implements; its hide was used as a covering for his teepee, and for robes, leggings, beds, bow-strings, and sacks; the hair was woven into ropes and belts; and the dried droppings of the animals, known among the plainsmen as "buffalo chips," were used for fuel. Following the great herds from place to place the plains warrior studied painstakingly every peculiarity and habit of the animals for his advantage in times of need, and gained not only prowess but pleasure and excitement from the chase. Yet, as much as he loved it, he killed only what was necessary for home consumption and barter, and angrily censured white hunters who wantonly slaughtered for sport.

The Indian's favorite method of hunting the buffalo was to dash upon a herd, astride his wiry mustang, and bring down his game with bow and arrow, before the great lumbering creatures could get under way. He would generally approach the animal selected for slaughter from the rear and aim his shaft at the vulnerable spot between the protruding hip bone and the last rib. Many times the force of the driven arrow would carry it completely through the body. Upon the twang of the bow-string, the horse was taught to swerve from its victim, for the rider well knew that a wounded bison would quickly turn and attempt to gore its assailant. Sometimes the horse made its turn too late, and, when it was bowled over by the enraged bison, its rider would be thrown violently to the ground. In such instances the hunter occasionally suffered a broken limb; and since the savages knew nothing about bone setting, the sufferer would languish for weeks, and sometimes months, until death released him from his lingering pain. Many times on such hunts the Indians would throw a cordon of hunters about a small herd and kill large numbers of them before they could escape, the outer guard turning back those seeking to break away.

The Indians had various other ways of killing buffaloes. In winter, when, because of the depth of snow, the animals were unable

4. Thomas C. Battey, *A Quaker Among the Indians*, p. 17.

to move rapidly, they fell easy victims to the hunters, who, upon snowshoes, dispatched them with bow and arrow, or drove their lances into their bodies. But probably the most novel method was that explained by J. A. Allen, a scientist who visited their country in the early seventies.

This mode of hunting was to select one of the most active and fleet young men, who, disguised with a buffalo-skin fastened about his body, with the horns and ears so secured as to deceive the buffalo, placed himself at a convenient distance between the herd of buffalo and some of the river precipices, which sometimes extend for miles. His companions, in the meantime, get in the rear and along the flanks of the herd and, showing themselves at a given signal, advance upon the herd. The herd, thus alarmed, runs from the hunters toward the river. The Indian, who thus acts as decoy, when the precipice is reached, suddenly secures himself in some crevice of the cliff previously selected, leaving the herd on the brink. It is then impossible for the foremost of the herd to retreat or to turn aside, being pressed on by those behind, and they tumble headlong off the cliff, strewing the shore with their bodies.[5]

In later years, when the great herds were fast disappearing, the plains Indians complained that white hunters were destroying their chief food supply; yet, from statistical data which have been made available by the fur-trading companies of the West, it is evident that the Indians, too, were slaying them by hundreds of thousands each year. As indicated above, they killed not only for food, but also for commercial purposes. In 1845 General John C. Fremont gave out some figures of the American Fur Company, showing that the Indians on the Upper Missouri alone had been selling 90,000 robes annually, for a decade. Since buffalo hides were good for robes only four months in the year, it was estimated that in this area not less than 120,000 animals were being killed which, over a period of ten years, would give a grand total of 1,200,000. These figures, of course, did not include those slaughtered on the southern plains. Indeed, one observer estimated that each year on the Great Plains, the Indians slaughtered more than 500,000 buffaloes, a total of 5,000,000 for the years 1835 to 1845. Because the

5. J. A. Allen, "History of the American Bison," in *Ninth Annual Report of the United States Geological and Geographical Survey*, 1875, p. 519 *et sqq.*

Indian could exchange a skin for a pint of liquor, or for several robes could procure a gun and ammunition, he, too, found profit in the slaughter of the great herds.

Just how early white hunters began to make serious inroads on the southern herd would be difficult to determine. Josiah Gregg, in 1835, referred to the reckless slaughter of bison by white hunters, and stated that it might be well to take precautions against it. W. B. Parker, who accompanied Captain R. B. Marcy on his reconnoissance through Texas in 1854, said that "this animal is rapidly disappearing from the plains," and Marcy himself a short time later stated that "multitudes of these animals which have hitherto darkened the surface of the great prairies on the west of the 'Father of Waters' are fast wasting away under the fierce assaults made upon them by the white men as well as the savages."[6]

The projection of railways across the Great Plains and the discovery of a process for tanning "flint" hides were the main reasons for the final destruction of the two great herds. When the Union Pacific, the Missouri, Kansas and Texas, the Atchison, Topeka and Santa Fe, and the Texas and Pacific were built across the southern plains every small town and station became a point from which buffalo parties were outfitted and sent out on the range. The roads found it quite profitable to advertise the fact that passengers could shoot buffaloes from car windows, and posters boosting the sport placarded every vantage point along highways and railroads near the frontier. In the autumn of 1862 railroad hunting excursions from such cities as Cincinnati, Chicago, and St. Louis were advertised as follows:

RAILWAY EXCURSION
AND
BUFFALO HUNT

An excursion train will leave Leavenworth, at 8 A. M.
and Lawrence at 10 A. M. for

SHERIDAN

On Tuesday, October 27, 1868, and return on Friday.

6. For statements of two men, see W. B. Parker, *Notes Taken During the Expedition Commanded by R. B. Marcy, U.S.A., Through Unexplored Texas in the Summer and Fall of 1854*, 101-2; and R. B. Marcy, *Thirty Years of Army Life on the Border*, p. 338.

This train will stop at the principal stations both
going and returning.

Ample time will be had for a grand buffalo

HUNT ON THE PLAINS

Buffaloes are so numerous along the road that they
are shot from the cars nearly every day. On our last
excursion our party killed twenty buffaloes in a hunt
of six hours.

All passengers can have refreshments on the cars at
reasonable prices.

Tickets of round trip from Leavenworth, $10.00[7]

A passenger on such an excursion between Wallace and Sheridan,
Kansas, over the Kansas Pacific, wrote to the Denver *Rocky Mountain News*, on February 1, 1871:

> We were favored by one of those grand reviews, consisting of
> a herd of buffalo of at least 5,000. The passengers turned out
> *en masse* to welcome their approach, saluting them as they
> passed with about forty shots. Judging from the amount of
> carcasses lying near the tracks, they must receive salutes of that
> kind very often. The buffalo, when killed in this way, are soon
> disposed of by wolves and ravens, which abound on the plains.

In 1871, John W. Mooar sold a consignment of fifty-seven flint
hides to a Pennsylvania tanner for the sum of $3.50 each. This is
said to have been the first transaction of the kind ever made in
America. The hides were bought for experimental purposes, and so
successful was the tanning test that a great demand for hides followed. Then hunting parties were organized on a commercial basis,
and the period of the great slaughter had begun.

The most successful hunting party consisted of one hunter and
about six "strippers," or skinners, although there were many
smaller parties. The party would usually be organized at some railway town, where it bought a hunting outfit, including wagon, team,
guns, cartridges, reloading sets for shells, and supplies. The latter
consisted of a large "Dutch" oven, frying pans, coffee pots, camp
kettles, coffee mill, tin cups, tin plates, knives, forks, spoons, pot
hooks, meat broilers, shovels, spades, axes, mess box, and such
foods as flour, bacon, canned fruits, potatoes, and onions. For

7. Keim, *op. cit.*, p. 76.

protection against predatory animals considerable quantities of poison were also taken along to be used on hides after they had been staked out and were being dried. So thriving was the trade in outfitting hunters at frontier towns that unusual quantities of goods were sold. On January 14, 1877, the F. E. Conrad general merchandise stores at Fort Griffin reported its sales for the day at $4,000, $2,500 of this amount representing sales of guns and ammunition.

The life of a buffalo hunter was not so adventurous as is sometimes believed. His daily routine was one of arduous toil and filth. His bloody work kept him so occupied that he had little time for sanitation, and his camp as well as his person naturally became foul. A visitor to a buffalo camp on the southern plains wrote:

In place of the buckskin suit of the Rocky Mountain hunter, the buffalo hunter goes clad in a coarse dress of canvass, stiffened with blood and grease. His hair often goes uncut and uncombed for months together, and his hands are frequently unwashed for many days. The culinary apparatus of the whole party consists of a single large coffee pot, a "Dutch" oven, and a skillet, and the table set, of a tin cup to each man, and the latter vessel often consisting merely of a battered fruit can. Each man's hunting knife not only does duty in butchering the buffalo, but is the sole implement used in dispatching his food, supplying the places of spoon and fork as well as knife. The bill of fare consists of strong coffee, often without milk or sugar, "yeast-powder bread," and buffalo meat fried in buffalo tallow. When the meal is cooked, the party encircles the skillet, dip their bread in the fat, and eat their meat with their fingers. When bread fails, as often happens, "buffalo straight," or buffalo meat alone, affords them nourishing sustenance. Occasionally, however, the fare is varied with the addition of potatoes and canned fruits. They sleep generally in the open air, in winter as well as in summer, subjected to every inclemency of the weather. As may be imagined, a buffalo hunter, at the end of the season, is by no means prepossessing in appearance, being, in addition to his filthy aspect, a paradise for hordes of nameless parasites. They are yet a rollicking set, and occasionally include men of intelligence who formerly possessed an ordinary degree of refinement.[8]

8. Allen, *op. cit.*, 561-62.

THE HUNTER'S PARADISE

During the closing years of the seventies from five hundred to fifteen hundred hunters invaded the buffalo country of the southern plains. At all hours of the day on the prairies, long trains of wagons, drawn generally by ox and mule teams, were to be seen making their way eastward to market, over dim trails or roads. On each wagon were great bales of buffalo hides, piled one upon another, at times making it difficult for teams to pull them. About the hunters' camps were huge piles of cured hides, while others littered the ground staked out for drying.

The wanton slaughter of the buffalo carried with it a touch of pathos. Where once, unmolested, he roamed at will over vast prairies, now near every water hole and running stream, behind every clump of trees or tall grass, on his right or left, in front or behind, he could expect his hidden foes with their deadly "big fifties." Colonel Dodge thus described his pitiful fate:

> Every approach of the buffaloes to water was met with rifle bullets, and one or more bit the dust. Care was taken not to permit the others to drink, for then they would not return. Tortured with thirst, the poor brutes approach again and again, always to be met by bullets, always to lose some of their herd. . . . They are driven from one water hole to meet death at another. No sooner do they stop to feed than the sharp crack of a rifle warns them to change position. Every drink of water, every mouthful of grass, is at the expense of life, and the miserable animals, continually harrassed, are driven far from their natural haunts, anywhere to avoid the unceasing pursuit.[9]

So bloody was the slaughter from 1872 to 1874 that 1,373,359 hides, 6,751,200 pounds of meat, and 32, 380,650 pounds of bones were shipped to eastern markets over the Atchison, Topeka and Santa Fe, the Union Pacific, and the Kansas Pacific railroads. Over the Atchison, Topeka and Santa Fe alone, in the year 1873, 754,-529 hides were shipped to market. From 1870 to 1880 not far short of 7,500,000 buffaloes were slaughtered on the southern plains. By 1879, there was only a small remnant of the great herds grazing the area south of the Brazos, and after the passing of two years the herd was entirely gone.

9. Richard Irving Dodge, *Hunting Grounds of the Great West*, 133-34.

III

Next in interest among the animals of the southern plains was the mustang. Wild horses were a subject of comment for all travelers in this region during the early days. In herds of tens, twenties, and sometimes as many as a thousand—bay, roan, sorrel, milk-white, pinto, and black in color—these superb creatures made an inspiring sight as they dashed across the rolling plains or leaped gullies and small streams in their mad flight.

Historians who have delved into the records of the early days of Spanish penetration have proved that the wild horses were not native to America, but descended from the famous Arabian steeds and animals in use in Spain at that time. Before the coming of the Spaniard, the Indian tribes inhabiting the area were footmen, depending on dogs and squaws to drag their camp equipment from place to place. After the horses had once found freedom on the great sweeping plains, they multiplied rapidly and, with the passing of decades, became wild.

By the close of the eighteenth century the fame of the wild horses of the southern plains had spread to the eastern seaboard, and more particularly the south. In the densely timbered areas of the latter region, means of communication were few, roads were bad; and dim trails were sometimes the only kind of highways found in the country. Accordingly, riding horseback was the usual mode of travel; good horses were eagerly sought for; horse racing was popular; and an animal which was a fast, sure traveler was much prized. During this period, Southerners became much interested in the wild horses; and traders drove thousands of them from the Spanish province of Texas to southern markets.

An example of the attitude of the Southerner toward this traffic is found in an interesting incident of the year 1798. On June 24 Thomas Jefferson wrote a letter to Philip Nolan of New Orleans, requesting information on wild horses in the province of Texas, as well as on the varieties of animal and plant life found there. Nolan was so interested in the enquiry that shortly thereafter he visited Jefferson at Philadelphia, carrying a letter of recommendation signed by James Wilkinson, and stating that Nolan could give him "details of a country, the soil, clime, population, and improvements and productions of which are so little known to us." It is not certain whether this visit led to Nolan's famous expedition into Texas, but in October, 1800, with a party of twenty-four Americans, Mexicans, Negroes, and Creoles, he crossed the international boundary into the province of Texas. By the spring of 1801 he had captured more than three hundred animals, and it seemed that considerable success attended his work until he was attacked by a detachment of Spanish troops. In the fight, Nolan was killed and his small party was scattered. The Spaniards captured ten men, one of whom died a short time later. In February, 1807, an order came from the King of Spain to put to death one out of every five men captured. Since there were nine men left, Spanish officials decided that the death of one would satisfy the order of the King. The nine men cast dice to determine who should die, and Ephriam Blackburn threw the unlucky low number. He was executed at Chihuahua, Mexico, on November 11, 1807; and the other men of the party were imprisoned. Ellis P. Bean was the only man to make his return to the United States from this ill-starred adventure, and in his memoirs he later told the story of the thrilling enterprise.

Four decades later George Catlin, the artist, passed through the range of the wild horse and was much impressed with the large herds which he found. Concerning the beauty of the animals, he wrote:

The tract of country which we passed, between the False Washita and this place (western Kansas) is stocked, not only with buffaloes, but with numerous bands of wild horses, many of which we saw every day. There is no other animal on the prairies so wild and so sagacious as the horse; and none other so difficult to come up with. So remarkably keen is their eye, that they will generally run "at the sight," when they are a mile distant; being, no doubt, able to distinguish the character of the enemy that is approaching when at that distance, and when in motion, will seldom stop short of three or four miles. I made many attempts to approach them by stealth, when they were grazing and playing their gambols, without ever having been more than once able to succeed. In this instance, I left my horse, and with my friend, Chadwick, skulked through a ravine for a couple of miles; until we were at length brought within gunshot of a fine herd of them, when I used my pencil for some time, while we were under cover of a little hedge of bushes which effectually screened us from their view. In this herd we saw all the colours, nearly, that can be seen in a kennel of English hounds. Some were milk-white, some jet black—others were sorrel, and bay, and cream-coloured—many were of an iron gray, and others pied, containing a variety of colours on the same animal. Their manes were very profuse, and hanging in the wildest profusion over their necks and faces—and their long tails swept the ground.[10]

On account of the shyness mentioned by Catlin, wild horses were hard to approach, and difficult to capture. Hunters generally employed one of four methods in taking them: "creasing," roping, corralling, and running them down. To crease a horse was to lie in wait near a water hole, or some other favored resort of the animal, until the herd approached. The hunter would then shoot the horse through the muscular part of the neck, above its vertebrae. If the shot was successful, the horse would drop to the ground, paralyzed for a few moments. This brief interval would be sufficient for the hunter to approach, place his rope about it, and side-line it before it could regain control of its limbs. If, however, the shot was too low, there was danger of breaking the animal's neck, a misfortune which the horse hunter encountered more than once. The Indian hunter did not often use this method of capture; he was more successful in roping. Because of his ability to approach closely a herd, by taking advantage of screening ravines, hills, or trees, he could suddenly dash among the mustangs, astride his pony, before they were aware of his presence. He could then expertly cast his rope about the neck of a horse, and begin his struggle to make it a captive. When the noose of the rope would settle about the horse's neck, the hunter would leap from the back of his mount, and, on foot, so maneuver the leaping, frantic animal as to wear away its strength. Again and again the horse would attempt to escape, strike its tormentor with its sharp hoofs, or run him down, but the agile Indian would frustrate its every effort. Finally, after a long period of strenuous effort, the hunter would shorten his rope, foot by foot, until he would stand immediately before his captive. Anglo-American horse hunters, who have observed these unusual struggles, say that when this stage was

10. George Catlin, *North American Indians*, II, 64.

reached, the Indian captor would then do a very extraordinary thing. When he had at last approached the head of the animal, he would blow his breath into its distended nostrils, after which it would lose its fear of the captor, allow him to put a half-hitch about its lower jaw, mount its back and ride it into camp.

Corralling and "running down" were the methods of capture generally employed by Anglo-Americans. Strong pole corrals, with V-shaped entrances, were built, and into these wild herds were driven. It was then comparatively easy for the hunters to rope, side-line them, and begin the process of taming their captives. The fourth method employed was a very novel one indeed. It was introduced after the corralling system had been in use for many years. A herd was first located by a member of a hunting party, who would make careful observations as to its range and watering place. The hunters would pitch camp near the center of the range, preparing for a stay of several days. A rider would then start out in search of the herd. When he would come in contact with it, it was his custom to follow leisurely the fleeing animals, at a gait which would not exhaust his own mount but would give the wild horses little time to feed or drink. Again and again the tireless rider would overtake the herd, and again and again it would dash away before him, but always in a wide circle of fifteen or twenty miles in diameter. When the rider and mount tired of their exertions, a relay would be furnished and the pursuit would go on. Sometimes it required two days of ceaseless riding to wear down the animals, but this stage of the chase was finally reached. The hunters could then place the ropes about their necks, yoke them together, and take all necessary precautions for conquering their proud spirits when once they recovered from their fatigue.

Many of the wild horses were unmistakably descendants of the species known as the Barb, brought to America during the days of conquest. In winter, they were of an unprepossessing appearance. Their bodies were covered with long, shaggy hair; their stomachs were distended with cottonwood bark which they were often forced to eat for sustenance; their eyes were lusterless; and their every characteristic bespoke sluggishness and physical poverty. But with the coming of spring, they went through a surprising transformation: they would shed their winter coats; their eyes would brighten with a new life; and their small keenly pointed ears would seem to move this way and that to catch the faintest sound of an approaching enemy. It is also quite probable that some of the wild animals were descendants of Anglo-American horses which were brought into the country near the beginning of the nineteenth century. Among these herds, however, were the offspring of a far better type of animal—the famous Arabian steed. Stallions of such ancestry were generally the guardians of the herds with which they ran; and some of them were much sought for by the hunters. Catlin had the misfortune of killing one of these while attempting to crease it; and George Wilkins Kendall, in his *Narrative of the Texan Santa Fe Expedition*, tells of a Mexican rider, trained to the business of capturing wild horses, tiring down "no less than three race nags," in his efforts to capture the much-talked-of "White Steed of the Prairies." So much desired was he that large sums had been offered for his capture, and attempts were frequently made, but no hunter was able to approach close enough to throw a lasso over his head. After Kendall had returned to New Orleans, he wrote: "Since my return, I have been informed, by a Texan gentleman, that a horse in many respects answering the description of the 'White Steed of the Prairies' has been caught, after a hard chase, between the headwaters of the Trinity and Brazos. He lived but a short time, however, the excessive fatigue of the race causing his death."[11]

IV

The antelope (pronghorn) of the plains was found in herds almost as large as those of the buffalo. A visitor to the Concho River country of southwestern Texas, in 1868, stated that he saw one herd of these beautiful creatures which he estimated to contain 100,000 animals. A passenger on an excursion over the Kansas Pacific in 1871 wrote: "We saw more antelope on this trip than was ever seen before—so said the railroad men anyhow—and it must be so for the road was lined with them all day, and nearly all of them within gunshot from the train."[12]

11. P. 89.
12. *Rocky Mountain News* (Denver, Colorado), February 1, 1871. A medical officer of the army stationed at Fort Concho during this same period made the following entry in his post record: "Zoology: Bison, vast herds; cotton-tailed deer; antelope in herds almost as large as buffalo herds; mustangs; two or three varieties of wild cats or lynx; black bear;

*Upper, in camp after a deer hunt; lower, 40,000 buffalo hides piled
in yards of Rath and Wright, Dodge City, Kansas, 1877,
ready for shipment*

THE HUNTER'S PARADISE

The antelope was a small, timid, fleet animal, and for the hunter who did not have a knowledge of its fatal weakness of curiosity, it was very difficult to kill or capture. The plains hunter, however, was usually able to slay as many as he desired by resorting to a simple expedient. When he chanced to spy a herd, he would crawl on hands and knees as close as he could approach without exciting the fear of the animals. Then he would lie prostrate in the tall prairie grass, or hide behind a clump of bushes, and make his preliminary preparations. He would tie a handkerchief—preferably a red one—to a rod and slowly raise it above his hiding place. As a rule it would be spied immediately, and the startled herd would go bounding away, but after a short run would stop and face about in order to examine the cause of its fright. The hunter would slowly wave his bunting to and fro, still without showing his body above his place of concealment. Its curiosity now thoroughly aroused, the antelope would gradually approach by wide circles the object of its interest. The hunter had only to exercise enough patience to allow the herd to come within range of his rifle, when he could carefully aim at and shoot down the animal of his choice before the remainder of the herd could flee.

Closely akin to the antelope was the deer, large numbers and several species of which were also found on the southern plains. And they, like the bison and antelope, disappeared with the passing of the frontier. They were not so important a source of food to the red man as they were to the white settler. Like the antelope, they were difficult to approach, and sometimes novel means were employed to slay them. The hunter often used dogs in the chase for deer, while he would station himself at some vantage point, near which he had good reason to believe the deer would run, and pick it off with his rifle as it approached his stand. Then, again, he would lie in wait near a favorite watering place and shoot down his game as it came for its evening or morning drink. But probably the most unusual method was called "fire hunting." An English sportsman who came to the southern plains during the second quarter of the nineteenth century thus explains this practice:

---

lobo wolf; coyote; musk-hogs; prairie-dogs; several varieties of squirrel; mule-eared rabbit; large hare; cotton-tailed rabbit; skunk; turkey; bald-eagle; Mexican eagle; buzzard; raven; crow; black bird; mocking bird; two varieties of quail; ducks; swans; plover; larks; paradise birds; and many other kinds." MSS, found in *Medical History of Fort Concho*, CCV (December, 1867, to December, 1872), 55, Old Records Division, Adjutant General's Office, War Department, Washington, D. C.

Fire hunting is perhaps the most destructive method of killing deer known. It is pursued in the following manner:—An old frying-pan is riveted onto four or five upright pieces of hoop iron, whilst a circular piece runs round the top to hold in the fire. The handle of the pan is lashed on to a stout stick some six or seven feet long, which is carried on the left shoulder, the pan being some three feet behind the head of the hunter. The light meeting the eyes of any animal, is reflected back, or, in hunters' language, "shines their eyes," and so amazed or fascinated are the deer by the blaze, that up-wind they are often approached within a few feet. The darker the night, too, for this murdering work (for it is not sport), the better. In our case, a supply of food for "the hands" was the justification.[13]

The party with which the English hunter was associated killed thirty-five deer during one night's hunting.

To the average frontiersman, a fried steak, a roast, or a rib barbecue of young, fat venison was a rare delicacy. Even the head of the animal came in for its share of consideration as is evidenced by the following account of its preparation by a hunter-cook:

Before stretching myself for the night, I proceeded to put the head of the deer I had killed into a condition to serve me for a breakfast in the morning. As the process, I believe, is neither understood nor practiced on this side the Atlantic, I will give the recipe, for the benefit of future cookery-book manufacturers. Having dug a hole about eighteen inches deep and about the same in diameter with your hunting-knife, you rake some of the cinders from the fire at which your supper is preparing, to kindle another fire in what is to be your oven, and you build in and over this hole a large fire, which you allow to burn down gradually as you eat your supper, drink your coffee, and smoke— that luxury to the solitary hunter—a pipe. Then before "turning in," all the fire is raked away, the cinders scratched out of the oven as well as possible and some damp prairie grass laid at the bottom, upon which is placed the head, unskinned, and just as it is cut from the carcass; then more prairie grass is put over that, the cinders are brought back, and another fire is built over all. In the morning, after a bath in the creek, the ashes are removed, the head, beautifully baked, is brought to light, the skin peels off neatly, and there upon a piece of bark before you a dish fit for the queen. First, there is some good picking on the jaws; then

13. "Adventure in Texas," in *Leisure Hour*, XII, 60.

comes the tongue; and last, the daintiest of all, the brains, seasoned with red pepper and salt and washed down with a tin mug of *café noir* followed by a pipe. Such a repast leaves the hunter in the happiest frame, and makes him wish that "all the world and the rest of mankind" had laid as good a foundation for the pleasures or toils of the day as he has.

V

On the southern plains predatory animals were almost as prolific as game. Ravenous packs of wolves, in hundreds and thousands—gray, black, lobo, and coyote—ranged over the country in search of food; and bears, panthers, and wild cats were found in the sparse timberlands along the streams. Before the end of the nineteenth century trappers had taken thousands of beavers and otters; wolf hunters had destroyed the great packs by scattering poisoned meat over the prairies; and immigrant farmers had destroyed millions of prairie dogs, and transformed their "towns" into well cultivated fields. These little rodents were enemies of the farmers' crops, therefore they had to go. They were trapped, poisoned, and slain in such large numbers that by the end of the nineteenth century they were confined to small patches of pasture land here and there, and to undeveloped ranch properties. In this ruthless slaughter of the wild life of the prairies, the Anglo-Saxon invader was actuated by little sentiment. If it was a choice between his welfare and that of the wild animals, his mind was made up—the wild life must be destroyed. To this end, bounties were offered for the killing of predatory animals; organizations were formed; and even the timid mule-eared rabbits were rounded up in community "drives" and slaughtered by the hundreds, because they fed on growing corn and wheat.

From the foregoing pages of this chapter it is not difficult to see how hunting on the treeless, semi-arid plains called for adaptations not necessary in other regions of the United States. Novel techniques, not used in the forested areas east of the Mississippi, were employed in hunting, capturing and killing the wild animals of the plains, all of which helped to lend color to the folkways of the early settlers.

Today "the hunter's paradise" does not exist. It vanished with the passing of the frontier. Yet memories of the "good old days," when the southern plains was the mecca of the hunters of the world, are still fondly cherished by frontiersmen. Sitting about the fire during the long winter evenings, they often regale their grandsons and granddaughters with stirring tales of adventure in the early days, and their eyes kindle and their faces glow as they relive the past. Speaking of early hardships and suffering, they sometimes justify their destruction of the "hunter's paradise," and point out that during this period plains culture was in its swaddling clothes and that before it could grow to maturity it had to recreate its environment.

2

"THE LAND OF MILK AND HONEY"

I

SINCE the days when Moses led the hosts of Israel across the Red Sea in search of a new home, the people of the world have been searching for the "Promised Land." This ancient quest brought the Phoenicians from their eastern Mediterranean homes to the northern shores of Africa, where, about 822 B. C., they established the mighty city of Carthage; it led the Golden Horde of Mongols to invade and exploit eastern Europe in the first half of the thirteenth century; it launched the Vikings on their career of depredations and colonial plantations in the ninth and tenth centuries, resulting in important changes in the political organization of Europe; and it finally found expression in the pioneering movement in the United States. "The Land of Milk and Honey!" What magic this will-o'-the-wisp held for the land-hungry Anglo-American during the nineteenth century! It led him to subject his wife and children to the arduous toil of a long journey through dense forests and across uncharted prairies, exposing them to the starvation period of pioneering in a new land, to the scalping knife of the savage foe who lurked in the forest or tall prairie grass, to the fate of captivity in an Indian camp, and even to death in a strange land where physicians were scarce. This magic quest carried the American flag to the blue waters of the Pacific; it wiped out, by 1890, the last American frontier; and it led to the reclamation of hundreds of thousands of acres of desert land in the Rocky Mountain area. And unmistakably it stamped its influence on the cultural growth of the nation. For its democratic offspring liberalized the state constitutions of the eastern seaboard; its literary heritage found expression in the songs, poetry, and folklore of the nation; and its drama has been reproduced on the stage.

In 1865 a human tide of homeseekers swept over the undulating prairies of the southern plains. It swelled rapidly with the passing of years until by 1890 it had flooded the millions of acres of un-occupied tillable land. To bring about this marvelous result, every agency of the country cooperated. Newspapers, magazines, and handbills, state advertising organizations and land companies, joined in a mighty chorus of praise for the southern plains as a land of opportunity. No other part of the United States had been more effectively advertised. Even state and territorial officials in their annual reports would depart from their stereotyped phrases when referring to the southern plains, and burst forth into expressions of exultation. The spirit of "boom-town" and "free-home" opti-mism swept the country like a prairie fire. It was irresistible and irrepressible; and its unconquerable force soon quickened the lifeblood of the nation.

In the occupation of our public domain shortly after the close of the American Revolution, the states and territories north of the Mason and Dixon Line and the Ohio River were the first to be well settled. The northern tier of states had the advantage of Atlantic seaports, and canals and railways which brought them in contact with the interior. By 1865, the southern states came to see that they were falling behind in this movement, and in various ways they sought to overcome their handicap—not without success.

A novel scheme for the settlement of the western part of Texas by immigrants was evolved in the early summer of 1866, when delegates from some fifteen or twenty counties met in Galveston.[1] The convention put itself on record as recommending that, follow-ing the procedure of other pioneering states, good wages should be offered to laborers, lands at low prices and in suitable tracts to purchasers, and advantageous leases of lands to those who wished to lease. Moreover, it urged that a company be organized to collect necessary information on Texas soil, climate, production, and social, religious and educational advantages, and that com-petent agents be appointed to carry this information abroad. In order to accomplish these ends, the executive committee proposed

1. *The Texas Almanac for 1867*, 272-73. The annual report of the Texas Secretary of State, entitled *Texas Secretary of State, 1879-1880*, pp. 18-26, lists other immigration socie-ties, with the capitalization of each. They are as follows: San Antonio Immigration Aid Association, capital, $100,000, charter filed November 24, 1879; Galveston and Santa Fe Land and Immigration Company, capital, $100,000, charter filed March 19, 1880; South-western Immigration Company, Austin, Texas, capital, $100,000, charter filed July 19, 1880; and Texas Land and Colonization Company, Tyler, Texas, capital $250,000, charter filed July 22, 1880.

to issue 2,000 shares of preferred stock, on condition that five dollars a share should be paid on subscribing, five dollars more on the final organization of the company, ten dollars in two months after, ten in four months, ten in six months, and ten in eight months. The remainder of the stock was to be issued for the purchase of lands to be sold to immigrants, and for the payment of their transportation and other expenses. Any profits which might accrue from the purchase and sale of lands were to be equally divided. The state legislature granted the organization its charter, but no considerable benefits ever came to its members. It did, however, point the way to the Texas Bureau of Immigration, which was to meet with a large measure of success.

Four years later, the legislature created a Bureau of Immigration, with Gustav Loeffler as its first superintendent. Agents were appointed to work in cooperation with him in England and France. An eastern agency was established at Atlanta, Georgia, under the charge of C. W. Mathews, to carry on active work among the homeseekers of the South; and a western agency at St. Louis, Missouri, under the supervision of W. G. Kingsbury. Texas itself was divided into two districts and agents appointed to represent the interests of the Bureau in each district.[2]

Other states and territories of the southern plains watched with much interest the progress of Texas, and sought to emulate its example. That the New Mexico Territory was not to allow this Texas challenge to go unanswered is intimated in *Memorial No. 2* of its legislature:

> Thirty years have elapsed since the ratification of the treaty of Guadaloupe Hildalgo and yet its obligations have not been fulfilled. A mighty tide of emigration has passed over the broad plains to the rich mountains of New Mexico, seeking more distant homes toward the setting sun, because of the unsettled state of the land titles of the Territory. Neither the grant owner nor the settler can have that security in their possessions as would prompt them to that expenditure of labor and capital in improvements which would insure the development and prosperity of the country.[3]

2. *Annual Report of the Superintendent of Immigration,* December 31, 1873. For provisions of act, see Jacob Kuechler papers, MS, I, 1804-72, report of Representative Ira H. Evans, Archives, Library, University of Texas.

3. Broadsides collection, Division of Manuscripts, Library of Congress, Washington, D. C.

In order to retain a fair share of this immigration in New Mexico, a Bureau of Immigration under William G. Rich was created on February 27, 1882. As was expected, the superintendent became an active propagandist for the Territory. In a report made two years later, he stated that he had prepared for publication four editions of *Illustrated New Mexico*, totalling 16,000 copies, and averaging 150 octavo pages to the edition. In addition to this general publication, Commissioner G. W. Prichard had prepared and published 1,000 copies of a sixteen-page pamphlet on San Miguel County; and Commissioner A. J. Fontain had issued a similar publication for Dona Ana County, making a grand total of 2,450,000 pages. To distribute this publicity among travelers, many expedients were used. In the principal towns, it was handed out to visitors; coaches of passenger trains passing through the country were regularly boarded by agents of the Bureau; and thousands of circulars and booklets were handed to visitors at picnics and fairs, such as the Denver Exposition of 1882 and the Santa Fe Tri-Centenary Exposition of July, 1884.[4]

Kansas also lent its official sanction to the immigration movement. In 1868, Governor Crawford urged the legislature to take some steps toward encouraging immigrants to settle in the state. He warned: "Kansas cannot afford to remain idle while other states are using every honorable means in their power to encourage immigrants to settle within their borders." In calling the attention of the legislature to what he had expected for the preceding year, he stated that the "immigration for 1867 was only 50,000 and it should have been 100,000."[5] This spirit of anxiety was reflected not only in the statement of the Governor, but also in the annual reports of his officials. In 1870 the Adjutant General visioned the possibilities of the western part of the state when he wrote that "large tracts of land which at the present time are pastures for vast herds of buffalo, will be brought into cultivation; domesticated animals will take the place of the buffalo, revenue will flow into our treasury, and the settler can work in peaceful security without hearing the yells of bloodthirsty savages intent on plunder and

4. Report of the Bureau of Immigration, February 16, 1884, p. 5, *passim*.

5. John S. Dawson, "The Legislature for 1868," in *Kansas State Historical Collections*, X (1907-8), 257.

murder." Unquestionably, the state was willing to do all it could to attract the human tide flowing toward the West.

II

Although state agencies did much to encourage immigration, they were not as important as private enterprises. In fact, land-grant railways rendered the greatest service in settling the country. They established extensive advertising agencies; they scattered their agents through the states east of the Mississippi River; and they offered homeseekers material inducements such as free transportation to their lands, temporary housing facilities, and conveyance from railway stations to lands beyond convenient travel.

Chief among the roads which sought the foreign immigrant was the Atchison, Topeka, and Santa Fe. Under the able leadership of A. E. Touzalin, it tried to dispose of 3,000,000 acres in Kansas. His four-story office building at Topeka was a hive of industry, to which land agents, newspaper reporters, advertising solicitors, and homeseekers flocked; and Mr. Touzalin was said to be the "king bee" of them all. Imbued with his optimism, C. B. Schmidt, head of the foreign immigration department, went to Russia in search of settlers. Although he encountered the jealous opposition of Russian officials, he succeeded in returning to the western plains of Kansas, in 1875, with 1,900 German Mennonites from the Crimea and the coasts of the Black Sea and the Sea of Azov. These German-Russian colonists bought 60,000 acres of land; and by 1883, more than 15,000 kinsmen had been settled on other large blocks of land.[6] Indeed, by the close of the century, this tide of foreign home-builders approached the one hundred thousand mark. In 1869, the Union Pacific located a Swedish colony under the leadership of S. G. Larson, S. P. Lindgren, and Dan Lindahl, on 16,000 acres of its land in the southern part of Saline County.

Colorado and Oklahoma passed through the same experience. Many of the land-seekers who came to these regions migrated from the mother colonies in Kansas; and others hailed from various parts of the Union. The Denver *Rocky Mountain News* of February

6. C. B. Schmidt, "Reminiscences of Foreign Immigration Work for Kansas," in *ibid.*, IX (1905-6), 485-97.

16, 1870, called attention to an advance party of the German Colonization Society, 175 strong and well equipped with all the necessities for establishing homes, which had reached St. Louis, en route to the Wet Mountain Valley. At the same time, other colonists were moving into the eastern plains area of Colorado, which was occupied by the conclusion of the immigrant movement in western Kansas. A discussion of the Oklahoma settlement will be found in Chapter XVI.

In each state and territory of the southern plains, immigration societies and land companies flooded the country with tons of extravagant literature. Homeseekers were told that this region was the long-sought-for "land of milk and honey." The *Texas Almanac for 1867* reasoned that "those who have money to purchase lands can buy the very best, ready improved or unimproved, in every county in the state, at prices so low that every acre will pay for itself twice over by the crop it produces the first year." For him who wished to engage in the cattle business, the *Almanac* stated that he could "have pasturage of as many thousand acres as he pleases, without money and without price." In an oration on Texas, delivered at the Philadelphia Centennial, on September 11, 1876, Governor Hubbard described his country as a region of "fertile lands, rich mines—mocking the wealth of the Indies—underlaid by measureless fields of coal and iron, unnumbered herds of cattle scattered over countless plains, a genial clime opening to the hand of man the facile culture of all the products of other lands," and declared that "cotton, wheat, corn, rye, oats, rice, barley, and sugar *grow side by side on the same fertile fields.*"

In brief, the propaganda artist used his rosiest hues in painting his brilliant picture of the southern plains. He took the country, dressed in its finest robes of spring, summer, fall, and winter, and held it up to the gaze of an admiring public, as it occasionally was. Here and there it did have its limpid, cool streams, its fields of ripe golden grain, its orchards of luscious fruits, and its vast green, velvety pasture lands, covered with fat, sleek horses, cattle, and sheep; but every part of the country was not so adaptable to occupation, and every year could not promise such extravagant returns in climate and produce. The propagandist neglected to warn the immigrant against adversities and tribulations. He said little about occasional drouths, visitations of clouds of grasshoppers which sometimes destroyed all growing vegetation, cold northers, and blizzards which took a heavy toll of both man and beast, the lack of a water supply in some parts of the country, and many other handicaps which made the accumulation of considerable wealth by a large percentage of the settlers highly improbable. When such subjects were mentioned, they were treated as inconsequential.

III

The homeseekers' hearty response to the effective advertising of these various agencies led to the rapid occupation of the country. In 1870 the southern plains was the favored range of vast herds of bisons, and the hunting ground of wild Indian tribes. By 1890, it was fairly well checker-boarded with farms and ranches. The immigrants came walking, on horseback, in ox-wagons, and in vehicles drawn by horses and mules; they came in large and small parties, and in ones and twos. Well-traveled highways soon took the places of dim buffalo trails; and well-built railways offered a means of transportation which was a great improvement over the rough roads of freight caravan and stage coach days. Finally, along these railways were built numerous *termini* towns, some of which sprang into full growth within a day's time and sank into insignificance with the passing of the boom. Others were large tent towns in the beginning and grew into still larger cities and towns of a substantial character after a decade.

Many a "boom town" of this period was conceived in the brain of a land speculator, and built on the uncertain basis of "boom" optimism. Its day of prosperity was the heyday of the gunman, gambler, and promoter, who found temporary abodes in its tents and shanties, and moved on to similar places when law and order, and stable institutions, made their appearance. Fortunes were quickly made and lost in the wild speculation which accompanied the excitement of town building. In many instances, large residential districts were organized on plots of ground near the towns, lots were marked off and sold at fabulous prices, graveled and hard-surfaced streets were laid down, and other conveniences for lot owners were provided. But more than once all this preliminary work was for naught; the growth of the town was abruptly halted, residences did not materialize, and lot owners—and sometimes real estate organizers and planners—were left with worthless property on their hands.

Towns located in the same trade territory would often become jealous rivals, and each would sponsor arterial road building and local bond elections and public subscriptions to finance various construction projects or to attract railway builders and factory owners. Even the editors of the local newspapers would engage in friendly banter—and in rivalry which sometimes was not friendly— pointing out the shortcomings of the citizenship of the other town and the progressiveness of their own. This spirit was transmitted to other business organizations, and each sought to win the trade territory of the other. "County seat wars" have resulted in the abandonment of more than one town on the southern plains, and in a few instances the centers of towns have been moved several miles through successful manipulations of cliques, parties, or land owners—as in the case of Amarillo, Texas, and Denver, Colorado.

IV

After 1875, the growth in population of the southern plains was quite rapid. In 1873, the Superintendent of the Texas Bureau of Immigration reported that 125,000 homeseekers had come into the state in that year—75,000 by land, and 50,000 by way of the Gulf of Mexico. Two years later, he reported the annual number increased to 300,000; and by 1877, it was estimated that the rising tide had reached 400,000. These settlers added greatly to the population of the state. In 1850, it had little better than 200,000; in 1860, it had increased to 604,215; and by 1880 it had risen to 1,591,749. The new population included representatives of almost all parts of the Union, and several of the nations of Europe.

The development of the country was well publicized in the newspapers. Since cities like Austin, Denison, and Dallas held important positions in relation to the unoccupied lands of the state, it is interesting to notice the kind of articles which appeared daily. On March 27, 1873, the Denison *News* stated that there was "a perfect rush for Texas from the north, east, west, and south"; and its issue of May 15, 1874, reported that 50,000 Alabamans had recently settled in the northern part of the state. The Dallas weekly *Herald* of January 3, 1874, called attention to the fact that "frontier counties are filling up"; on October 17, it stated that a Mr. William Van Dyke, Esquire, was in that vicinity to purchase 30,000 acres of land upon which he proposed to settle a colony of Hollanders; on November 14, it reported a Mr. Richard Couch of Pana, Illinois, in town with an excursion party of fifty-six home-seekers from the North; and on December 22, 1877, it announced the arrival of a representative from New York and New Jersey with a colony of one hundred and twenty-five families wishing to purchase 80,000 acres of land. The Austin *Tri-Weekly Statesman* was equally enthusiastic and as early as December 14, 1872, pro-claimed that "thousands of immigrants were pouring into the state."

In Kansas and Colorado the same kind of news was pouring from the press. The Denver *Rocky Mountain News* and the Topeka *Commonwealth* gave column after column to stories of the arrival of settlers; and as early as the seventies the Santa Fe *Daily New Mexican* was also joining in the gladsome chorus, although the Territory had no great accessions during this early period. The population of Kansas in 1875 was 528,349; after five years it rose to 996,096; in another five years to 1,268,562; and in 1890 to 1,423,585. When its government lands were occupied, the overflow spread to the eastern plains of Colorado, and constituted one of the urgent reasons for opening the unassigned lands in Oklahoma in 1889.

The southern plains frontier was a crucible in which its citizen-ship was refined. Thousands of immigrants who could not stand the test soon returned to the country from whence they came. They found that they had not come to a land of "milk and honey"; that to stay required arduous toil, resourcefulness, and the solution of economic problems not encountered in their old environments. It was no uncommon thing to find immigrant wagons, which had hastened westward during a good year, slowly moving eastward at the end of a drouth year. "Back to God's Country" was some-times crudely scrawled on the bellying wagon covers, and many of the returning homesteaders in their disappointment, ardently sub-scribed to its sentiment. Often about their campfires, at the close of a hard day's journey, they would contrast their life in an arid country with that which they had formerly known in their old homes; and in anticipation they would wax enthusiastic as they spoke of bubbling springs, stone-curbed wells and moss-covered buckets, green fields, spacious lawns, and wide-spreading trees providing comfortable shade.

There were other immigrants who learned that they really had come to a "land of milk and honey," providing—as a writer of the period put it—they brought along with them "good milch cows and bees." Stout physiques and hopeful courage, softened with the attributes of optimism and neighborliness, were necessary for success in the new land. These settlers found that sometimes the country would promise little and give much, and again would promise much and give little. After years of experience, therefore, they came to depend, to some degree, on averages. When their crops were poor they looked toward a better year, and when they were good they held in reserve a surplus to tide them over the lean years. Since land was cheaper on the southern plains than it was east of the Mississippi River, and more arable on account of scarcity of weeds and grass; and since western farms did not have to be fertilized, the settler found that he could have occasional drouths, scourges of grasshoppers, and other handicaps, and still do as well as he did in his old environment. And he discovered that cheerfulness was a far more effective weapon than discouragement in combating occasional adversities.

When the immigrant had learned these truths, he had been changed into a plainsman—a type not superior but distinctive. The southern plains was not the "land of milk and honey" sought by the dreamy-eyed wanderer. But willing workers and men of faith remained and those who did not care to pay the price moved on to other regions.

3

SHIPS OF THE PLAINS

I

FOR more than three centuries following the eventful voyage of Christopher Columbus in 1492 the world was in the throes of a "commercial revolution." In no prior age could nations boast of such bold and resourceful sailors as now voyaged on the high seas. The ships of Spain, Portugal, England, and France penetrated to every clime. There were one-masted vessels and three-masted vessels; single-decked ships and three-decked ships; sloops, caravels, barks, clippers, and galleons—engaged in transporting the commodities of Europe to every land. The period was one of adventure and romance, of courage and hardship. Nations struggled with each other for trade concessions and spheres of influence; and the spirit of their trade wars was transmitted to their mariners, who vied with one another in deeds of daring, determined achievement, and seamanship.

On the wind-swept expanse of the southern plains during the first half of the nineteenth century were many circumstances to remind one of the sea. Anglo-American travelers of the time frequently noted the resemblances. In the early spring of the year the plains were covered with tall billowing grass, bending in the wind; and like the mariner, the prairie traveler could watch the sweep of the wind for a great distance under the blue dome of the sky. Above this billowing mass of green the prairie hawk would float on the balmy air, darting down at intervals after its prey, like the sea gull. Here and there were green copses, like islands, offering a haven of rest.

When the forces of civilization had finally made their appearance in the West, the cumbersome covered wagon or "prairie schooner" plowed the prairie like a ship of the plains. In the distance, topping the swell of the prairie with its canvas cover bellying and flapping in the wind, the wagon looked like a sailing vessel. Shortly after the

〚 31 〛

Civil War, when the wagon was still the most common means of transportation in the West, an observer wrote of seeing "its white top, now and then, far ahead for a while, and presently far behind, diminishing to a speck, and finally no longer distinguishable from the little piles of bones which dot the distance." Another traveler of the time in an account of stirring scenes on the southern plains, pictured the freight wagons in similar terms: "These latter are of immense size, and from the circumstance are sometimes called "prairie schooners"; and, in truth, when a train of them is winding its way over the plains, the white covers flecking its surface like sails, the sight is not unlike a fleet coming into port."[1] When captains of caravans chanced to meet on the plains, it was not uncommon for them "to greet one another and exchange news, like captains of ships hailing at sea."

Plains caravan traffic during the pioneering period was of huge proportions. Thousands of people crossed the plains annually. A visitor to the West in 1860 estimated that 20,000 freight wagons were in use at that time, requiring approximately 100,000 oxen and 40,000 mules. From the early years of the Santa Fe trade, the southern plains were the center of the caravan and freighting trade of the entire West. Figures from the books of freighting firms in Atchison, Kansas, indicate that in 1865 this place was the principal point on the Missouri River from which freight was forwarded to the West, including Colorado, Utah, and Montana. At this place 4,480 wagons were loaded, drawn by 4,310 mules and 29,720 oxen. To control and drive these trains an army of 5,610 men was employed. The freight transported amounted to 27,000 tons. Assuming that the traffic was as great in the remaining areas of the southern plains—and there is every reason to believe that it was greater— the added amount of shipping from other points in Texas, New Mexico, and Colorado would more than double these figures. In the years which followed the close of the Civil War, as might naturally be supposed, this traffic was greatly augmented; and by 1875 it had increased more than one hundred per cent.

There are numerous examples of individual enterprises during the days of caravan traffic which reveal the astonishing proportions of prairie transportation. When John Butterfield and his associates

1. The first quotation is from A. C. Wheeler's *The Iron Trail*, p. 20; and the second from W. E. Webb, *Buffalo Land*, p. 143.

put into operation the Overland Mail line in 1858, they used more than one thousand freight wagons to haul supplies to the numerous stations along the trail. In the same year the firm of Russell, Majors and Waddell was given a government contract to supply General Albert Sidney Johnston's army operating against Mormons of Utah. Supplies were hauled a distance of one thousand miles from western Kansas to the war zone. To move more than 16,000,-000 pounds of supplies the firm used 3,500 wagons, 40,000 oxen, and over 4,000 men. When the Union Pacific railway was under construction toward the West, General Nelson A. Miles stated that 25,000 workmen and 6,000 teams were ceaselessly at work on the road, and that 600 tons of freight were daily forwarded from either end of the track.

During these days of transition, many towns of the southern plains served as "ports of entry and debarkation" for the prairie schooners. Chief among these termini were Abilene, Dodge City, Denver, Las Animas, Albuquerque, Santa Fe, Dallas, Fort Worth, and San Antonio. Their streets were generally crowded with great wagons, ready to take on cargoes for distant points or piled high with goods to be unloaded; and the medley of noises produced by the groaning and creaking of the vehicles, the raucous voices of swearing teamsters, the braying of mules, and the bellowing of cattle, approached in annoyance the din and confusion of a modern city when traffic is heaviest.

Wagons were first used in the Santa Fe trade by William Becknell about 1822 "four years before Ashley took his wheeled cannon to the Salt Lake valley, ..." according to Hiram Chittenden. In a table included by Josiah Gregg in his *Commerce of the Prairies*, wagons are shown not to have been used until 1824, at which time twenty-four vehicles were listed, although it is quite probable that the writer overlooked three wagons which Becknell used on his second trip. In the period from 1824 to 1843, Gregg lists a grand total of 1558 wagons which hauled 2,895,000 pounds of freight over this famous trail.[2]

II

The caravan traffic at the height of the Santa Fe trade exhibits

2. R. G. Thwaites, *Early Western Travels*, XX, 222.

the "ships of the plains" in what was probably their most colorful phase. The Missouri points of departure were Franklin and Independence; and the route of travel ran thence via Council Grove to the Great Bend of the Arkansas River. From this point it followed along the north bank of the river for about fifty miles, then crossed to the south bank near where Dodge City was later established, and thence in a southwesterly direction across the Cimarron "desert" to Las Vegas, and on to Santa Fe. Those who did not wish to cross the arid wastes of the Cimarron country had the choice of traveling up the Arkansas to Bent's Fort, and thence via Trinidad and Las Vegas to Santa Fe. Both of these routes were frequented by the caravans; and many a story of hardships, Indian attacks, and arduous toil is encountered in the narratives of the traders.

The organization and daily routine of a caravan were as interesting as anything of the sort in the records of sea adventure. The usual starting place was Council Grove, since dangers of Indian attack east of that point were inconsiderable. Here, R. L. Duffus says, "the company would elect a captain, a first lieutenant, a second lieutenant, a clerk, a pilot, a court of three members, a commander of the guard and perhaps a chaplain."[3]

A train of twenty-five or twenty-six large "Murphy wagons" constituted a caravan of respectable size. Each wagon would ordinarily carry from three to three and one half tons of freight, protected from rain and snow by three sheets of thin ducking, and was pulled by six pairs of oxen with from twenty to thirty spare animals driven along behind. The average distance traveled was from twelve to fifteen miles a day for loaded wagons and twenty miles for empty wagons. In traveling toward the west captains were very careful in choosing camping sites, taking into consideration defensive needs in case of Indian attack, grass for the animals, and water for both man and beast. When the caravan stopped for the night, an oblong corral was formed by turning out the tongue of each wagon, and chaining the fore-wheel of each to the rear wheel of the one immediately in front. In this manner the animals could be penned for the night without fear of a stampede, and an adequate defense could be had in the event of a night attack by the Indians.

After 1830, oxen were used extensively in prairie traffic. Handling

3. R. L. Duffus, *The Santa Fe Trail*, 135-36.

the trains and keeping them moving required considerable skill on the part of wagonmasters, or "bullwhackers." On this point Alexander Majors, a celebrated plains freighter, writes:

> However, the distance traveled depended much upon the skill of the wagonmasters who had them in charge. For if the master was not skilled in handling the animals and men, they could not make anything like good headway and success. To make everything work expeditiously, thorough discipline was required, each man performing his duty and being in the place assigned him without confusion or delay. I remember once of timing my teamsters when they commenced to yoke their teams after the cattle had been driven into their corral and allowed to stand long enough to become quiet. I gave the word to the men to commence yoking, and held my watch in my hand while they did so, and in sixteen minutes from the time they commenced, each man had yoked six pairs of oxen and had them hitched to their wagons ready to move. I state this that the reader may see how quickly the men who are thoroughly disciplined could be ready to "pop the whip" and move out, when unskilled men were often more than an hour doing the same work. The discipline and rules by which my trains were governed were perfect, and as quick as the men learned each one his place and duty, it became a very pleasant and easy thing for him to do. Good moral conduct was required of them, and no offense from man to man was allowed, thus keeping them good-natured and working together harmoniously. They were formed into what they called "messes," there being from six to eight men in a mess, each mess selecting the man best fitted to serve as cook, and the others carrying the water, fuel, and standing guard, so that the cook's sole business when in camp was to get his utensils ready and cook the meals.[4]

When a caravan was extended across the plains, on its way to or from Santa Fe, it presented an interesting spectacle. Sometimes, because of the rough country over which it was forced to travel, it would move in a long sinuous line; and again in crossing a broad level prairie, it would often proceed in four parallel columns, the perspiring teamsters walking beside their teams, and the captain and his under-officers riding in advance and alongside of the slowly-moving wagons. Often the entire caravan would be enveloped in a

4. Alexander Majors, *Seventy Years on the Frontier*, 103-4.

cloud of dust. In 1846, George F. Ruxton, a member of the Royal Geographical Society of England, made a trip through the northern states of Mexico, and parts of our own Southwest. When he arrived at Valverde, New Mexico, he found encamped a caravan of Missourians, whom he describes as follows:

> The traders had been lying here many weeks, and the bottom where they were encamped presented quite a picturesque appearance. The timber extends half a mile from the river, and the cotton-wood trees are of a large size, without any undergrowth of bushes. Amongst the trees, in open spaces, were drawn up the waggons, formed into a corral or square, and close together, so that the whole made a most formidable fort, and, when filled with some hundred rifles, could defy the attacks of Indians or Mexicans. Scattered about were the tents and shanties of logs and branches of every conceivable form, round which lounged wild-looking Missourians, some cooking at the camp-fires, some cleaning their rifles or firing at targets—blazes cut in the trees, with a bull's-eye made with wet powder on the white bark. From morning till night the camp resounded with the popping rifles, firing at marks for prizes of tobacco, or at any living creature which presented itself. The oxen, horses, and mules were sent out at daylight to pasture on the grass of the prairie, and at sunset made their appearance, driven in by the Mexican herders, and were secured for the night in the corrals.
>
> . . . .The traders, mostly young men from the eastern cities, were fine hearty fellows, who employ their capital in this trade because it combines pleasure with profit, and the excitement and danger of the journey through the Indian country are more agreeable than the monotonous life of a city merchant.[5]

III

Although each caravan had its captain, the most characteristic figure of prairie freighting days was the "bullwhacker." He could not claim any particular nationality; there were Missourians, wanderers from other parts of the United States, Mexicans (sometimes called "Greasers"), Irishmen, Germans, and sons of old France and Spain—all making up a motley array of personalities and colorful attire. The Missourian was often dressed in his buck-

5. George F. Ruxton, *Adventures in Mexico and the Rocky Mountains*, 174-75.

skin suit and coonskin cap; the Mexican wore his tight-fitting trousers, *sarape*, and *sombrero*; the recently arrived Irishman and German were dressed in old-country style; and the city-bred merchant clothed himself in a fustian frock "with a multitude of pockets capable of accommodating a variety of extra tackling." Indeed they possessed only two characteristics in common: the average teamster could use his whip expertly, and under adverse circumstances, he could swear as luridly as the mariner. Concerning this propensity of a Missouri "bullwhacker," Ruxton wrote: "We broke camp at daybreak, leaving our friend wo-ha-ing his cattle through the sandy bottom, and 'cussing the darned country' at every step."[6] Twenty years after Ruxton made this statement, another observer contributed to *Harper's New Monthly Magazine* the following description of the teamster: "Usually he is a well-built man, bronzed by constant exposure to the weather, his hirsute and unclean appearance indicating a cat-like aversion to water. He is more profane than the mate of a Mississippi River packet, and, we have his word for it, 'ken drink more whiskey.' Accompanying this assertion were seven of the most astounding oaths that ever fell on an ear used to the strong language with which the army teamster encourages his mules."

Although the handle of the ordinary whip of the "bullwhacker" was seldom more than three feet in length, the lash, of braided rawhide, was seldom less than twenty. From the handle, which was sometimes ten inches in circumference, the whip gradually tapered toward the end until it formed a ribbon-shaped thong. With this "persuader" the teamster could cause a lazy sleepy-eyed ox to awaken from his bovine reverie, and display amazing energy. The accuracy with which the "bullwhacker" could throw his lash was astonishing. It was reported that a favorite pastime was the cutting of a coin from the top of a stake thrust loosely into the ground, the teamster winning only if he knocked the coin from its position without disturbing the stake. A traveler in the southern plains country in the late sixties reported the following amusing incident:

A Bullwhacker noted for the accuracy with which he threw his lash, bet a comrade a pint of whiskey he could cut the seat of his pantaloons without cutting the skin beneath. The bet was

6. *Ibid.*, p. 188.

accepted. The blow was delivered at the stooping form of the acceptor of the wager, who is said to have executed the tallest jump on record, at the sight of which the thrower of the lash remarked, "Thunder I've lost the whiskey." The other party was minus a strip of skin as well as a large fragment of breeches.[7]

The teamster was of necessity a resourceful man. Often he was confronted with problems of an unusual character, the solution of which required skill, quick decision, and good judgment. When the sudden blizzard of winter, the subtle attack of Indians, a broken-down waggon, or the crossing of a swollen stream required attention, the "bullwhacker" must be ready for the emergency. J. Wright Mooar tells how a Kansas caravan extricated itself from a blizzard. The freighters were traveling over the government road from Dodge City to Camp Supply, when suddenly the cold wind swooped down upon them and soon covered both men and teams with snow and ice.

. . . .The Government road along here for miles was a wide and deeply beaten trench from one to two feet deep. The howling gale drove the snow across this, banking it on the other side, and leaving a plain trail for the teams to follow, but at length we came to the mouth of the Creek Valley (Mulberry Creek) as it debouched into the wide valley of the Arkansas, and the trail shallowed, and was soon apparently lost.

Another council was held, and it was agreed to stick together and try to reach John Hunt's ranch at a point on the trail. Here a saloon, store, and ranch houses would afford shelter that was rapidly becoming a necessity if we were to survive. Ice formed on our beards, eyebrows, and eyelashes until we could scarcely see our way.

At last the lead team, driven by Levi Richardson, stopped, bringing the whole cavalcade to a halt. Staggering back through the howling gale to the other drivers, he announced that one of his mules was frozen to death. John Mooar saw that Richardson was completely blinded by the ice that had formed on his beard and eyelashes. Cupping his hands around his own mouth and over Richardson's eyes, he blew his warm breath on the matted ice until he could brush it away and Richardson could see.[8]

The caravan thus battled through the swirling snow and ice until

7. *Harper's New Monthly Magazine*, July, 1867, p. 138 *et sqq.*
8. James Winford Hunt, "Buffalo Days," in *Holland's Magazine*, February, 1933, p. 10.

it at last arrived safely at a ranch house where the frozen men found food and a warm fire, and the teams a shelter.

Yet not all the experiences of the freighters were of the humdrum and arduous kind. Sometimes, after they had established themselves in their camp for the evening, they gave themselves up to story telling, games, or dancing. Such an occasion is thus described by a notable English visitor to the southern plains during these early days:

About a hundred yards from the wagons, the goods of these Mexicans and Pueblo-Indians were lying scattered about in a semi-circle; the moon shone brightly down on the vast plain; all was still, except that there now and then came from afar the howl of a prairie wolf, faintly heard in our camp, where men of various races were sauntering negligently about. The beauty of the night seemed somehow to awaken the music in the soul of an American waggoner of our party; and having found himself the highest and most convenient place he could on the top of the luggage, he brought out an old cracked fiddle, which he had laboriously conveyed from his distant home, and began to draw from it some extraordinary sounds. The shrill notes, however, no sooner reached the ears of the company, than a crowd gathered round the amateur, who proud of the sensation he was producing, worked away more and more vigorously upon the dusty jingling strings, negro melodies alternating with "Hail Columbia!" and "Yankee Doodle." Those were tunes which found their way straight to every man's heart.

Logs of wood were flung on the fire to make a fresh blaze, and bearded Americans, yellow descendants of Spain, and half-naked Pueblos, all armed from head to foot, and in attire that bore the marks of long and painful travel, began to foot it as if possessed.

Here two long Americans seized each other, and jumped and whirled round together in mad circles; there a Mexican was seen waltzing with an Indian; on one side were two Kentucky men performing an energetic jig, and a little way off two Irishmen, in the uniform of the United States infantry, were working energetically at a national dance, and shouting "Ould Ireland for ever!" and "Oh if we had but plenty of whiskey!"

Even the sentinel leaning on his musket grew sentimental and musical, and murmured to himself,

"J'aime à revoir ma Normandie"

while the musician, from his lofty throne, looked calmly down on the commotion, and fiddled away unweariedly, triumphantly remarking, that all the dances in the world might be danced in time to his tunes; and the songs of every nation on the earth carried on amicably together. He played through half the night, till a thick cloud of dust hid his face and his violin, and the exhausted dancers sank down beside their luggage, or betook themselves to their rest, to try to gather, from a few hours' sleep, strength and spirits for the march of the following day.[9]

In the varied experiences of the prairie traveler the spring and summer months were as formidable as the winter months. When the streams were filled with the flood waters of spring, it was difficult for a caravan to cross them. To plunge into the swift, turbid stream required a great deal of courage and determination. On such occasions oxen were herded into the water and forced to swim to the opposite bank, directed by two men riding horses on either side, or a single rider leading the way. In order that the wagons might float, water kegs would be tied underneath and used for pontoons, and carefully each vehicle was thus ferried across. Such attempts to cross swollen streams were not without danger. In relating his experiences in prairie travel on General S. W. Kearny's New Mexico expedition, which were not unlike those of other plainsmen during that period, Lieutenant J. W. Abert described one such instance which ended fatally. "During the afternoon a man by the name of Hughes was drowned in attempting to cross the stream; there were two men with him at the time, but the current was so violent that it soon swept him out of reach."

Physical ailments also tended to discourage plains freighting. Scourges of smallpox, cholera, and dysentery were common in the camps of the teamsters. Against such enemies the "bullwhackers" were at a great disadvantage. They sometimes carried with them simple remedies such as liquor, quinine, and calomel, yet in the event of serious illness they were exposed to contagion and death. In speaking of an epidemic of dysentery which broke out in Kearny's army, Abert wrote that "First one then another of the party became ill, and several were seized with a severe vomiting." When he, too, became a victim of the dreaded scourge, he thus described his situation:

9. W. F. Ainsworth (ed.), *All Round the World*, 611-12.

Tuesday, July 21st.—This morning we presented quite a sorry looking array of human faces. At day-break I was seized with a vomiting, which lasted for some time; I was obliged to send for the doctor. I however determined to push forward, in compliance with the order of Lieutenant Emory, who was with General Kearny, and committed myself to the waggoner's care, while Lieutenant Peck took command of the camp. Lying here, my eye roved over but a confined prospect; under me were bundles of bedding, with blankets, red, blue, and white; near me a sick man languidly gazing upward; above me, the bended bows of the wagon that supported a large white cover, through which the sun beat with intense heat. . . .[10]

When the "ships of the plains" arrived in Santa Fe, the "bull-whacker" sought to forget all his experiences on the road. Although the town was little more than a collection of mud-dried huts grouped about a dusty square, here the weary traveler could find rest, food, drink, and entertainment. When once he had shifted the burden of responsibility for his goods to the shoulders of the Mexican customs officials, he gave himself up to drinking, card playing, and dancing; or he sauntered about among the hucksters, market-going women and children, and wood sellers thronging the plaza. After briefly enjoying the benefits of the white man's civilization, the trader turned his attention to the serious business of barter and satisfying the customs officials. When he began to be charged the blanket tax of $500 he realized more profit by changing to a larger type of wagon, or trekking on southward to the distant Mexican city of Chihuahua, where customs officials were more liberally disposed, or where he could find a fairer profit. In the end, however, when the time came for him to turn his face towards Missouri once more, he was generally eager to start on his return journey.

IV

After the pioneering days of the Santa Fe traders, the "ships of the plains" were the chief conveyance for immigrants. Although these caravans were usually smaller, they were far more numerous

10. W. H. Emory, *Notes of a Military Reconnoissance, from Fort Leavenworth, in Missouri, to San Diego, in California, Including Parts of the Arkansas, Del Norte, and Gila Rivers,* in *Senate Executive Document,* Thirtieth Congress, first session, No. 7, p. 404.

than those employed in the freighting business. Sometimes they were the only homes of the plains travelers who migrated here and there in search of a bonanza. Every well-known highway was crowded with them. In 1865, the white covered emigrant trains, moving along the south bank of the Platte River, together with immense freight caravans, traveled in a long unbroken line. As far as the eye could see, to the east and to the west, they rolled along, with their iron-tired wheels groaning and clucking on their greased axles, piled high with a great assortment of mining tools, machinery, agricultural implements, and other articles. Frequently wagons carried, in addition to their normal loads, whimpering, tousled children and tired, scolding mothers, as well as grandfathers and grandmothers who were too feeble to walk. Where the load was too heavy, it was not uncommon for the husband, together with all able bodied members of the family, to trudge along beside the laboring teams, enveloped in clouds of dust. At times a herd of cattle, sheep, or goats would follow the wagon, driven by a mounted youth who was equipped with a rawhide whip or a lash improvised from a willow bough or other timber growing scantily along the prairie streams. If one of his charges sought to stray from the line of march, he drove it back to the main herd with lusty shouts and the flourishing of his whip. Yet the travelers were not always morose and depressed; the flower-splashed landscapes of spring, the sunburned meadows and hills of summer and fall, were a never failing source of pleasure. The strange quietude of the great open spaces, the scurrying wild birds and animals, and the ever changing panorama unfolding before their advance, acted as a powerful elixir of youth and adventure which lifted them from the drab toil of the open road.

The California roads crossing the southern plains area or the numerous immigrant trails of the country were crowded with the great lumbering wagons of the "movers." Because of deprivations, hardships, and weary travel, each of these early roads was "a trail of tears." The marked and unmarked graves of men, women, and children, and occasionally the bleaching bones of those who had met with violent deaths, were grim reminders of the dangers which lurked beside the way. But even for the "movers" all was not toil and sorrow. Occasionally they found a camping site near a clear-running stream and by the flickering light of their campfire, they would eat their simple fare of cornbread, fat bacon, and potatoes, and forget their toilsome experiences of the day. When time came to retire for the night, they would seek their pallets of blankets and quilts, and gaze into the star-spangled heavens until sleep claimed their weary bodies.

Long after the coming of railways and the disappearance of the stage coach, these "ghosts of former days"were sometimes seen making their way toward the west or east, their restless drivers peering from beneath the covers of the wagons, seemingly searching for that which they never found. Indeed, the "ships of the plains" have played a major role in every stage of frontier development; even in the days of railways, hard-surfaced roads, and automobiles they still provide the farmers with a means of transportation for his farm products and at moving time. They were not so elegant and comfortable as the stage coach, which next claims our attention, but unquestionably they served the country well.

4

STAGECOACH DAYS

I

FROM the foregoing account of the "prairie schooner" it is evident that the clumsy wagon was better suited to transportation than to travel. On the raw frontier it met the demands for heavy freighting and the moving of immigrants and their household effects. But the stagecoach was to furnish a more expedited service for government mail and passenger travel. Indeed, when the stagecoach came in, so considerable were demands for rapid transit to and across the southern plains that it was not uncommon for travelers to find no riding space in coaches for days at a time. Shortly after the Civil War, a Texas traveler was unable to secure accommodations on a line running from Houston to Austin and complained that "no seats were to be had within less than a week, owing to the pressure of travel towards the capital."

General conditions bringing about this state of affairs were largely premised on a series of western developments beginning with the migration of Mormons to the Salt Lake Basin in 1847 and the discovery of gold in California in the following year. The human tide which poured across the southern plains from this early time until the disappearance of the last American frontier reached astonishing proportions. Agent William Bent of the Kiowas and Comanches wrote to the Commissioner of Indian Affairs in 1858: "I estimate the number of whites traversing the plains across the central belt to have exceeded 60,000 during the present season:" and as late as August 31, 1864, George K. Otis, general superintendent of the Overland Mail Line, wrote to Commissioner of Indian Affairs William P. Dole, that records kept at Fort Laramie since July 9 of that year showed that 19,000 emigrants had passed that place bound westward; and, counting those passing through Cheyenne Pass, "the aggregate amount of this emigration cannot have been less than 50,000 souls."[1] In fact, from 1849 to 1885, every trail and highway leading to or across the plains was crowded with wagons and other vehicles; and hundreds of thousands of people were moving here and there, looking for adventure, gold, and homes, or running from the law.

This ever increasing concourse of people passing across the plains made it imperative that some adequate means of communication and transportation be provided to encourage the development of the western domain. Under an act approved by Congress in 1853, an appropriation of $150,000 was made to be spent in the survey of possible routes for a railway to be built from the Mississippi Valley to the Pacific Coast. Under the direction of the Secretary of War, Jefferson Davis, five surveys were made running from east to west across the Great Plains and the Rocky Mountains, the northernmost paralleling the Canadian boundary and the southernmost running just north of the Mexican boundary. When Davis, a Southerner, recommended the southern route, a political storm broke which was to frustrate completely all efforts to build a railroad at the time. Anti-slave agitators and politicians maintained that the South was seeking a line of projection into the Mexican Cession for its institution of slavery; and Southern alarmists were equally positive that a railway built across the plains farther to the north would materially aid the Free States in settling the western domain. In the end, no road was built during this period, and the West was left to flounder about for a solution of its problem.

When Secretary Davis saw that the construction of a railroad across this region would have to be postponed, he recommended to Congress, on December 1, 1853, the purchase of camels to be used as beasts of burden on the arid trails of the Southwest. In spite of the novelty of the proposal, Congress appropriated the sum of $30,000 for the purpose; and Lieutenant David D. Porter of the navy and Major Henry C. Wayne of the army were dispatched to the Levant to make the purchases. As a result of their trip, some seventy-five camels were imported into Texas and stationed at Camp Verde, not far from San Antonio. For a time it seemed that these peculiar animals were to meet a long-felt need. They could travel for hours without water; they could carry huge burdens; and they could travel much faster over broken country than other

1. *Annual Report of the Commissioner of Indian Affairs for 1859*, pp. 137-39; *ibid.*, 1864, p. 254.

beasts of burden. Yet, by the time of the outbreak of the Civil War, the experiment was abandoned and the animals sold. No good reasons were given by the Secretary of War for taking this step; but in all probability the experiment was regarded as too revolutionary to succeed. Not only did those in charge of the venture find it difficult to convince army officials of the feasibility of using camels, but even residents in the vicinity of the post remained skeptical until the end.

While the camel experiment was under way another unique program was being sponsored by Postmaster-General Aaron V. Brown. Congress had authorized him to provide for a mail service to run from the Mississippi basin to the Pacific Coast. To this end, a contract was awarded John Butterfield and associates[2] to operate a semi-weekly stagecoach mail service between Missouri and California, with the understanding that passengers could also be accommodated. The cities of Memphis and St. Louis were to be the eastern termini of the road; the northernmost terminus was Tipton, Missouri, connected by rail with St. Louis; and the western end of the line was San Francisco, 2795 miles from St. Louis. The two eastern lines were to converge at Little Rock,[3] Arkansas; and thence the route would extend southwestward across the Red River near Preston, along the frontier line of settlements in Texas, and on via El Paso, Fort Yuma, and San Diego, to San Francisco. Along this long semi-circular route were to be nine divisions, ranging from 160 miles to 462 miles in length, under the care of a superintendent, assisted by freighters, drivers, stock tenders, and station keepers.

To make all necessary preliminary preparations and to operate this long stage line was a stupendous undertaking. At some places on the route the contractors must grade the road, and at others provide crossings for streams; while at convenient distances along the way they must erect more than a hundred stations, with appurtenant barns, stables, and corrals. Hundreds of freight wagons, more than a hundred Concord coaches, above two thousand horses, mules, and oxen, and a large number of employees were in constant

2. Others associated with him were G. Fargo, Hamilton Spencer, W. B. Dinsmore, J. V. P. Gardner, Marcus L. Kinyon, and Alexander Holland.

3. The agreement was later so amended that the Memphis and St. Louis branches converged at Fort Smith, Arkansas.

〖 46 〗

service. The original investment of the company must have approximated a million dollars; and other expenditures were made from time to time to keep the line in repair.

The contract signed by Butterfield and his associates called for the beginning of mail service not later than September 26, 1858, but eleven days before the date named a stagecoach moved out from San Francisco towards the east, having as its sole passenger G. Bailey, an inspector of the Post Office Department. The actual traveling time of this coach was twenty-four days, eighteen hours, and thirty-five minutes. President James Buchanan telegraphed the contractor his congratulations, saying that "it is a glorious triumph for civilization and the Union"; and in his report for 1858 Postmaster-General Brown announced that the service was a "conclusive and triumphant success." But this optimism was soon changed to pessimism. At the end of the first year of operation, the government had paid $572,771.06 more than its receipts from the line, and Brown was forced to admit that his experiment had failed.

The vehicle first used by the contractors was a spring wagon built at Concord, New Hampshire, but it was soon supplanted by the Abbott-Downing coach, built at the same place. This was generally regarded as the acme of elegance and comfort in stage travel. The body was slung on stout leather braces to prevent violent jolts on rough roads. In an emergency four passengers could ride on top of the coach with the driver, and nine could be crowded inside. Since passengers must travel both night and day, with only a few minutes of rest at stage stations, it was necessary for them to sleep on the coach. If there were but few passengers, the seats inside could be so arranged as to provide beds, and the weary travelers could take their turn at sleeping; if, however, the coach carried its maximum load, this was hard to do. In the latter case, moreover, those who rode on top of the coach were subjected to the varying fortunes of the weather, those inside being sheltered by leather curtains. Many times, however, an extra load or violent storms would necessitate the carrying of mail pouches inside the coach, and its swaying and rolling over uneven roads, together with the buffeting of the unwieldy bags, made even inside travel unpleasant. But ordinarily both mail and baggage were carried in a leather-covered "boot" projecting from the rear of the coach, and as a precaution against overloading no passenger was allowed more than twenty-five pounds of baggage.

Further inconveniences of stagecoach travel were noted by W. L. Ormsby, a correspondent of the *New York Herald*, who in October, 1858, was sole passenger on a west-bound coach, and as he journeyed from place to place, wrote accounts of his experiences, which he sent to the *Herald* by east-bound coaches. At Phantom Hill, Texas, he wrote of the danger of attack by Indians, whose frequent raids made it difficult for station keepers to retain good horses:

> The station is directly on the trail of the Northern Comanches, as they run down into Texas on their marauding expeditions. To leave this and other stations on the route so exposed is trifling with human life, and inviting an attack on the helpless defenders of the mail. As I have already said, there will be designing white men as well as Indians, whose cupidity must be overawed by adequate military protection. Let but this be afforded, and I predict for the mail route a complete success, as well as a rapid settlement of the many fertile and desirable spots along the line.

On the following morning, at Mountain Pass, some thirty-five miles southwest of Phantom Hill, Ormsby ate breakfast prepared by a buxom negro woman. Not only was he dissatisfied with his cornbread, bacon, and coffee without sugar, but he was not particularly pleased with his hostess. For, as he told his readers, if "cleanliness was next to Godliness, she would have little chance of entering the portals of Heaven." In spite of these objections, he spoke enthusiastically of his trip before an impromptu gathering at San Francisco, and declared that if he had not just traveled over the road he would be glad to return to New York the same way. Instead, however, he took passage to New York on a ship around the Horn—several thousand miles out of his way.

The approach of the Civil War brought to an end operations on the Butterfield Southern Overland Mail. Indeed, its abandonment was foreshadowed by the beginning of the "Pony Express," in April, 1860, fostered by the Central Overland California and Pike's Peak Express Company. This organization advertised that it would inaugurate a twelve-day mail from San Francisco to New York. In order to provide for such an expedited service, a system of

*Upper, a caravan in camp formation, on Holladay Street, between
F and G Streets, Denver, Colorado, Autumn of 1866;
lower, a southern plains stagecoach*

relay pony express riders was introduced. The company employed a large number of sturdy, fast horses, and experienced riders and tenders and constructed numerous relay stations along the way. When once the new service was introduced, it was so much faster than that provided by Butterfield that the southern route soon lost much of its letter-carrying business. Finally, on March 2, 1861, Congress approved an act which authorized the Postmaster-General to discontinue the Butterfield service over the southern route, since a part of it ran through Confederate territory; but, in order that the contractors might not lose their investments entirely, they were to be offered a contract for a six-times-a-week schedule over the central route, which, as later amended, was to begin at Atchison and end at Placerville. After the Civil War the Butterfield Overland route was again used in part by smaller companies, but never again did it enjoy national prominence.

Although the Butterfield line was the longest route operated in the West during this period, it was not the only major project of its kind. In the summer of 1849, a service was put into operation between Independence, Missouri, and Santa Fe. About the same time another line was projected westward to Salt Lake City; and the Mormons also provided for their own needs by organizing the "Great Salt Lake Valley Carrying Company." In each instance, however, relay and supply stations were not constructed along the way; and it was necessary for coaches to travel during the day and stop at night by the roadside to allow teams, drivers, and passengers to sleep and recruit their energies.

II

In 1858 thousands of people started across the southern plains for Denver, Colorado, to seek their fortunes in the newly discovered gold field. In the winter of this year, W. H. Russell (of the freighting firm of Russell, Majors, and Waddell) and John S. Jones sought to persuade Alexander Majors to enter into an agreement with them for the operation of a stage line from the Missouri River to the gold fields. When Majors refused to enter the compact, they decided to proceed without him in their organization. They bought one thousand Kentucky mules and a sufficient number of Concord coaches to begin operations. Since they did not have ready cash, they made their purchases on ninety days credit. When their notes came due, they were unable to pay, and the firm of Russell, Majors, and Waddell took them over.

The new firm reorganized the line, which had been given a charter by the Kansas legislature under the name of the Leavenworth and Pike's Peak Express Company. The starting point was changed from Leavenworth to Atchison and the end of the route was Denver. A daily service was continued and every effort was made to provide for the comfort and welfare of the passengers. Stations were established along the line under the direction of divisional superintendents who had under them the usual employees, including drivers, station keepers, animal tenders, and freighters; and each station was provided with forage for the teams and food for drivers and passengers. By running day and night, the coaches made the trip of 687 miles in six days. The arrival of the first coach on May 17, 1859 was the occasion of a gala celebration by the citizens of Denver.

To expand their interests and to pay expenses, the company also took over the Hockaday and Liggett line. This route was from Atchison to Fort Kearney to Fort Laramie, and thence up the Sweetwater route and South Pass on to Salt Lake City. The added responsibility was not all the new owners could desire. The few stages which were owned by Hockaday and Liggett were light and cheap; there were few teams of either horses or mules; and there were no stations along the way to make possible an immediately expedited service. Indeed, Majors had traveled over the line from Kansas to Salt Lake City in the fall of 1858, and he later complained that the trip consumed twenty-one days, when under the reorganized schedule it was made in ten days. Then still a third contract was awarded by the government to the Russell, Majors and Waddell firm in 1860, who were given the old Chorpenning contract between Salt Lake City and Placerville. The new owners, however, changed the weekly schedule to a semi-weekly service. Thus, by the time of the outbreak of the Civil War, they had been given contracts for handling the government mail over the central route from Kansas to California.

Yet, try as they might, the contractors reaped no profits from their triple organization, and a short time later the firm failed. Ben Holladay, an energetic Missourian, who was its chief creditor, then purchased its equipment at public sale, and re-established the lines on a more substantial basis. After October, 1862, his organization was given a charter by the Colorado legislature as the Overland State line, and Denver was made the center of his extensive interests. His line of stages began at Atchison, on the Missouri River; its first section extended across the plains to Denver, 687 miles; from this point it ran westward another 600 miles to Salt Lake City, passing over the Rocky Mountains at Bridger's Pass. From Salt Lake City to Nevada and California, about 750 miles farther, the stage line was owned by an eastern company, and was under the management of Wells, Fargo and Company, express carriers. From Salt Lake City, Holladay ran a tri-weekly coach line north and west 950 miles through Idaho to the Dalles on the Columbia River in northern Oregon, and branching off at Fort Hall, a tri-weekly line to Virginia City in Montana, 400 miles more. From Denver he ran a subsidiary line to Central City and Nevada.

Over all these routes Holladay carried the mail, for which he was paid $650,000 a year by the federal government. Over his far-flung lines of 2760 miles, he used 6000 horses and mules and 260 coaches. At intervals of ten to fifteen miles he built stations. To administer his extensive interests required an expenditure of considerable sums of money. Corn for his teams was transported from the Missouri River, and hay was hauled hundreds of miles to many remote points. Indian attacks in 1864 alone resulted in an estimated loss of $500,000, in station houses, barns, vehicles, and supplies. Holladay's general superintendent, William Reynolds, who resided at Atchison, was paid a salary of $10,000 a year; divisional superintendents received $2,500; and drivers and stock tenders, $75 a month. In addition it was necessary to keep roads in repair, build bridges, and buy new equipment.

To meet these expenses it was necessary for Holladay to charge heavy fares. From Atchison to Denver, the fare was $175; to Salt Lake City, $350; to Nevada, $500; to California, $500; to Idaho, $500; and to Montana, $500. Samuel Bowles, editor of the Springfield (Massachusetts) *Republican*, who in 1865 traveled over the line in company with Schuyler Colfax, reported that Westerners were complaining of exorbitant prices. Probably the basis of this dissatisfaction was a report, current along the frontier, that Holladay had amassed a fortune of about $5,000,000. Certain it was that he lived in New York City, employed John E. Russell as his confidential secretary and financier at a high salary; and owned in addition to his extensive stage interests Pacific steamship lines from San Francisco north to Oregon and British Columbia, and south to Mazatlan, Mexico, with mail contracts from the American and Mexican governments on both routes.

Twice a year Holladay made an inspection tour of his stage lines. On these trips every effort was made to provide for his speed and comfort. Indeed the fastest time ever made by a stage coach in the West was made over his line between San Francisco and Atchison. This was during the Civil War, following the sinking of his ship the *Golden Gate* off the west coast, carrying with it his partner, Edward Rust Flint. After the disaster, Holladay traveled the distance of 1220 miles in only twelve days and two hours, at an estimated cost to himself of $20,000.

There were probably two reasons why Holladay was successful in his operations, while other contractors met with failure or only moderate success. First, he was reared on the Missouri frontier, and knew well its hardships and handicaps, as well as its opportunities, in stagecoach operations. In this connection he had gained considerable experience as a government contractor during the days of the Mexican War, hauling vast quantities of supplies to Colonel Stephen W. Kearny, and Colonel A. W. Doniphan in New Mexico. After the war he sold to the Mormons large quantities of materials which he had bought from the government at a bargain price. Secondly, with the fortune he had amassed, he was able to buy the best of horses and equipment for the lines under his operation and to make all necessary improvements. Editor Bowles said of Holladay: "I am inclined to reckon him high among the agencies that are so fast developing the great western Territories of the Republic, and to doubt if many others in the community are doing their share in the work more fairly to the public than he is."

III

After 1865 stage operations became extensive on the southern plains. It grew to large proportions until the railways were built across the region, north and south, east and west. Among the successful operators of this time was Ben Ficklin, a former employee of Alexander Majors during freight caravan days. *The Texas Almanac for 1871* advertised three stages operated by him: (1) a tri-weekly service between San Antonio and El Paso over a 650 mile stretch of barren country; (2) a fast forty-eight hour service between Sherman, Texas, and Fort Smith, Arkansas; and (3) a tri-weekly service between San Antonio and Eagle Pass. The following advertisement in the Santa Fe *Daily New Mexican* of August 21, 1872, is an indication that good stage connections were to be found in all parts of the country during this period:

J. F. Bennett and Company's
Southern Overland Mail and Express Line
of First Class Concord Coaches between
Santa Fe, New Mexico, El Paso, Texas, and
Tucson, Arizona,
Makes uninterrupted connections with
coaches for
Denver, and Kit Carson, Colorado, Texas,
the City of Chihuahua, Mexico and all
points in California.

In these days of extensive stage coaching the names of John Butterfield, G. Fargo, Alexander Majors, Ben Holladay, and Ben Ficklin loom large in the annals of the southern plains. As a rule they were men of vision, strong determination, and heroic achievement. To their employees they were generous and kindly disposed; and to their friends and patrons they were courteous and accommodating. They had enough faith in the development of the country to invest their means as well as their lives in their professions; and they carried into their arduous work a spirit of adventure which buoyed them up above the many trying experiences of the road.

No less meritorious were the services performed by the stage drivers who were daily on the road. Of necessity, the best driver was he who could handle horses efficiently; who was thoroughly acquainted with the country over which he drove this stage; who was willing to remain in his seat for long hours of wearisome travel, sometimes battling manfully with wild mules or prancing horses; who had nerves of steel and was not afraid of Indians or road agents; and who generally sought to run his stage on time. The death toll among them from the attacks of red and white thieves was heavy. Particularly was this true in the period before the Civil War. In 1856, Frederick Law Olmsted visited the Texas part of the southern plains frontier. In his account of his interesting experiences, he points out the many hazards of stage travel, especially as they related to the driver. When he arrived at Fort Duncan he found a mail train on its way from San Antonio to El Paso and Santa Fe. The train consisted of two heavy wagons and a hack for passengers, who were carried to El Paso, a distance of seven hundred miles, for one hundred dollars. The contractors advertised that "Passengers are allowed forty pounds of baggage, and not required to stand guard" when the stage stopped by the roadside at night. Each vehicle was drawn by four mules, with one spare mule led behind each wagon. As to the routine and the hazards of travel, he wrote:

> The train is attended by a mounted guard of six men, armed with Sharp's rifles and Colt's repeaters. Their pay is forty dollars a month. A man is lost on nearly every trip out and back, but usually through his own indiscretion. After passing Fort Inge, there is no change of team for more than five hundred miles. The train usually camps from ten o'clock at night till four in the morning. At eight o'clock, a stop of an hour or more is made, to graze the mules, and for breakfast. Another halt is made between three o'clock and sunset. The average distance accomplished in a day is over fifty miles. No government officer or functionary goes with the mail. The commander was an old Texan ranger captain, and the guard, we understood, was composed of old rangers. They had, however, so much the appearance of drunken ruffians, that we felt no disposition to join the party.[4]

Often Indians or white outlaws killed both the driver and passengers. About the same time that Olmsted made his trip across the lower part of the southern plains, Alexander Majors traveled over the Santa Fe Trail from Missouri to New Mexico. When he arrived at Wagon Mound, beyond the borders of New Mexico, he came upon the ruins of a burned stage coach. Near the charred débris, he found the bones of the horses, as well as the skeletons of ten men who had been murdered by Indians. He lamented that "not one escaped to tell the story, and they were, I think, a party of ten

4. Frederick Law Olmsted, *A Journey Through Texas*, 286-87.

as brave men as could be found anywhere."[5] Records kept by army officers stationed at frontier forts are replete with accounts of this kind. Dramatically, in terse sentences, they portray the cool heroism of stage drivers. Shortly after the Civil War, according to the record of an officer stationed at Fort Concho, Ficklin's stagecoach was attacked near Johnson's Station by a band of Indians, and the driver made his escape by jumping into a cluster of prickly pears by the roadside, although his mules were taken, and the coach and mail destroyed.[6]

Flooded streams, severe blizzards, and snow-covered roads delayed but did not daunt experienced drivers. Knowing how much depended on unfailing service, the seasoned driver seemed to be obsessed with the idea of operating his stage on schedule. If his stage overturned—as often occurred— he would call on passengers to help in righting it again; if unruly teams ran away with the coach and damaged it he sought to mend the broken parts from available materials. Whatever the exigency, the driver was generally equal to it, and performed his tasks well. The hardihood of a Texas driver—as well as his humor—on the occasion of a runaway, is thus described by a passenger:

. . . . Upon reaching the scene of the disaster, I found the Yankee trader badly frightened but uninjured; the doctor somewhat painfully bruised; the driver knocked senseless; and Johnson sitting on the ground bewailing his ruined rifle, which was smashed beyond redemption. The most serious case seemed to be that of the driver. He was apparently very badly injured. Upon examination we could find no wound. The injury was, doubtless, internal. The poor fellow breathed heavily, occasionally gasping as if for air. Badly as the doctor was bruised, he forgot his own injuries, and manifested the greatest concern about the unfortunate driver. "Gentlemen," he said, "I'll have to bleed him, or he'll die," and forthwith he pulled out his lancet,

5. Alexander Majors, *Seventy Years on the Frontier*, p. 138. Stage travel in New Mexico during this period was unusually hazardous. A passenger on a Concord coach plying between Santa Fe and Fort Bliss in 1867 wrote that "two or three mails have been destroyed by the Indians." As to his own misgivings, he said: "I frequently passed through some of the deep canyons especially in the night with fear and trembling and with a revolver in each hand, for I was the only passenger and robbers are exceedingly numerous and bold and between them and the Indians a man stands a good many chances of being overhauled in going the 330 miles between here and Santa Fe." O. M. Knapp to his mother, Fort Bliss, March 16, 1867, MS, in O. M. Knapp papers, Archives, Library, University of Texas.

6. *Medical History of Fort Concho*, MSS, CCV, 269, in Old Records Division, Adjutant General's Office, War Department.

and began to bare the man's arm. "Doctor," whispered the driver in a faint voice, and slowly opening his eyes, "don't bleed me. I'll be alright presently. Give me a—little—pull at the brandy. It's only a kind of fainting spell—brandy always sets me right." Of course the medicine was administered. The effect was miraculous. Colonel Wash got up, shook himself, gave a yell to test the strength and purity of his voice, and set to work like a man to clear the wreck and get the horses on their feet.[7]

IV

The arrival of the stage meant much in the life of a frontier community, as it was not uncommon for an isolated town to be without news from the outside world for weeks at a time. To the inhabitants the coach brought letters from distant loved ones, news of daily happenings over the nation, and information about conditions along the frontier. Of an outpost town of this kind, the chronicler of Fort Concho, in 1873, wrote:

We have been without mail during the last three or four weeks, and but little hope is entertained of getting in possession of it for some time to come; all the animals of the different stage routes are affected and sick from the Epizoutic and therefore unable to travel, which causes great disturbance in business circles.—This is rather disagreeable to everybody, as the arrival of the United States Mail forms part of the little excitement on this isolated post and the mail is always eagerly expected.[8]

The foregoing discussion of the stagecoach is not intended to leave the impression that elegance, ease, and rapid transit were provided generally by stagecoach companies operating in the West. Service of this type was the exception rather than the rule. Only a few companies furnished high grade transportation. One of these was the Ficklin line, operating between Sherman, Texas, and Fort Smith, Arkansas, which advertised Concord coaches, four-horse teams, and rapid travel. In times of desperate need operators were known to use wild horses and mules. Harnessing these animals was a difficult task. After they had been roped, cuffed, and beaten, they could then be held in line and harnessed to the coach, until

7. The *Overland Monthly*, July, 1868, pp. 160-61.
8. *Medical History of Fort Concho*, MSS, CCVI, 81, *loc. cit.*

the driver gathered up his reins, and the passengers were in their places. Then, the driver would shout, "Go!" and the tenders would release their holds. And "Go!" they would, often upsetting the coach and maiming the occupants, or so buffeting them about as to cause them to leap from the careening vehicle.

On some lines coaches were used far beyond their natural lifetime. These were frowsy, dingy, and ill-conditioned, with something of the "dreariness of premature decay superadded." They had the average number of decrepit springs below, squeaking and protesting, and the customary number of leathern straps above, swaying and beckoning in a spectral fashion amid the half-light of the dim interior, as the coaches bumped, jounced, and jolted on their way. Racks for packages, over the windows, would sometimes unceremoniously empty their contents on the heads of the passengers, who were too busy holding on desperately to a wildly swaying coach to ward off the attack.

When continued rains filled streams with a swirling flood of turbid water, and depressions in the road were converted into quagmires, it was not uncommon for the stagecoach to discharge its passengers from their seats at regular intervals, to plod and flounder onward beside the laboring conveyance—a wretched crew of grumbling pedestrians, on whose feet mud accumulated in great balls. On a trip over the Butterfield line, when the roads were slippery and filled with mud and water, a passenger complained that his coach capsized three times in a distance of only a few miles. Again and again both drivers and passengers were forced to camp beside a raging torrent until the waters would subside, and generally without camp equipment to make their forced stay a pleasant one.

When all such inconveniences, however, are balanced against the merits of stage travel, the fact remains that this kind of service was of great importance in developing the frontier. Before the day of railways and "steam cars" there was no other means of transporting government mail and passengers quite so satisfactory as the stage coach. Even the driver, with his weather-beaten face and unique character, whose choice of roads and horsemanship was not always in favor of his passengers, still remains a heroic figure to those who lived during these early days.

5

THE SETTLER'S HOME

I

THE resourcefulness of the American frontiersman has been one of the most interesting phases of western civilization. With him, probably to a greater extent than with any other group in our nation, necessity has been the "mother of invention," in the matter of food, clothing, and shelter.

In the construction of his dwelling he used materials that were at hand—trees in a wooded country; stones in a broken, rock-strewn area; adobe brick, as did Mexican settlers before him, in the semi-arid regions of the Big Bend district of Texas or eastern New Mexico; or blocks of thickly-matted grass root sod cut from the level grass plains. And sometimes he burrowed in the ground, like the prairie dog and coyote, and made a dugout for his family.

Often, when running streams were not available, he used his turning plow and shovel to scoop from the ground a shallow tank which would catch sufficient water from spring rains to meet his needs for stock and household purposes, or with a cylindrical drill he bored a deep hole into the earth to reach a sub-stream, hidden by many strata of thick rock and clay. In this new country, wherever he turned, he encountered problems so singular that they taxed to the utmost his native skill and resourcefulness. In the course of time, accordingly, the southern plains developed a separate and distinct way of living.

Bordering the southern plains on the east, from the Arkansas River on the north to the Brazos River on the south—four hundred miles in length—was a comparatively narrow strip of woods, known as the "Cross Timbers."[1] This extensive belt of post oaks and black-jacks forms one of the most prominent features of the country. Until the close of the seventies, it marked the line of outpost settle-

1. The "Cross Timbers" ranged from thirty miles to five miles in width. *Cf.* R. B. Marcy, *Exploration of the Red River of Louisiana, in the Year 1852*, pp. 84-85.

ments. The region west of this wooded area was a prairie land occupied by wild Indians and animals. Here the boldest spirits of the frontier had established themselves, built their cabins, cleared away the timber from patches of ground, and sought to coax a living from the soil. Since the region was a buffer between the timberlands of the east and the western plains (often called the prairies during the frontier days), it is natural to suppose that its homes would reflect the characteristics of both sections; and such was the case. The walls were usually made of logs, and the roof was sometimes covered with brush and sod or roughly made shingles, held in place by weighted poles. Windows and doors were generally covered with stout timbers which could be barred from within when hostile Indians appeared; but sometimes flint-hides of buffaloes or cows were used. These were also used as chair bottoms and table tops. Puncheon tables, chairs, bedsteads, and shelves completed the furnishings.

Travelers in the "Cross Timbers" during the frontier period were familiar with the one-room cabin. It was seldom more than fourteen by fourteen feet in dimensions, with no floor except the native soil, packed hard by constant use. Crevices between the roughly hewn logs were chinked with mud or a mortar of sand and lime. If the house was well constructed, it was comfortable enough in all kinds of weather; but in these early days of border life, few houses were well built. Reasons for poor construction are not hard to find; indifference born of hardship, lack of price, and, more often, poverty and the scarcity of building materials. Sometimes the settler allowed the crevices between the logs to go unchinked, and depended on a booming fire in the great open chimney to drive away the chill in inclement weather; and sometimes he put forth little effort to keep out either insects or "varmints." Yet in a cabin of this kind, occupied by a family of seven or eight, a stranger could find a night's lodging, not always adequate to the needs of the most exacting traveler, but sufficient to protect him from a raw and stormy night. An English lady who visited the southern part of the "Cross Timbers" after the Civil War wrote that "a Texan generally has three or four beds in his principal sitting room," adding facetiously, "It would not be properly furnished without them, ..."[2]

2. Mary K. Jaques, *Texan Ranch Life*, p. 96.

Occasionally, more pretentious homes of two, three, four or five rooms were found. Mrs. Elizabeth B. Custer, wife of General George Custer, and a visitor to the Texas frontier in 1867, describes a home of the better type:

> It was a long one-storied, log building, consisting of a parlor, dining-room, bed room, and two small "no-count" rooms, as the servants said, all opening into one another upon the porch. The first surprise upon entering was, that the roof did not fit down snugly on the side of the wall. A strip of the blue sky was visible on three sides, while the partitions of the dining room only came up part of the way. . . . The walls were roughly plastered, but this space just under the roof was for ventilation, and I fancied they would get enough of it during a norther.[3]

An English traveler in Texas describes another log house, on the banks of a creek. It consisted of two rooms, boarded in all around and divided from each other by a kind of hall, open at both ends, in which the meals were taken. Running the entire length and breadth of the exterior was a "gallery" in which were hung saddles, lassoes, fishing nets, and hunting gear. Detached from the house, on either side were two other log buildings, one used as a kitchen and the other as a smoke house, with hides of leopard cats, deer, Mexican hogs, and otters on the outer walls stretched and nailed up to dry. Through the house, and around it, wandered large numbers of dogs, turkeys, ducks, and chickens, fraternizing freely with the family.[4]

II

Sometimes before the "Cross Timbers" belt was occupied by settlers, evidences of white habitation were found on the upper part of the southern plains. About 1826, Charles, William, George, and Robert Bent, together with Ceran St. Vrain, led a band of trappers from the Upper Misssouri region to the headwaters of the Arkansas. Here, between what is now Pueblo and the mountains, they erected a temporary stockade and opened trade with the Cheyenne Indians. In 1828 they began the erection of a permanent

3. Elizabeth B. Custer, *Tenting on the Plains, or General Custer in Kansas and Texas*, p. 143.
4. "Adventures in Texas," in *Leisure Hour*, XII, 91 *et sqq.*

post, which was complete after two years of hard work. Quite unlike the general type of building found later on the plains, the post was made of adobe. The use of adobe seems to have been the idea of Charles Bent, who believed that it was more durable than other available materials; that its thick walls would offer a greater measure of protection against Indian attacks and the blizzards of winter; and that the interior would be cooler in the hot days of July and August. In order to insure the best results he made a visit to New Mexico, where he secured skilled Mexican laborers to make the brick, and purchased a large quantity of wool to mix with the adobe mud for greater durability. When finished, the post constituted the only white habitation in the entire region—according to the late George B. Grinnell, a post five hundred miles from the nearest frontier settlement.[5]

The new post was so well built that it provided an adequate defense for the traders in the event of an Indian attack. The floors of the building were of beaten clay, and the roof was made in the fashion that long prevailed in adobe architecture. Poles were laid from the front walls to the rear, slightly inclining toward the front. Over these were placed brush, twigs, and grass, and over the brush clay was spread and trampled down hard. Finally, the roof was covered with gravel, which had a tendency to harden with rains. At two corners of the structure were bastions or round towers, thirty feet in height and ten feet in diameter, with loopholes for muskets and openings for cannons; and above the ponderous gate was a watchtower which contained a single room, with windows on all sides, furnished with a chair and bed. Mounted on a pivot was an old fashioned telescope or spyglass, used by the watchman when suspicions of danger were aroused.

John T. Hughes, of the First Regiment of Missouri Cavalry, accompanying the Doniphan expedition to New Mexico in the summer of 1846, thus describes the post, with an accompanying drawing:

Fort Bent is situated on the north bank of the Arkansas, 650 miles west of Fort Leavenworth, in latitude 38° 2′ north and 103° 3′ west from Greenwich. The exterior walls of this fort, whose figure is that of an oblong square, are 15 feet high and

5. George B. Grinnell, "Bent's Old Fort and its Builders," in *Kansas State Historical Collections*, XV (1919-22), 28.

4 feet thick. It is 180 feet long and 135 feet wide and is divided into various compartments, the whole built of adobes, or sun-dried brick. It has been converted into a Government depot.[6]

After this post was established—sometime before 1840—the traders, desiring to open traffic with the Comanche and Kiowa tribes south of them, established Adobe Fort on the South Canadian River, in what is now Hutchinson County, Texas. It is not known just how large the post was, but it probably was smaller than the post on the Arkansas. After twenty years, both posts were abandoned and soon fell into ruins. Indeed, the fort on the Arkansas was blown up by its builders when they abandoned it.

III

But, the pioneer work of Anglo-American habitation accomplished, other dwellings followed. Events hastened the occupation of the entire country. The discovery of gold in Colorado brought across the plains a concourse of people, some of whom stopped to establish homes; the settlement of Kansas, after the passage of the Kansas-Nebraska Act of 1854, brought homeseekers to the western part of the territory; and the enactment of the Homestead Bill of 1862, made possible the acquisition of a home on the prairies for him who cared to meet the requirements of the law.

At first only temporary homes were established. The average homesteader was poor, and could not make pretentious improvements. Sometimes the "move on" spirit dominated him; and a ten-by-twelve shack of the cheapest material, poorly constructed and scantily furnished, was his first home. He did not care to make permanent improvements because he had established his homestead as an investment which he proposed to sell as soon as he could prove up his claim. But sometimes he was unable to make considerable improvements until the income from his land would justify such expenditures. Mrs. Emily Haines Harrison tells of helping to establish such a temporary home in Ottawa County, Kansas, in 1866, with her nephew, Henry H. Tucker, and her son, Waldo W. Haines. When they arrived at the Saline River, they found collected along its banks huge drifts of cottonwood timber,

6. John T. Hughes, *Doniphan's Expedition*, p. 33.

which, together with green timber cut from the banks of the stream, they used to build their new home. Their hut was covered with earth, and the interior was decorated with keepsakes and "little luxurious appointments," which Mrs. Harrison says were brought from her old home. But an unfortunate occurrence brought distress to the household:

> Then a heavy rain came, ran through the loose earth with which the roof was covered, and poured in rivulets over my furnishings, and rained mud three days after the sky was bright without. By that time my keepsakes were ruined and the earth firmly packed on the roof, so that we had little trouble of that kind again. I remember of frying pancakes on my stove while Mr. Tucker held the umbrella over me and the stove.[7]

W. E. Webb, in 1872, wrote of a similar experience, which was as amusing as it was unfortunate. During a sudden rain at Sheridan, being obliged to turn out early one morning to protect some goods, he discovered that the neighboring habitation had dissolved into a mound of mud. As he gazed at the ruins, fearful for the safety of the occupant, the object of his thoughts suddenly came spluttering through the top of the roof, like a dirty gnome, clad in a brief night shirt. While the latter stood there in the cleansing rain, he said: "Lucky that houses are dirt-cheap here, stranger, for I reckon this one's sort o' washed."[8] Similar experiences, some even more alarming, could be multiplied. More than one housewife found her cabin inhabited by a rattlesnake which had fallen from the dirt roof; and scorpions and centipedes were common visitors.

As a rule, when the eaves of the house protected its sides from dashing rains, and when the proper precautions were taken to keep the roof from leaking, a sod house was durable enough. William D. Street gives a good account of the construction of a schoolhouse in Western Kansas.

> The pioneers brought with them a desire for education and the hope of religion. Schoolhouses of rude pattern, built of logs or sod, sprang up everywhere. They were used for the dual purpose of education during the week and devotional exercises on Sunday. The log and sod schoolhouses have given place to

7. Mrs. Emily Haines Harrison, "Reminiscences of Early Days in Ottawa County," in *Kansas State Historical Collections*, X (1907-8), 622-23.
8. *Buffalo Land*, 385-86.

new and modern houses of education, and nearly every county-seat has a county high school and graded schools of high character. Many churches of commodious size and excellent design take the place of the former house of worship. The building of the schoolhouse in any neighborhood was an event of more than passing interest. They frequently built before a regular organized district was set apart and before any taxes were levied for schools or for school buildings.

In such cases work would be donated by some and funds by others. On occasions persons were asked to contribute enough to buy a joint of stove-pipe or a board from which to manufacture a seat. The building of the sod schoolhouses was an event from which occurrences were reckoned, as happening before the schoolhouse was built or after. The site being decided upon, the neighborhood gathered with horses, plows, and wagons. A piece of virgin prairie sod would be selected, the sod-breaking plow would be started; the sharp share would cut the grass roots and slice out a long piece of the sod from two to four inches in thickness, by twelve to fourteen inches in width. After the sod had turned and the place where the edifice of learning was to be reared had been cleaned of the buffalo-grass down to the bare soil, men with sharp spades would cut the long furrows of sod into convenient lengths to be handled. These bricks of sod would then be loaded into wagons and taken to the building site, the foundation laid, the door frames set in at once, and as the work progressed and the walls had reached the height of a foot or such a matter, the window frames were set in and the building continued to the required height. Great care would be taken to break joints with the sods and also to put in binders, soft mud or fine soil. The latter was used more frequently to stop up every crevice or vacuum in the walls until they would be almost airtight. Then the roof, sometimes of lumber, but more frequently of dirt, would be put on. To put on a dirt roof, a large log, the length of the building was selected, or two, if one long enough could not be secured from the native lumber sparsely scattered along the streams. This log would be put on lengthwise —a ridge log, it was termed. Shorter and smaller poles were then cut and laid from the sides of the walls to the ridge log. Over these would be placed small willow brush; then sod would be carefully laid over the willows; later to receive a layer of fine dirt carefully smoothen over the entire roof, which completed the job. The floor, usually of dirt was sprinkled with water to

An early western Indian Territory half-dugout

lay the dust, and as this process was continued the dirt floor became hard-packed and easily kept in order.[9]

About fourteen miles north of Hamlin, Texas, near the Double Mountains Fork of the Brazos River, broken liquor bottles, battered fruit cans, and mounds of earth mark the site of a thriving buffalo hide town of the late seventies, built entirely of sod. Here, more than a hundred miles from civilization, was a wild community, made up of hide buyers, gamblers, lewd women, hunters, and an occasional cowboy who visited the place to buy liquor and supplies. It is estimated that a million hides were hauled down the dusty streets of this remote town by big bull trains on their way to Fort Worth. The hides were bought, sorted, and stacked here before they were finally shipped east. A stage driver who carried the mail from Fort Griffin to Reynolds, thus describes the town during its heyday:

 . . . . As to Reynolds, it had one large store about 30 by 100 feet, canvass roof; on the west end were three rooms, cook house, and sleeping rooms; and west of it was a small house about 12 by 16, belonging to a Chinaman and his wife. They ran a laundry. They came down there from Fort Elliott with the Rath supply train. East of the store was a small house about 10 by 12, belonging to James Knight. He worked for Lee, Reynolds and Rath in the hide yard. West across the street was a big saloon and dance hall run by a man named Fleming from Fort Elliott. It was about 30 by 80 feet. West of the dance hall was George Akens' saloon and Restaurant, it was about 30 by 80 feet; and about 100 yards west was a big sod corral, about 100 yards square. All the buildings were sod and had dirt roofs. There was a little house on the northwest corner of the corral, about 10 by 12; it was a bunk house.[10]

Although the sod house was more common, the dugout was frequently found in the northern part of the southern plains. This type of building was usually constructed by digging into a hill, which formed the back side of the dwelling. The front was made of logs or spare lumber, and the roof of sticks, on which was laid grass or prairie hay, covered with a thick layer of earth. A fireplace and flue

9. William D. Street, "The Victory of the Plow," in *Kansas State Historical Collections*, IX (1905-6), 38-39.
10. James W. Steele to C. C. Rister, March 3, 1929.

were dug at the rear end or side of the excavation, and a chimney was projected above the roof by means of stones or sticks plastered with mud. Such homes were more comfortable than they appeared to be. During the severe blizzard which struck western Kansas, the Indian Territory, and eastern Colorado, in December 1886, thousands of settlers escaped with their lives by living comfortably housed in dugouts. O. P. Byers, of Hutchinson, a survivor, later stated that as soon as possible after the storm, a systematic search was made of dugouts, shanties, and sod houses in order to ascertain the condition of the settlers. In some of the shacks, a number of people were found frozen to death, and those who were still alive were in bed. In northwestern Kansas, a settler and his team of two horses were found frozen to death within fifty feet of his dugout. As for those who were in dugouts, Byers said: "The uninviting dugout, of rattlesnake and other reptile legend, alone could provide security in such a storm. Families living in them, having sufficient provisions and fuel, suffered but little discomfort."

In the lower portion of the southern plains, the most common types of habitation during the early period were the dugout and the adobe house, the one introduced by the Anglo-American rancher and settler; the other by the Mexican. By far the greater number of temporary ranch homes were rudely constructed dugouts, and even after permanent buildings of adobe and stone were provided, the former were still used as winter homes by line riders and stock tenders. When farmers came in to establish their small properties, they, too, built this primitive type of home, occasionally modifying it by constructing a "half-dugout," which was a frame structure of the basement order, covered with shingles.

Along the exposed frontier settlers used their dugouts for defense. The Indians seldom attacked when they were thus protected. The *Rocky Mountain News* of June 22, 1870, carried an interesting account of an eastern Colorado pioneer woman relative to her dugout home. "I think I never knew any one," she said, "who was more unwilling to go into a hole in the ground (as I called it) than I was myself." But she explained that this means of security from Indian attack helped to overcome her objections. "Frank has had three forts built, or rather dug," she explained, "for out here the forts [homes] are all under ground and covered with sod, the port holes being just above the level of the plain. One is large, one on each side of the large one, are smaller. In one of these smaller forts we sleep and you have no idea how comfortable we rest." Moreover, she and her husband had little fear of Indians for they were adequately armed with carbines, Colt's revolvers, and had an abundant supply of ammunition.

As the Mexican ranching and trading interests developed in New Mexico, the inhabitants of this area pushed out eastward to meet the Anglo-American settlers coming westward. The latter found that in this semi-arid country adobe buildings were more satisfactory than the kinds of dwellings with which they were familiar. Although not so prepossessing as either frame or stone structure, they were cool in summer and easily heated in winter; and their thick walls and roofs provided a durability which could not always be had in other plains dwellings.

One of the best known, and at the same time most remote, cattle towns of the Panhandle of Texas was Tascosa, for all practical purposes the county seat of Oldham, Hartly, Sherman, Moore, Potter, Randall, Dallam, Deaf Smith, and Castro counties—the Panhandle. In 1877, on the side of what was to become Tascosa, arrived Don Casimero Romero and two Mexican friends, who began the construction of adobe homes. Others soon followed; and when cowmen, gamblers, merchants, and saloon operators arrived, "the wickedest town on the plains" had sprung into being. Primarily because of Mexican influence, Tascosa was almost as distinctively an adobe town as Reynolds City had been a sod town. Its unique and interesting history was given to the world by C. F. Rudolph, through the columns of his newspaper, the Tascosa *Pioneer*. By 1887, the editor could boast of a well-established town of saloons, dance halls, restaurants, cowboy-outfitting stores, and blacksmith shops. And so respectable became each of these in the eyes of the citizens that Jim East, proprietor of one of the seven saloons, was also sheriff of Oldham County for two terms.

IV

The story of how the early homes of the southern plains were furnished is soon told. The settler of the timbered country, as previously stated, found an abundance of wood from which he could roughly make his bedsteads, dressers, tables, chairs, and shelves; but he who came to the treeless plains found little he could use for such purposes. Sometimes the housewife insisted on putting in the immigrant wagon, to be hauled to her new home, such heirlooms as a cumbersome bedstead, a dresser, or table, made of walnut or other hard wood. But when the furniture arrived at its journey's end it was considerably the worse for the wear. The jolting and lurching of the wagon over the rough and roadless journey often scratched the varnish badly, and otherwise seriously abused the treasures. Many times, enlarged and framed photographs of loved ones who had died, of a wandering boy, or of aged parents in an eastern home were carefully wrapped in quilts and blankets and carried along to adorn the walls of the new home. In all instances, however, there were many things needed which could not be brought in the immigrant wagon; some things which the home-builders could not anticipate until they arrived at their new homesite, and others which had such small intrinsic value as to make their transportation for any considerable distance quite unprofitable.

The settler, however, was not to be denied the common necessities of a frontier home. Along the numerous creeks and branches were found scanty patches of willows, which proved adequate for making chairs, settees, and tables; and wooden boxes, in which the mover had transported clothing, quilts, and other odds and ends from his old home, were also used for the same purposes. Odd bits of colored cloth, silk and lace, were used to cover rudely fashioned mantels, shelves, and settees; and even the drab walls of the sod house or dugout were made more presentable when plastered with newspapers and leaves of old magazines or covered with sheeting. General W. T. Sherman, who was frequently entertained in such primitive homes as those described, later wrote that he could see in memory a beautiful young city-bred lady who had married a poor second lieutenant and followed him to his post on the plains, and had found that his quarters were in a dugout, with a dirt roof, ten feet by fifteen and seven feet high, four feet of the wall being of earth and the other three of sod, with holes for windows and corn sacks for curtains. Yet, by means of her Saratoga trunk used for a sofa, a rug on the dirt floor, a few candle boxes covered with red cotton calico for seats, a table improvised out of a barrel head, and a chimney excavated out of the back of the wall, she soon transformed her first home in the West into a most attractive place.

It mattered little to the average housewife whether her bedstead was scratched and battered, or whether her mirror was cracked, as long as she could have them in her new home.

It is difficult to generalize in regard to the furnishings of southern plains homes, since conditions were not always the same. But this one fact is well established by early records: the average settler had little means with which to equip his habitation with desirable furniture and decorations, and squalor was everywhere in evidence. The settler's goal was the comfort of his family in inclement weather, rather than luxurious appointments; a place where he could "get along," rather than pleasurable surroundings. Housewife and daughters must be content to look to the future to supply all their needs, and they must have enough faith in the new country to work hard toward that end. That the pioneer woman was practical is proven by early records. A Kansan writing in 1872, said: "The sod house of far western Kansas, the cabin of Texas, and the adobe of Colorado and New Mexico generally proclaim afar off their occupancy by women by a planted vine, a draped window, or a swept path in front of the door."[11]

11. James W. Steele, "Women Under Difficulties," in *Kansas Magazine*, II (September, 1872), No. 3, p. 225.

6

ABOUT THE FIRESIDE

I

HERE and there on the southern plains sparse growths of timber furnished firewood. Along the larger streams could be found hackberry, elm, cottonwood, pecan, and walnut trees; in the "Cross Timbers" belt, post oak and blackjack; and in much of the southern part of the area, stunted mesquite, which was excellent fuel. Curiously enough, in parts of the treeless Staked Plains roots could be had for the digging, and sometimes had to be cleared out before the sod could be plowed under. These stumps and roots are indubitable evidence that at one time timber grew here also, but was probably burned away by prairie fires, which frequently came racing across the plains with leaping flames of from twenty-five to thirty feet in height.[1] And on these stumps and roots immigrant farmers often depended for their winter's supply of fuel as long as they could be found.

In these areas the chimney, made of stone or of mud and sticks, was considered an indispensable household fixture; and on still, frosty mornings, the smoke lazily drifting on the air symbolized the domestic tranquility within as the housewife prepared the noonday meal. Suspended from an iron hook, over the glowing embers on the hearthstone, an iron pot might send forth delicious odors of cooking turnip greens, potatoes, or beans. On the other side of the fireplace might be a Dutch oven, in which a venison or buffalo roast was slowly becoming "brown to a turn." And on still other coals a kettle filled with water might be simmering with iron-throated music. Completing the iron equipment of the hearth,

1. Obadiah Knapp, an officer stationed at Fort Bliss after the Civil War, tells of more than one party of men sent out from the fort to dig mesquite roots for firewood. Entry of January 8, 1867, in his manuscript diary, the O. M. Knapp papers, Archives, Library, University of Texas.

a shovel, tongs, and a rake generally leaned against the stone front of the fireplace. Yet not all cabins of the early days were so well equipped. Sometimes a single pot or Dutch oven served every cooking purpose; in it the vegetables were boiled, the meat was cooked, and the water was heated for washing the dishes. And sometimes, about a single vessel of this kind, the members of the family would gather, after the potatoes, turnip greens, or roast had been cooked, and take their turns dipping their bread into the contents, or using their spoons.

During frontier days many pleasurable hours were spent about the fireside. On wintry nights, when the day's toil was ended, the family would sit about the open hearth on puncheon benches or rawhide-bottomed chairs and watch the crackling flames leap up the chimney and pour their mellow light into every part of the room. The picture is one of comfort and peace not exceeded even in our modern homes. Curled up on the hearthstone was a drowsing cat, and lying within the fireside circle was a dog—not a pedigreed animal with a silver mounted leather neck-band, its body perfumed and carefully bathed, but just a mongrel, flea-bitten, faithful—its head resting on its paws, blinking at the glowing fire. The members of the family would be engaged in various tasks: the mother knitting, sewing, or darning; the father mending broken harness, sharpening a knife, or half-soling a shoe; and the children playing simple games or carrying on an animated conversation about their experiences of the day—killing a skunk which had got into the coop and had eaten several of the baby chicks, running from a prairie lobo which had shown its bristles at them, or finding the roosting place of wild turkeys. Even when bedtime came all were reluctant to abandon their cozy places for the night; but tasks of a new day, which called for their awakening at four or four-thirty o'clock in the morning usually summoned them to a needed rest.

This picture of domestic tranquility, to be sure, holds good only for the better type of frontier home. It does not include the hundreds of cases in which the house was poorly constructed, and therefore difficult to heat; and in which children often went to bed hungry. Sometimes wood was scarce and other kinds of fuel could be had only by great industry and hard labor; and sometimes the head of the household was too shiftless to provide for the ordinary needs of his family. Sometimes, instead of one dog, he had a dozen or more long-eared hounds, with insatiable appetites, which rendered little service in return for the enormous quantities of food they consumed, or could consume when it was available. As a rule, then, the difference between one type of home and another was a matter of ambition. But occasionally sickness in the family, severe droughts, scourges of grasshoppers, or lack of a market brought poverty and discomfort to the frontiersman and his family. And such cheery scenes about the glowing hearth were certainly not found in thousands of dugouts, sod houses, and adobe structures where the only available fuel was cow chips,[2] roots, and—with the coming of the railroad—coal.

These poorly constructed houses were shaken from foundation to roof by northers and blizzards. Many of these winds were little more than dust storms, or "sand storms" as they were popularly known on the southern plains, which filled houses with dust so as to make breathing difficult. But many times the winds sent their frigid blasts whistling through crevices and poorly-framed windows, forcing the family to seek warmth about the fire on the hearth or in the sheet-iron stove, or, on rare occasions, to go to bed. After the passing of a sand storm the women would busy themselves sweeping great quantities of sand from the floors and dusting it from curtains, mantels, and window sills, to make the interior presentable again; while the father and sons would inspect their farm to see what damage had been done to fences, outhouses, and even growing crops. The norther would come suddenly and with terrific force, causing a sharp drop in temperature for a few hours, and then would leave the sky balmy and clear.

The accounts of the sufferings of thousands of southern plainsmen during severe winters are sometimes challenged by those who have not experienced similar hardships, but there is an abundance of documentary proof to establish many of the extraordinary tales told. No doubt the severity seemed more intense because of greater exposure. Many pioneers still living assert that blizzards are not so severe now as they once were—weather bureau records to the contrary notwithstanding—the reason for this erroneous belief being that today homes are better constructed, winter travel is better safeguarded against cold, the average plainsman is more comfor-

2. Cow chips are dried cow dung.

tably dressed in the winter months, and our nearest weather station heralds the approach of a blizzard many hours before its coming, thus enabling us to prepare for it.

II

Many settlers on the southern plains used the primitive campfire for cooking, especially during the heat of mid-summer, when housewives did not care to build a fire in the open hearth. Thus they learned to prepare most of the foods enjoyed by early plains travelers, as well as some which were not so well enjoyed by any one. They learned how to use the flame, hot coals, or ashes in preparing various dishes, without burning the food or cooking it too quickly.

Newcomers often hesitated to use buffalo chips or cow chips for fuel, particularly in cooking, as one southern plains traveler indicates:

> I am not Professor Blot; but yet consider myself a cook of no mean order. There is not a section of the country in which I have not hunted or fished, making use of the best means at hand to cook the game thus secured. This experience entitles me to consideration when I affirm that there is no better broiling fuel than a perfectly dry "buffalo chip." That a doubt arose as the smoke curled up from the newly-lighted pile, as to the judiciousness of depositing a juicy venison steak on those coals, it is useless to deny. The appearance of a bright red coal with an ash of almost snowy whiteness soon became apparent. The steak was quickly deposited on the fire, notwithstanding the expostulations of the chip-gatherers, who would have found a gridiron, if such an article had formed a portion of the stock-herders cave.[3]

Not only primitive fuel but primitive cooking methods were employed. One primitive way of cooking small game, such as rabbit, quail, or fish, was to skewer it. The game was properly "dressed," or stripped of its skin, entrails, feet and head, and washed clean in a pond or stream; and salt—if available—was thoroughly rubbed into the flesh. Then the meat was impaled on a sharpened stick and held over the glowing coals until it was cooked on one side, the cooked meat was flecked from the bones and eaten, and the raw side was placed back over the coals and

3. *Harper's New Monthly Magazine*, July, 1867, p. 141.

similarly served.[4] Bread was often cooked in the same manner. When the dough had been kneaded, it was wrapped about a stick and held over the coals until ready. A Texas Ranger who served on the frontier during early days declares that food cooked in this manner was delicious, retaining all the natural juices.

On the open hearth or over a camp fire on the open prairie bread was usually baked in a Dutch oven. This was a flat-bottomed, cast-iron vessel, whose lid had a rim around it to keep coals spread over its surface from falling off. Glowing embers were also placed under the oven. Bread dough was "raised" with baking powder or by mixing it with sour dough and adding a little soda, and sometimes with only the latter ingredient. Usually, after the lapse of ten or fifteen minutes the biscuits were nicely browned and ready to serve.

One should not infer, however, that all bread thus prepared and cooked was palatable. In spite of the thrill of camping out on the great open prairie, with the mysterious darkness hovering about the flickering camp fire, some travelers found it difficult to eat bread prepared in this way. One of these was J. S. Campion, an Englishman:

> Supper was being prepared, and the blaze, from what our *chef de cuisine* coarsely but forcibly designated as "that portable h—," made the surrounding darkness appear almost solid, and brought into ruddy relief Jack's flannel-shirted buckskin-breached figure, as he stooped over the portable aforesaid to bake what he called a "pome"—that is to say, he had achieved a lump of dough, grease, and sceleratus, half as thick as a brick, twice as large, and about as digestable, which aid to suicide he was placing, by means of a shovel extemporized out of the top of a candle-box, into a large bed of red-hot wood-coals, ...[5]

In this connection it might be noted that soldiers patrolling the border and furnished with small portable Dutch ovens, flour, soda, and salt, for cooking their own bread, suffered stomach disorders as a natural consequence of using too much soda and salt or pond water.[6]

4. Frederick Law Olmsted, *A Journey Through Texas*, p. 307.
5. J. S. Campion, *On the Frontier*, p. 11.
6. For experiences of federal troops stationed on the Texas frontier see *Report of an Inspection of the Eighth Military District*, by Colonel W. G. Freeman, April 23, 1853, MS, Old Records Division, Adjutant General's Office, War Department, Washington, D. C.

Housewives of the pioneer period cooked corn pones on the heated rocks of the hearthstones. Often these pones were made simply by mixing salt and scalding water with coarse meal, which had been ground in a coffee mill attached to the wall of the cabin. Since no soda, milk, or grease was added, the bread was heavy, yet, strange as it may seem, palatable and digestible—when one was ravenously hungry. Indeed, one of the popular meals of frontier days in this region consisted of corn pone, turnip greens, and buttermilk, or "pot-likker"—a nourishing soup made by boiling turnip greens with salt pork for an hour or more in the inevitable cast-iron pot.

The average frontiersman lived a simple life and subsisted on a simple fare. If he had cornbread, salt pork, molasses, dried fruits, and occasionally game to eat and coffee and milk to drink, he had little cause to grumble, and indeed was quite content. Flour bread or biscuit was considered a luxury to be enjoyed only on week-end occasions, and cakes and pies were seldom seen on frontier tables. Molasses usually came in keg containers, if it was shipped from the cane-growing areas of Louisiana or eastern Texas, and was not generally available for all southern plains homes. A frequent substitute was a syrup put up in gallon buckets and strongly impregnated with chemicals and coloring matter. When allowed to stand for any length of time in a warm room it became sour and unsavory; yet because it was all that was to be had, it was eaten in large quantities. Furthermore, if allowed to stand in an open pitcher or bucket on the table of a careless housewife, it gathered an assortment of flies and ants. These were carefully skimmed from the vessel, if discovered; otherwise, they were left to be disposed of by him who ate the molasses. "Lasses" or "lick," as the syrup was sometimes called by illiterate settlers, was often the only kind of sugar-food to be had, except here and there where fruits could be grown, or were found in their wild state along the streams. It was used to sweeten coffee, and occasionally to make cakes and pies, but more commonly it was eaten with butter and bread, and was not entirely unsavory in this form. In the absence of usual ingredients, frontier women came to use expertly what they had, even though it might be a substitute, and were quite successful in preparing delicious meals.

Although the southern plains did not grow such an abundance of edible plants as the well-watered timbered areas of the nation, there were many to be had if the immigrant knew what to look for. In the early springtime, there were wild onions which when stripped of their woody, fibrous coverings, disclosed a tender white bulb pleasant to the taste. Artichokes also grew in southwestern Kansas and eastern Colorado; and an excellent substitute for tea was made from the crisp, bright green leaves of a small bushy shrub with white flowers, found in the upper part of the region. "Lamb's quarter," which had tender leaves in the early spring, was cooked and eaten like spinach, as was pokeweed, which grew along many of the running streams. Wild plums, black and red haws, and "possum" grapes were wild fruits which added variety to the summer diets of many frontier inhabitants. During the fall of the year pecans, walnuts, and persimmons grew along the streams and in sparsely timbered areas. These were usually gathered after the first frost and eaten about the fireside at night.

Indeed, where members of the family were industrious, self-sufficiency and contentment were almost as much in evidence here as in the "Cross Timbers" belt. During the season of cold nights, it was not uncommon to find members of the family, as they sat about the fireside, engaged in popping corn, roasting sweet " 'taters" in the ashes of the fireplace or in the sheet-iron stove, or parching pecans and walnuts. Probably it was with the idea of having these advantages as well as a perennial water supply that the immigrants first occupied the public domain stretching along running streams. Here they could find, in addition to the foods mentioned, abundant fuel and wild game, such as squirrels, turkeys, ducks and geese.

One would naturally suppose that with the coming of the railroad, the diet of the settler would be more varied, but little change was made. The primary problem was a lack not so much of transportation facilities as of money. In 1869 bacon sold for twenty-five cents a pound; lard, twenty-five cents; butter, sixty-five cents; coffee, thirty-five cents; corn, four cents; meal, five cents; flour, six to nine dollars a hundred pounds; potatoes, three cents; sugar, twenty-five cents; molasses, two dollars to two dollars and fifty cents a gallon; teas, two dollars to two dollars and fifty cents; and beef, twelve and one-half cents to twenty cents. Yet board could be had at from five to ten dollars a week.[7]

7. Frederick B. Goddard, *Where to Emigrate and Why. Homes and Fortunes in the Boundless West and the Sunny South*, 172-73.

ABOUT THE FIRESIDE

Early travelers on the southern plains and settlers who have recorded their impressions of these frontier days have written in complimentary terms of the food served in some of the homes. On some tables, to be sure, were biscuits, heavy and brown-specked because of too much soda; fat bacon, "swimming in an ocean of grease"; and coffee more "water than Java." But other trifles presented a more appetizing aspect. A Texas traveler writes of being entertained in a "long, cool kitchen; a swart girl standing at one end and a swart boy at the other. Each agitates a long stick adorned with strips of paper, and thus a breeze is kept up and the flies are driven off. Buttermilk, corn-bread, excellent meat, and the inevitable coffee are the concomitants of the meal."[8] A Kansas traveler also reports that on one occasion the wild turkey served was fat and very rich in flavor, and the antelope steaks were more delicious than venison, although condensed milk was used. Even hunting parties were often supplied with coffee, sugar, salt, soda, molasses, lard, and occasionally canned fruits.

III

Much of the time spent about the fireside by the mother and adult daughters was used for making clothing for the family. Many of those who migrated to the southern plains before or soon after the Civil War brought with them in their capacious wagons, cards, spinning wheels, check reels, warping bars, and looms, or else these articles were made soon after arriving. When once they were set up in the new home, the women industriously busied themselves in carding wool and cotton, spinning it into thread, and weaving thread into cloth which they then made into clothing for the family. Sometimes the thread was colored with dye made from native herbs, barks, and roots, for the designers to fashion into beautiful patterns of striped, checked, or plaid cloth. They also knitted socks and stockings, large and heavy in appearance, but comfortable enough in the winter months.

The family footwear was often made by the father, or the local cobbler, on a homemade last, from leather tanned in a local vat, and put together with wooden pegs made from pecan or other timber. When they were available, metal brads were put on the

8. Edward King, *The Southern States of North America*, 143-44.

heels. Shoes thus made—usually known on the frontier as "brogans"—were rough and heavy; and not infrequently wooden pegs would work their way through the soles of the shoes and give the wearers much discomfort. Sometimes, to make the leather soft and pliable as well as waterproof, shoes were soaked in oil or rubbed vigorously with tallow, which added to their ungainly appearance. The head covering sometimes consisted of home-braided straw hats in summer, and cloth or felt caps and bonnets in winter.

In these early days jeans, calico, gingham, and "hickory" shirting were favored by the frontier family. Men and boys usually wore "hickory" shirts and jeans trousers of home manufacture because these could better withstand the rough usage of out-of-doors life. Sometimes both man and boy were provided with large roomy shirts, with sleeves too long or too short; dull-gray jeans trousers which bagged at the knees and failed to make connection with the shoe tops, with long cavernous pockets, both fore and aft. Yet the wearer must endure uncomplainingly, because there was no other clothing to be had—and sometimes he knew of nothing better.

Equally uncouth was the attire of the women. The "split-bonnet" somewhat resembled the forepart of a covered wagon. The shape of the body was often completely lost in the spacious garments. Ten or more yards of cloth were used in making a dress, the body tight-fitting or loose-fitting as the styles dictated, and the skirt long and canopy-like. From beneath the forepart of the skirt modestly peeped the rough brogan shoes. The roominess of the skirt was unduly accentuated by the four or five petticoats worn—when they could be had.

As railroads crossed and re-crossed the southern plains and towns sprang up here and there, homespun and brogan shoes gave way to store-bought and factory-made apparel. Even then, however, one reads of shirts for boys being fashioned out of flour sacks, and trousers from duck or bed ticking. Women could now purchase calico, gingham, muslin, or even silk from home town merchants, and shoes had of a more presentable manufacture. On March 26, 1874, the enterprising editor of the Dallas *Herald* published the following fashion note:

> Texas ladies are fully up to the average of their sex. In the item of dress, both as to quality, material, trimmings, lace, and all the little *et ceteras* that go to make up a lady's toilet, they are

evidently as expensive to their husbands and fathers as their sisters at the north, and are equally as profuse in the display of fine jewelry, diamonds, chains, bracelets, etc. The dress of a young lady who rode with the gossiping editor through the Texas wilds was a black silk, closely fitting, with sprays of flowers worked with black beads across the breast and slightly over the shoulders. Her dress was close up to the throat, and a stiff white standing collar, turned down at the points, was encircled by a blue silk scarf, worn precisely as a gentleman wears a cravat, tied in a bow in front. This gave to her a fine form, an exquisite finish while her clear complexion and the healthy bloom on her cheeks were sufficient to soften the heart of an anchorite.

According to the editor of the *News* of Denison, a frontier town of the "Cross Timbers" area, writing on April 17, 1873, fine Leghorn and split straw hats would be held in indiscriminate favor during the coming season; and broad and often high crowns would be the rule, with every variety of brim. The chief difference between the styles of that and the previous year was the way of wearing them. Sailor hats and high English turbans and *Henri Quatre* hats were alike worn off the brow, leaving the face and front hair fully exposed. The only difference between hats and bonnets was that the latter had strings. The highest, largest crowned English hat was tilted backwards, the brim turned up in front like a coronet, or the back was turned up with a facing of silk and bunch of drooping loops and ribbons, the strings tied down over the ears. In some shapes the narrow brim came closely about the face, but was caught up at the left with a bunch of flowers under it in very pretty fashion, "as a Spanish woman hangs roses behind her ears."

Men bought factory-made suits of clothes, derby hats, and sharp-pointed shoes. Shirts and cravats were of all patterns and styles. The editor of the *News* issued a warning on July 10 of the same year that men "who wear the open-in-the-back shirts, and go without coats, should never forget their vests," there being nothing at all poetic in the appearance of a man all split up behind like a locust gone to seed; and besides, he said, "it isn't nice. If the ladies wanted to dress so, of course we'd have to let 'em—if it was the fashion; but men should be more particular."

In general the scenes about the fireside, and all domestic relations of the southern plains country, compare favorably with those of other regions of the nation during the pioneering period. Families were sometimes large—one writer speaks of sixteen sleeping in a one-roomed sod house—and resources were sometimes scant, but there was little suffering from lack of nourishment and clothing when the provider for the home was resourceful and diligent in looking after the wants of his family. In fact, many of those who were reared in dugouts and sod houses still look back to the "good old days" when on cold wintry nights they sat about the fireside and enjoyed the pleasant associations of the family circle. They stoutly maintain that food cooked on the electric or gas range is not half so good as that cooked in the cast-iron kettle or Dutch oven over the glowing coals of the hearth, or even in the wood stove; and that "store bought clothes" cannot compare with those woven on the looms of the frontier homes. During the eighties and nineties, however, the new order of things was rapidly approaching and scenes about the fireside became increasingly "modern."

7

BORDER HOSPITALITY

I

THE early settler on the southern plains found himself in
an inhospitable environment. The perversities of its
climate, a large part of its wild life, and its devastating
prairie fires were formidable adversaries. Yet in a land where
nature did not always deal with him kindly he was hospitable to
strangers who occasionally visited his home, and he enjoyed greatly
the companionship of his neighbors. As a rule, he lived an isolated
and lonely life. Since his nearest neighbor often was twenty-five or
more miles distant, he could afford to make but few social calls.
Bad roads, inadequate conveyance, and the dangers of travel were
further deterrents. Accordingly, an occasional camp meeting,
picnic, wedding, or funeral was an event of great importance. And
if two or three times a year he were able to visit a distant town to
procure supplies, he was more fortunate than some of his neighbors; while, if on these occasions he could find at the post office
a letter, weekly newspaper, or magazine awaiting him, he considered himself exceedingly fortunate. Periodicals and books were
read over and over in order to glean some bit of news or information which might have been overlooked in the first reading; and
passers-by who brought news from the outside world were questioned at considerable length.

Colonel R. B. Marcy, who was often entertained in the homes
of settlers on the southern plains frontier and had many opportunities to observe its folkways, accounted for the peculiar traits
of the people by the fact that their sparsely settled habitations,
far removed from towns and villages and seldom visited by travelers, almost entirely excluded them from intercourse with the
civilized world; and as a result they were nearly as ignorant of
what was happening outside of their own immediate sphere as the
savages themselves. They seldom or never saw a newspaper, and

could not read it if they did; "and," he added, "I honestly believe that many of them could not tell whether General Jackson, Mr. Lincoln, or Mr. Johnson is President of the United States at the present time."[1] The majority of the earliest settlers, it is true, were illiterate and poor, but at the other extreme there were many well-educated, intelligent people.

The early settler of the region possessed the same restless urge which drove men like John Sevier, James Robertson, and Daniel Boone into the wildernesses of Watauga and Kentucky. He was not satisfied with being confined to the limits of a small government allotment, and therefore moved westward where he could have access to the wide sweeping reaches of the prairies. During the fall of 1892 the *St. Louis Globe-Democrat* sent Walter B. Stevens, one of its most experienced and reliable special correspondents, to Texas with instructions to stay as long as he pleased and record his observations. Having traveled the length and breadth of the frontier region of this state, and studied the peculiar characteristics of its people, he wrote: "The Texan has been raised to distances. His elbows stick out. He wants plenty of room, and in laying out his farm he has taken it. But he doesn't call it a farm. He calls it a ranch. And a ranch of less than 1,000 acres is hardly worth mentioning."

This predilection for "the great open spaces" was not peculiar to the American people, for foreigners, individually or in colonies, were impelled by the same motive. A Texas immigrant guide book for 1878 gives the following interesting item in this connection:

At the head of the beautiful Lon Morris [Los Moros] Creek, a tributary of the San Saba river, having its source in Menard County, is situated what is known as "King Carlin's Ranche." The proprietor is Ernest Carlin, a French nobleman, born and bred in Paris, and who gave up the fascinating delights of the capital, its ease and comforts and entertainments, to build the great industry of sheep husbandry in Western Texas. His estate consists of 30,000 acres of splendid rolling prairie in one body; 30,000 sheep, with a present annual increase of 20,000 lambs; and a rock palace which is perhaps the finest residence in Western Texas.[2]

1. Colonel R. B. Marcy, *Thirty Years of Army Life on the Border*, p. 357.
2. James L. Rock and W. I. Smith, *Southern and Western Texas Guide for 1878*, p. 187.

BORDER HOSPITALITY

Although some of the border settlers were poor and some afflu-
ent, some illiterate and some cultured, all were friendly and hospitable. For frontier restlessness and isolation did not destroy family
and social life. In a report to Governor O. M. Roberts of Texas
concerning general conditions along the frontier, after an extensive
inspection tour, Adjutant General W. H. King, on November 25,
1881, stated that there were but two habitations on the road from
Colorado to Blanco Canyon, a distance of more than one hundred
miles; yet in one of these, which was merely a hole dug in the side of
a hill, he found a sweet-looking, bright-eyed, cheerful, and intelligent little woman, who had been living thus for three years. Her
husband was a cattleman, and she, "with a brave heart and willing
mind has followed him to that lonely spot to aid him in his efforts
to achieve success." When asked how she could be content so far
from her friends or any of the delights of social life, she replied
with a smile that she was not so badly off, for in different directions she had one neighbor only fifteen miles way and two others
at a distance of about twenty-five miles. At Fort Davis, on the
lower part of the southern plains, the Adjutant-General declared,
"he owed it to the hospitality of a Mr. Sender and his genial wife
that his stay at that place was made so agreeable." And he found
the home of a Mr. Crossland brightened by the presence of a fine-
looking hospitable wife, two pleasing chatty grown daughters, and
several handsome children.

In the same spirit George S. Denison, a young Vermont school
teacher, writing to his mother on June 7, 1855, said of the people
at San Antonio, and later of the frontier people of Texas in general:
"Everybody here is kind and hospitable and seem to understand
that there are such duties as *social* duties."[3] A traveler in southwestern Kansas in the late seventies observed that settlers there
were "sociable and well disposed toward strangers"; and a correspondent of the Topeka *Commonwealth*, about the same time, wrote
that the new arrivals in eastern Colorado were "hospitable to all."
Even in eastern New Mexico, where there were but few Anglo-
Americans during this period, ranchers were described as "courteous and friendly."

3. Denison letters, MSS, Division of Manuscripts, Library of Congress.

II

When the country was first settled, there were but few towns where hotel accommodations could be had; consequently, travelers passing through the region usually expected to spend the night in camp on the open prairie, or in the home of some settler. It was for this reason that settlers were generally expected to be hospitable. A traveler felt no hesitancy in asking for accommodations for the night, and he was seldom turned away; but occasionally he found his host mercenary and calculating.

A. B. Greenleaf, an Alabama traveler in Texas, cites an instance in which treatment accorded him in the home of a frontiersman was not all to be desired. On this occasion he found himself compelled to accept the hospitality of what, judging from the bustle and clamor about the premises, was a large family. When supper was announced, "the whole retinue simultaneously bolted for the kitchen in a double-quick step," and the guest brought up the rear. Upon his arrival at the table, however, he found that the host had reserved for him a place on his immediate right. But before he could get seated all the members of the family, including the head of the household, "were promiscuously grabbing at the huge boiled beef bones with the voraciousness of young ducks gobbling up a bran dough." After some hesitancy, he was compelled to select a large "mutilated shank," and to begin gnawing it after the prevailing fashion. The following morning he inquired of his host the price of his night's lodging, and was directed to "pay to the old umman." After some timid reconnoitering he found her at the cowpen.

On making known the object of my invasion, she said:

"What you bin payin' tother folks es you come along?"

As I had no desire to limit or restrict her price, I made an evasive answer, whereupon she said:

"We'all, ez I hez the rumatiz, an' needs a little bitters, an' tha axes a dollar an' a half fur whiskey, you may give me that."

I shelled out three eagle half dollars and exodusted with a dust.[4]

4. A. B. Greenleaf, *Ten Years in Texas*, 149-52.

Colonel Marcy tells of a similar experience. One night he and a
fellow traveler stopped at the home of a former Virginian, who
received them cordially enough and said that if he had known of
their coming, he would have given them"the biggest barbecue that
country had ever seen." But when on the following morning the
Colonel inquired the price of the night's entertainment, the host
replied, "Only six bits a piece, Cap." (Marcy states that the usual
price in that region was two bits.)

Sometimes unfavorable impressions were due to the uncouthness
of the settlers rather than their unfriendliness. Hospitality in a
ranch home along the frontier was often of a rough character.
On one occasion Frederick Law Olmsted, while on his tour through
Texas, spent the night at a ranch on the upper waters of the Trinity
River. He arrived about the same time as a cavalcade of cowboys,
who greeted him rather familiarly. Although he does not say that
the boys were rude and prankish, one is left to infer the fact from
the general tone of his account. After he had been told to unsaddle
his horse and place it in a rope corral, as the other riders had done,
he was allowed to wander at will about the premises. Soon, however, he was called to the supper table, where he was served fresh
beef, cornbread, and coffee. (The cowboys had slaughtered a steer
for the occasion.) After supper he was engaged in conversation by
his host, a former Kentuckian and a man of intelligence; but "his
sons and their friends were silly, rude, illiterate, and stupid, as perhaps might be expected from their isolation." Again one wonders
whether or not this summary appraisal was occasioned by a customary prank played on a "tenderfoot."

Olmsted's later impressions might have been influenced by the
bed bugs that were the frequent experience of travelers in the homes
of early settlers. "We were shown to a crowded loft to sleep, with
an apology for the absence of side-boarding under the roof, 'it was
difficult to procure lumber.'. . . . It was not the ventilation, however, but the insatiate bugs, of which we found reason to complain.
We rose exhausted at daylight, and were led, as usual to the common wash-basin upon the gallery."[5] A similar experience was that
of a Kansas traveler, who thus describes her battle with chinches:
"Here they come like a herd of homeopathic buffaloes, as if by a
preconcerted signal, making headquarters on the open prairie

5. Frederick Law Olmsted, *A Journey Through Texas*, 368-73.

between the high bluffs of your shoulder-blades—nice snug, table-land that—and 'catch me if you can' seems to be the taunt with which they set up anew their night's banquet at your expense."

But these unfavorable impressions of frontier hospitality were the exception rather than the rule. The weary traveler usually was saluted by such expressions as, "Howdy, stranger," " 'Light an' un-saddle yore hoss," " 'Light an' look at yore saddle," "Jist make yoreself at home," or their equivalent. At times the prospective host must know something about the antecedents of the traveler. Generally, when such questions as "Whar ye frum?" "Whar ye goin'?" and the like were answered satisfactorily, the settler was friendly enough and quite willing to share his rude fare with the visitor. Often such queries were intended as the basis of an after-dinner conversation, at which time the host expected to become thoroughly familiar with the affairs of his guest as well as the general news from "the old country." But sometimes the cautious settler sought to protect his family against lawless characters who rode about over the country and preyed upon the inhabitants; and if at times he was searching in some of his questions, he felt that law-abiding visitors should pardon this precaution.

III

Accommodations in frontier dugouts, sod houses, and other dwellings ranged from the scarcely tolerable to the sumptuous. One guest writes of being served at the supper table with mint julep, cakes, pies, "white fluffy bread, and several kinds of meats"; and another speaks of "fat salt-pork, corn-bread, and black bean-juice coffee." Some weary travelers slept on comfortable beds with "sweet-smelling, clean linen," others spent restless nights on pallets made of quilts, blankets, or buffalo robes, already occupied with one or more children, who "kicked like young mules." The ingenuity of poor housewives to provide for accommodations, and at the same time maintain modesty and social decorum, knew no limits. Often, where eight or ten men and women must sleep in a single room, a clever shifting of sexes would be resorted to. The men would retire to the friendly darkness of the great outdoors, until the women had made necessary changes and retired for the night; then the men would return to the room and make their preparations, also under cover of darkness. Sometimes this awkward emergency was avoided by the use of temporary screens for the beds, made of blankets, quilts, or sheets. Otherwise the most embarrassing moment came for those who overslept. In this case the mother and grown daughters would modestly busy themselves at the fireplace, cook stove, or dining table, while the male guest, using his bed covering as a tent, would sit up in bed awkwardly putting on his clothes; or, if the guest were a woman, the men of the household would modestly and conveniently retire until it was safe for them to return.

One such instance is recounted by a Kansas visitor. In cold weather, there being little to do at home, he and his brother Jack would often visit in the home of a neighbor, where sometimes they would be entertained for two or three days at a time, "tearing around," rabbit hunting, or sleigh riding with the neighbor boys. "At night," he says, "we were a little crowded, as there was only one room, and we numbered sixteen persons in all—viz., Mr. and Mrs. Quinn, eleven children, Jack and I, and a young man named John Clover, who owned the next farm, and who lived and worked with the Quinns." Yet they were arranged pretty comfortably; Mr. and Mrs. Quinn, and the two youngest children of the family occupied one bed, the four girls another, three or four boys a third, and the remainder slept on the earthen floor. In wet weather, however, they were not quite so comfortable as they might desire, for the sod roof leaked, and rain and snow came in pretty badly. Moreover, "one slight drawback was that the old man had a habit of chewing tobacco as he lay in bed, but it did not cause much inconvenience to those on the floor, as he was a pretty good shot, and generally managed to reach the fire-place with the juice."[6]

During these days of neighborly visits, it was not uncommon for a settler to load his family in a wagon and drive twenty or twenty-five miles for the purpose of spending the week-end with a neighbor, carrying along with him a quantity of fresh meat, a bushel of sweet potatoes, corn, or other suitable food supplies. Bedding down two families at night in one-, two-, or three-room huts was indeed a puzzling problem for the housewife, but she usually solved it by spreading quilt pallets and making other temporary arrangements. Such visits were more frequent particu-

6. Percy G. Ebbutt, *Emigrant Life in Kansas*, 50-51.

larly if the neighbor lived on a favorite fishing stream, near a frequented range of deer or other wild game, or near a meeting house where religious services were held by a visiting minister once a week, or twice a month. These visits were usually repaid, although sometimes a neighbor would plead that it was quite impossible for him to leave home because he had his livestock, chickens, and crop to look after, chores to do, and numerous routine duties to perform which would not permit an extended absence from home. The chronic week-end visitor was less thrifty, if more sociable and hospitable, than his stay-at-home neighbor.

The same hospitality manifested itself at picnics and other public gatherings. When settlers met on these occasions, they were generally prepared to have "dinner on the ground." But if there were some who had not brought along a basket of food they were invited to partake of the general repast, and were expected to accept the invitation. Thus it was not uncommon for the stranger to feel as free and easy at such a feast as those who had brought baskets with them.

In general, therefore, it may be said that southern plains hospitality during this pioneering period was a natural outpouring of souls hungry for the comradeship of their kind. It was born of loneliness, isolation, and hardship, and acted as a wholesome leaven for frontier society. It buoyed up the inhabitants above the drab routine of their daily lives, and gave them strength to lay the foundations of a virile civilization.

8

"MOONLIGHT RAIDS"

I

EARLY frontier days on the southern plains were filled with pathos and tragedy as well as adventure and romance. No border people of the nation have suffered more in establishing themselves in a new country, in the face of unusual hardships, constant struggles with natural obstacles, and an ever-present fear of Indian depredations. In battling against their red enemies, the southern plains settlers were pitted against a race fighting desperately to retain the last vestige of their once valuable hunting ground. The hostile Indians were largely composed of four major tribes—Comanches, Kiowas, Cheyennes, and Arapahoes. They were ruthless in warfare, and spent much of their time in plundering the frontier settlements. Trained by their elders to maintain a Spartanlike stoicism to pain and emotion, and to habituate themselves to endure the hardships of a prairie existence, Indian children developed into formidable foes of the white settlers.

It was these adversaries who presented the gravest problem for the frontier people to solve. As a rule, only an imaginary line separated the domain of the one from that of the other. Knowing the country as they did, the red men, in their kind of warfare, had a distinct advantage over the whites. They seldom attacked the settlements unless they were reasonably sure that conditions were propitious for the success of their foray. As the moon approached its full—the favorite time for raids—the settler learned to be watchful and prepared for possible Indian attacks. He bolted and barred the doors and windows of his cabin; and sought to protect his horses and mules behind the bars of their stalls. Hundreds of pioneers now living can remember these ghost-like nights when the eerie calls of the savages made known their presence to the frightened family. In the light of the moon the marauders could see how to direct their course in plundering and to take advantage of the topography of the country for their escape back to their wild retreats. They would generally leave their haunts in a large war party and proceed toward a favorite camping place within striking distance of the settlements. From this base they would carry out their raids in bands of fifteen or twenty warriors each, striking swiftly, driving their stolen animals before them back to their rendezvous and thence back to their prairie hunting grounds. They would kill and scalp the men, and make captives of women and children, if they could escape with them. Women prisoners were often used to satisfy the lust of the warriors, and children were made slaves until they could be adopted into the tribe or sold back to their kinsmen.

From the time that Stephen F. Austin brought his colony of Anglo-Americans into Texas down to 1881, the border people of this area suffered immeasurably from Indian forays; and from the time when Kansas and Colorado homesteaders first came to the upper part of the southern plains down to 1875, settlers in this area were also subjected to the horrors of Indian warfare. The federal government sought to protect the interests of its border people by projecting a line of posts along the frontier, and succeeded only partially. In the beginning, the Indians respected the power of the troops, but after years of contact with them they learned how to circumvent them in many ways. Since they knew better the country and its animal and plant life, they were generally successful in avoiding open battle with them. In this connection, Adjutant General F. L. Britton wrote Governor Edmund J. Davis of Texas, on December 14, 1872, that "The Comanches, Sioux, and Kiowas follow down Red River, cross into the northern counties, and under cover of the 'Cross Timbers' ravage the sparsely settled section of the northwest, even carrying their depredations into more thickly settled parts;"[1] and that the Kickapoos and Lipans raided the southwestern part of the state from bases in Mexico, crossing the Rio Grande above Eagle Pass.

Before the Civil War the southern plains region was largely unoccupied by white people; it was the hunting ground of the red

1. *Report of the Adjutant General of the State of Texas for the Year 1872.* Agent S. T. Walkley verified the Adjutant General's account by his own report to General W. B. Hazen, October 10, 1868, MS, in "Operations IV," Sheridan papers, Division of Manuscripts, Library of Congress.

men, and an area greatly desired by Anglo-American settlers who were extending their settlements from the east. It was therefore a land over which the two races contested, the red man seeking to retain it in its virgin state, and the white settler attempting to gain it as a future homesite. When nearly a million troops were mustered out of the army at the close of the Civil War, a large number of them turned their eyes toward this much desired area. As soon as they were able, they flocked to the plains, and according to General W. T. Sherman, they "were rather stimulated than retarded by the danger of an Indian war."[2]

Those who came to the southern plains at this time found little to encourage them. In Texas, the frontier settlements had been pushed in for a distance of more than one hundred miles. A Texas ranger who visited the frontier wrote in the San Antonio *Daily Express* of January 18, 1871, that "The sight of hundreds of lone chimneys now standing on the frontier from the Rio Grande to the Red River; the greatest number of decaying fences and houses; and the houses in this vicinity stained with blood of men, women, and children of all ages, is truly a shame to any nation on earth." R. B. Marcy, who passed over the same region on May 16 of this year, also noticed the desolate condition of the country, and wrote: "The remains of several ranches were observed today, the occupants of which have been either killed or driven off to the more dense settlements by the Indians. Indeed this rich and beautiful section does not contain today so many white people as it did when I visited it eighteen years ago, and if Indian marauders are not punished, the whole country seems to be in a fair way of becoming totally depopulated."[3]

That these two opinions were not the immature judgments of visiting inspectors is proved by abundant documentary evidence. As early as September 26, 1866, Governor J. W. Throckmorton telegraphed President Andrew Johnson that the frontiers of Texas were rapidly being depopulated by Indian depredations, and that he was requested by the legislature of the state to inform him that unless immediate assistance was afforded by the general govern-

2. "*Personal Memoirs of General W. T. Sherman*," II, 413-14.
3. "Extracts from Inspector-General Marcy's 'Journal' of an Inspection Tour while accompanying the General-in-Chief Sherman during the months of April, May, and June, 1871," MSS, in *Semi-Official Letters of General W. T. Sherman, 1866-1871*, Division of Manuscripts, Library of Congress.

ment, a force of one thousand state troops would be raised for the defense of the exposed settlements. This communication was placed in the hands of General Phil Sheridan, who had command of the Fifth Military District, composed of Louisiana and Texas. At first, the General believed that the representations of the Governor of Texas were based on "exaggerated reports," but when he once became convinced that they were true, he dispatched the Fourth Cavalry regiment to the defense of the settlements.

The annual reports of the Adjutant General of Kansas, the messages of the Governor, and federal frontier documents indicate that raids on the helpless settlements of Kansas were just as bad. In his report of March 13, 1869, Adjutant General Moorhouse stated that the savages were attacking the frontier settlements, "plundering and burning everything before them," and that it was impossible "to get the exact number killed, as reports are conflicting, but from the best information, sixteen persons in all were killed."[4] Several years of border warfare followed before order could be brought out of chaos. In his annual report of 1874, Adjutant General G. A. Morris stated that the "present year has been one of unusual danger and hardship to the frontier settlements, and for the number and atrocity of cold-blooded murders committed by Indians on defenseless citizens of the State, ... has scarcely a parallel in the State's history."[5] On June 16 of this year, a citizen named Warren was killed and scalped in Ford County, a short distance from Fort Dodge. On the same day a party of eleven Indians made a raid into Kiowa, in Barber County, and drove off five horses. On the next day, three settlers were murdered at different point on Medicine Lodge Creek, and Isaac Keim was killed on Cedar Creek; and on June 20, George Koons, a boy fourteen years of age was killed on Mule Creek, one and one-fourth miles east of the town of Smallwood, in Comanche County. In each instance the victims were scalped, and the bodies of some of them were mutilated.

II

In view of these incessant Indian attacks on the frontier settlements it is necessary to consider the causes of hostility. Federal

4. *Adjutant General's Report of the State of Kansas for the Year 1869*, p. 6.
5. *Ibid.*, 1874.

documents dealing with the problem are sometimes confusing. At times the Indians themselves were vague in their statements. In addressing a federal Indian commission at Fort Sill, Indian Territory, on August 20, 1869, Satanta, leading chief of the Kiowas, speaking for the Comanches, Cheyennes, Arapahoes, Wichitas, and Caddoes, in addition to his own tribe, complained bitterly of the reservation policy of the federal government. "We have tried the white man's road, and found it hard; we find on it nothing but a little corn, which hurts our teeth; no sugar; no coffee. But we want to walk in the white man's road. We want to have guns, breech-loading carbines, ammunition and caps. These are part of the white man's road, and yet you want us to go back to making arrow-heads, which are used only by bad, foolish Indians,. . . ."[6] When the federal commissioners refused to give to the turbulent tribesmen the guns and ammunition which they demanded, the latter held a medicine dance, about the time the cotton falls from the cottonwood trees, and decided to make war on the frontier. Lawrie Tatum, agent for the Kiowas and Comanches, was given the following reasons for their action: "1st, bcause they got so few annuity goods last fall; 2d, because so many of them got sick and died last summer and fall; 3d, because they are not allowed to purchase ammunition; 4th, dividing the land into reservations, instead of having all the Indian country in common, and liberty to roam over it at will."

When one weighs carefully all the available evidence, and liberally discounts bias reflected in conflicting reports of agents of the departments of War and Interior, five basic causes for Indian hostility are clearly revealed. First, the intrepid march westward of the white homeseeker was viewed with deep concern and resentment by the red man. He saw his white foe occupy the best of his hunting grounds, although he struggled desperately to prevent it. Second, the federal government resorted to an inconsistent policy, which deepened the hostility of the Indian. In an effort to meet the demands of the aggressive white settlers, the government shunted the bewildered Indian about from one reservation to another, always with assurances that his new home was to be reserved exclusively for him and for his posterity. There were times when

6. *Report of the Commissioner of Indian Affairs made to the Secretary of the Interior for the Year 1869*, p. 62.

such promises could not be fulfilled, yet commissioners, actuated by a policy of opportunism, would promise concessions which the hostile tribesmen would demand. Then, to add to the confusion, the War and Interior departments, jealous of each other's authority, followed divergent courses in dealing with the tribes, often at cross-purposes. Third, the red man found it quite impossible to make the transition from a wild, free, roving life to a sedentary existence, on a narrowly restricted government reserve, even when conditions were the best. To break with traditions, manners and customs which he had always observed, and with all those things which had contributed to his earlier well-being was quite impossible. To ask him to make his life conform to the white man's code of ethics, when the latter did not always so regulate his own conduct, and when the red man's ideas of life were in violent opposition, was asking of him the unreasonable. He did not like the "white man's road," and he refused to walk on it until he was forced to do so. Fourth, the vicious influence of white outlaws and illegal traders militated against all the wholesome policies the Commissioner of Indian Affairs and his agents could put in force. The former encouraged the Indians to prey on the settlements of the whites, offering to buy their plunder, and even lending the warriors horses, guns and ammunition with which to make their forays. Fifth, the red man could see that his wild, roving life was doomed by the destruction of the wild game of the prairies. The buffalo, deer, antelope, and other wild animals, were his commissary; their slaughter by white hunters added fuel to the mounting flame of Indian resentment. In general, therefore, the struggle which followed came as a result of an inevitable cultural conflict; a primitive existence pitted against a highly complex civilization.

Since the first three of these causes have been ably treated by other writers in the field, and since the fifth cause is discussed in an earlier chapter, the fourth demands brief notice at this point. In orienting an Indian policy on the southern plains federal agents and commissioners sought to prevent the Indians from securing liquor, guns and ammunition, for under the influence of the first they became fit subjects for any kind of deviltry, and with the last two they became formidable foes of the border settlers. Yet the Indians demanded that they be supplied with these forbidden commodities. Since federal agents and traders generally refused to

countenance their demands, although sometimes they were so un-
wise as to grant them, white outlaws and illicit traders defied government regulations, and supplied the wild tribes with all their
wants. As early as 1846, sub-agent Vaughan of the Osages, in Kansas, said that "for many years past the reports of superintendents,
agents, and sub-agents have teemed with complaints on the subject
of whiskey selling to the Indians. To defeat a course followed by
unprincipled white men—squatters on the Indian border—seems to
be, indeed, a hopeless task."[7] In the next year, Commissioner
Medill, in his report to the Secretary of War, W. L. Marcy, stated
that a part of the depredations of the Santa Fe trade were made
from New Mexico and that some of the attacks were instigated, if
not participated in, by white persons. Agent James C. Calhoun of
New Mexico corroborated this assertion on June 25, 1850, in his
statement that "the constant and unrestricted intercourse of
traders with the Indians of this territory is, perhaps, the greatest
curse upon it."[8] In Texas, Agent Robert S. Neighbors wrote the
Commissioner of Indian Affairs, in 1856: "There has been a very
extensive trade carried on during the summer. It can be proven
by Indians here, that at one time Jesse Chisholm and other traders
introduced and traded to those bands [Comanches] 75 rifles, ammunition, etc., of which they have since used in depredating on our
frontier."[9] In his report of the next year, Neighbors became more
bold and charged that an Indian agent of the federal government,
on the Arkansas River, was distributing arms and ammunition
among the Comanches and Kiowas. He reminded the Commissioner that he had previously called the other's attention to this
state of affairs but that nothing had been done to stop the abuse of
federal regulations.

Shortly after the Civil War, Acting Commissioner of Indian
Affairs, Charles E. Mix, wrote to Secretary of the Interior O. H.
Browning, that "a considerable trade is carried on by Mexicans
of New Mexico in cattle stolen from citizens of Texas by the
Comanches, the Mexicans lending them horses and pistols for the
purpose." Superintendent A. B. Norton of New Mexico wrote on
August 24, 1867: "Last year on my arrival here I found that

7. *Ibid.*, 1846, p. 307.
8. *Ibid.*, 1847, p. 744; and James S. Calhoun to Orlando Brown, in *The Official Correspondence of James C. Calhoun*, p. 105.
9. *Annual Report of the Commissioner of Indian Affairs for 1856*, p. 175.

an unrestrained commerce was being carried on between the Comanches and the Mexicans, and that thousands of cattle stolen by
the Comanches from the people of Texas were being traded for by
Mexicans having trade permits from General Carleton and from
my predecessor; in fact the territory was filled with Texas cattle."[10]
The Superintendent made a half-hearted attempt to stop this
illicit traffic by cancelling the trade permits of those guilty of
violations of federal regulations, but he said that an "ex-commis-
sioner granted licenses to four different citizens, and on those
licenses and those granted or sub-let by some of the parties holding
them, I am informed that hundreds of these Mexicans are again
trading with the Comanches, and matters are as bad as ever." Texas
ranchmen vigorously protested against this organized thieving, but
it was not until 1872 that much was done about it. In this year
General Renald S. MacKenzie led an expedition of three hundred
men from Fort Concho, into New Mexico with the avowed purpose
of breaking up the illicit traffic, but the thieves heard of his coming
and scattered to parts unknown. MacKenzie did, however, succeed in driving back into Texas more than ten thousand stolen
cattle.

It is not known whether those guilty of violating federal regulations in their dealings with the wild tribes were also involved in
the traffic in white prisoners of the Indians, but there are records
to prove that they sometimes assisted in restoring them to their
relatives. White kidnapping was a lucrative business for the red
men, as they could realize more in selling a captive than they
could from a stolen horse or mule. It is quite probable that white
outlaws also shared in this kind of traffic, although to what extent
is not known. Settlers who lived in the "Cross Timbers" belt of
Texas complained that some of the most formidable Indian raids
were led by a "red-headed, blue-eyed leader." Thomas C. Battey,
who spent more than a year as a Quaker school teacher among the
Kiowas, states that on one occasion the sheriff of one of the northwestern counties of Texas informed him that twice in his official
capacity he had called out a portion of the militia to put down
Indian depredations in his county, and in the ensuing skirmishes
one or two men had been killed, who proved to be white men,

10. *Ibid.*, 1867, pp 12, 194.

December the 13th A.D. 1860

Montague Montague County Texas
Mr J H Regan my Dear Sir I seat my self at this time to let you know that I am yet in the land of the living but from the news that we heare at this time I can not say how long I shall be in the land above mentioned the Indians came in to Jack county and killed several persons and burning thiere houses and every thing that thiere devlish thoughts could invent and then came in to Parker county one amongst the thickest settled county in the State and killed two women by treating one of them as bad as thiere devilish inclinations could invent and then wraping here hair around one of thiere hands and then cutting aroun here head below the eares and then pulling the whole skin of here head off and left here for dead and the was found and braught to Weatherford the county seat of Parker county and lived some three or four days and died such cruel treatment is enough to make the blood run cold in our veins

Page from a letter written by J. H. Cox to John H. Reagan, December 13, 1860, typifying the horrors of Indian raids on Texas frontier, Montague County

"so thoroughly disguised with false hair, masks, and Indian equipage, as to readily be mistaken for Indians."[11]

In dealing with the wild tribes of the Great Plains the federal government had early adopted a twofold program. First, it had sought to bind the Indians by definite treaty agreements to be satisfied with smaller reservations, for which they were to receive annuity gifts and money compensation, and to respect the rights of settlers on the frontier. Second, it sought to impress upon the minds of the Indians the power of the white race by establishing forts at strategic points along the frontier. At these posts troops were to be stationed and used in campaigns against those tribes which would not accept the government's program.

The shortcomings of the federal policy had clearly revealed themselves by the end of the first half of the nineteenth century. In 1851, after the discovery of gold in California, a vast stream of emigration was flowing over the Great Plains, which at that time was generally regarded as an Indian country. Seeing that the plains tribes were greatly disturbed by the intrusion and that depredations were perpetrated by these Indians on white settlers passing over the area, the Commissioner of Indian Affairs sent representatives among the tribes to negotiate a treaty which would give emigrants peaceful transit over their lands, and which would fix definite boundaries between the several tribes. A council was convened at Fort Laramie, on September 17 of that year, at which the Cheyennes, Arapahoes, Crows, Assiniboines, Gros Ventres, Mandans, and Arickarees were represented. An agreement was soon concluded which granted to the whites the right to establish roads and military and other posts in the Indian country, and peaceful transit over it, in consideration for which the federal government was to pay them $50,000 a year for fifty years, to be distributed among the respective tribes in proportion to the population.

At this council the Cheyennes and Arapahoes were allotted a part of the southern plains, including the large portion of the Territory of Colorado and most of the western part of Kansas, in their possession of which the federal government was pledged "to the aforesaid Indian nations against the commission of all depredations by the people of the United States after the ratification of this

11. Thomas C. Battey, *A Quaker Among the Indians*, p. 239.

treaty."[12] A short time later, however, gold and silver were discovered in the mountains of Colorado, and thousands of frenzied fortune hunters swarmed across the plains, occupied Indian lands in the mountain region, founded cities and established roads, and drove protesting red men down upon the waters of the Arkansas. Commissioners then concluded a second treaty with these tribes at Fort Wise, Kansas, on February 18, 1861, whereby the Indians were forced to abandon their former reserve, and to be content with a comparatively small area, lying on both sides of the Arkansas River, including the country about Fort Lyon, Colorado. To salve the feelings of the discouraged Indians, the commissioners pledged the federal government to pay each tribe $30,000 a year for fifteen years, to erect houses on the Indian lands, to break up and fence agricultural lands, to furnish them with stock animals and agricultural implements, to build mills, and to provide engineers, farmers, and mechanics to assist them in their journey on the "white man's road."

In the meantime, federal commissioners had also entered into contracts with the Comanches and Kiowas, the two powerful tribes which occupied the greater part of the southern plains. In 1853, Thomas Fitzpatrick, acting as sole commissioner for the United States, concluded a treaty with the Comanches, Kiowas, and Kiowa-Apaches, at Fort Atkinson (now Kansas), whereby these tribes were recognized in their claims to their hunting grounds south of the Arkansas River, but were pledged to refrain from depredating the emigration passing over this area, and to restore all captives which they had formerly taken. In compensation for this promise of peace and friendship, the federal government was to pay the Indians $18,000 a year during a period of ten years. Although the Indians promised to refrain from molesting emigrants passing through their territory, and to remain on friendly terms with all their neighbors, the frontiers of both Mexico and the United States contiguous to their hunting grounds were subjected to devastating forays.

At the close of the Civil War, on October 18, 1865, federal commissioners concluded a treaty with the same tribes at the council ground on the Little Arkansas River, eight miles from its mouth.

12. For all Indian treaties see C. J. Kappler, *Indian Affairs, Laws and Treaties*, II (treaties listed chronologically).

The terms of this treaty they evidently knew could not be carried out. As defined by the commissioners in this agreement, the boundaries included the major portion of the southern plains within Texas and western Oklahoma, notwithstanding the fact that Texas had reserved all her public lands when that state entered the Union. The unsettled relations between the two races had evidently been engendered by an unhappy Texas reservation experiment. Since the federal government had no control over the public lands of this state, two reservations had been provided by the Texas legislature for her Indian tribes. The first of these was located at Fort Belknap on the Brazos River, for the small bands of sedentary Indians located along the frontier; and the second was established at Camp Cooper, on the Clear Fork of the Brazos, near the present town of Albany, Texas, for the wandering Comanches. At both reservations there was constant friction between the Indians and the settlers, and a short time before the Civil War both experiments were abandoned and all the tribes located on them were moved north of the Red River.

During the stressful days of the sixties, therefore, Indian relations on the southern plains had reached a crisis. The Cheyennes and Arapahoes were dissatisfied with the terms of the treaty of 1861, and complained that white intruders were dispossessing them of their lands. Alarmed by their warlike activities, Governor John Evans of Colorado raised two regiments of state troops and put them in the field against those warriors who refused to assemble at two army posts which he designated. In the fall of 1865, five hundred men, women, and children of the Cheyenne tribe, gathered at Fort Lyon and asked the protection of Major E. W. Wynkoop. They were told that they would be protected if they would occupy a site near the post, which was pointed out to them; and this they did. Yet, on November 29, 1865, Colonel J. M. Chivington with troops from the two Colorado regiments attacked them at an early morning hour, and massacred almost half of those present. In a report to President Andrew Jackson, commissioners appointed under an act of Congress approved July 20, 1867, stated that when this massacre took place "a war ensued which cost the government $30,000,000, and carried conflagration and death to the border settlements. . . . . Fifteen or twenty Indians had been killed at an expense of more than a million dollars apiece, while hundreds of our soldiers had lost their lives, many of our border settlers had been butchered and much property destroyed."

When it was found that the federal government was fighting a costly war for little purpose, negotiations were again resumed. William S. Harney, John B. Sanborn, and others met representatives of the hostile tribes, in October, 1865, at the mouth of the Little Arkansas, and concluded a new treaty with them. At this council the Cheyennes and Arapahoes were induced to abandon their old home and accept a new reservation, partly in Kansas and partly in the Indian Territory, with the understanding that they could continue to hunt on their old range as long as the wild game lasted. But when the treaty came before the Senate, it was so amended that the Indians were denied any part of Kansas for a reserve, and were given only that part of the Indian Territory to which the Cherokees, who owned it, might consent. The confused Indians, therefore, found themselves without a home, except that temporary range defined under the treaty as their hunting ground.

At this stage of treaty making, affairs of the southern plains tribes were found to be so helplessly muddled that Congress at last demanded that an intelligent program be launched; and the "peace policy" was inaugurated. An important council was held by federal commissioners with representatives of the Cheyenne, Arapaho, Comanche, Kiowa, and Kiowa-Apache tribes, in October, 1867, on Medicine Lodge Creek, Kansas. As a result of this meeting, the Cheyennes and Arapahoes were confederated and placed on the Darlington Agency, which was taken from Cherokee lands, in the northwestern part of what is now Oklahoma; and the remaining three tribes were assigned a reservation south of them on what was called the Wichita Reserve. Thus, the final homes of more than six thousand wild Indians were fixed, and the program of teaching them how "to walk on the white man's road" was put under way once more. The Indians were to be maintained by the government, taught how to farm and how to raise horses and cattle, and trained in the schools of the white man.

Still, many of the warriors were not ready for the new life which the Washington authorities had planned for them, and continued their harrowing raids on the frontier, using their reserves as bases from which to operate. This practice necessitated extensive campaigns against them. In the winter of 1868, General Phil Sheridan

carried out a campaign against those bands camping along the
Washita River; and Colonel George Custer with a part of his force
struck the camp of Black Kettle and his band of Cheyennes and
destroyed it, killing men, women, and children. Sheridan then
forced other bands to go on their reserves, and it was thought that
Indian wars were at an end. But such was not the case; forays continued. One of the most extensive campaigns ever carried out
against plains tribes was inaugurated in 1874 by more than three
thousand troops under the command of Colonel Nelson A. Miles,
and other notable Indian fighters. More than fourteen battles were
fought, and the Indians were so thoroughly beaten that by the
summer of 1875 the last of the rebellious bands had come to Fort
Sill and were settled on their reservation.[13]

III

In this long period of disturbed relations, it is not difficult to see
that the angry tribesmen had some just grievances. In its efforts to
make room for the rapidly developing frontier, the federal government moved them about from reservation to reservation until they
were not sure that any of their former lands were to be left for
them. Then, the Indian agents carried out only those provisions
of treaties which best suited their needs, and wholly ignored others.
The Indians were told that they must give up their wild, roving
life; that they must depend on the bounty of the white race for
their subsistence; but when their agents withheld their annuities,
or furnished them with only half of what was needed to keep them
from starving, they were then forced to violate |provisions of their
treaties by hunting off their ranges or by depredating the settlements of the frontier, in order to add to their supplies. In each
instance, where federal commissioners and agents made serious
blunders, and thereby angered the savages, the settlements along
the frontier bore the brunt of Indian resentment. Indeed, the
charred remains of hundreds of homesteads, the destruction of
millions of dollars worth of property, and the scalped and mutilated

13. For detailed printed accounts of the two campaigns see *Personal Memoirs of P. H.
Sheridan*, II, chaps. xi-xiv; and *Personal Recollections* of General Nelson A. Miles, chaps.
ix-xii. Manuscript reports of Generals P. H. Sheridan, C. C. Augur, and John Pope, with
accompanying papers, are found in the Old Files Section, Adjutant General's Office, War
Department.

bodies of hundreds of men, women, and children were the fruits of a vacillating Indian program. For more than three decades the warring tribes showered the southern plains frontier with their "moonlight raids," causing untold suffering and destruction.

Since the federal posts scattered along the frontier did not offer adequate protection to the settlements, the frontier settlers were forced to take matters into their own hands. Protests which they made to state officials resulted in the organization of militia and ranger companies. It was this kind of troops which Governor Evans of Colorado put :n the field against the Cheyennes and Arapahoes in 1865, and which the Governor of Kansas furnished General Sheridan for his winter campaign of 1868. Texas had long maintained a ranger force on the frontier which had done effective service in patrolling the border, driving away marauding bands of Indians and outlaws, and making campaigns against the hostile Comanches and Kiowas into the very heart of their prairie ranges. In some instances the states furnished settlers with guns and ammunition for their own protection; and when raiders were reported in the community, a posse would quickly form and start in pursuit of the Indians. These forces were seldom successful in overtaking and punishing the marauders, but their activity undoubtedly aided in holding the Indians in check.

The bitterness aroused in the frontier people by Indian depredations was expressed in many newspapers of the country. Such publications as the Topeka *Commonwealth*, the Kansas *State Record*, the Wichita *Eagle*, the Dodge City *Messenger*, the Denver *Rocky Mountain News*, the Santa Fe *Daily New Mexican, Flake's Daily Bulletin* of Galveston, the Galveston *News*, the Dallas *Herald*, the San Antonio *Herald*, the San Antonio *Daily Express*, the Waco *Register*, and the Denison *News* carried frequent accounts of Indian atrocities, and criticisms of the federal program. These accounts gave the sordid details of the murder and scalping of men, women, and children, and the feeble efforts made by the settlers to protect themselves. The Waco *Register* of April 21, 1866, carried an account of two of its fellow townsmen who visited the northwestern frontier of the state and reported upon their return that the entire tier of counties through which they passed seemed to swarm with Indians; that "not more than one-fifth of the old ranches are occupied"; and that "the inhabitants remaining for the most part have run together and forted-up for self-preservation." *Flake's Daily Bulletin* charged the federal government with this state of affairs, and complained: "First we shoot half the warriors of a tribe, kill the squaws, and knock the papooses' brains out, and we give the others whiskey, blankets, rifles, and powder." That there was at least a basis for this complaint is seen from an account of an Indian foray in Medina County, in the San Antonio *Daily Express* for January 15, 1873, in which it was reported that the raiders were dressed "in United States Soldiers' overcoats and hats," and armed with the best of weapons. The depth of the frontiersmen's bitterness over their prolonged suffering is sounded in an article contributed to the *New York Times* on June 11, 1867, by a correspondent in Denver, Colorado. He wrote that a citizen of his town had offered ten dollars for every scalp of a hostile warrior brought to him; and that at a mass meeting of the citizens of Central City a fund of five thousand dollars was raised to buy Indian scalps at the rate of twenty-five dollars each. Numerous other instances might be given, over a period of more than twenty-five years but in general the story is the same; failure of the federal policy and destruction of property, ravishing of helpless women, and killing and scalping of innocent victims by the Indians were almost staple items of news carried by the frontier press.

It was to the credit of the frontiersman, however, that generally he remained at his post, brought order out of chaos, and reclaimed the entire region from a prairie wilderness. The federal government, too, finally awoke to the seriousness of the Indian problem on the frontier, and through the willing aid given by the plains states so controlled the wild tribes as to confine their activities within the limits of their reserves. By 1880 the last of the "moonlight raids" had occurred and the settlers were left in peaceful possession of the southern plains, over which they had been struggling with the wild tribes for three decades.

9

BORDER HEROINES

I

THE valorous deeds of pathfinders, hunters, and Indian fighters of the southern plains have been recorded by the historians of the nation. Students have long been familiar with the names of Zebulon Pike, William Bent, "Big Foot" Wallace, "Wild Bill" Hickok, "Buffalo Bill" Cody, Ewing Young, Josiah Gregg, "Kit" Carson, and their kind. But there is much that needs to be known concerning the heroism and fortitude of many obscure women of the border. Their lives were not so spectacular as those of their male contemporaries, but in general they were no less heroic. Indeed, if any distinction is to be made between the two, a less exacting order of courage and fortitude was required of him who followed the buffalo and Indian trails than of her who "carried on" with the monotonous routine of frontier drudgery, when she knew that the danger of an Indian raid was always imminent, that outlaws were robbing and murdering in the country, or that she was many miles from her nearest neighbor and cut off from society for weeks and months at a time. When the male defender of the home became restless or fearful of border trouble, he could find relief for his pent-up energies and emotions by hunting the wild game of the forests or prairies, by enlisting in a punitive expedition against the Indian or outlaw marauders, or by looking after the outdoor interests of his ranch or farm; but the average border woman had no such opportunity. While her husband or father was away, she sometimes had to wait long hours and days for his return, and she had no way of knowing that he was alive until he returned. As a result she must be possessed of patience, courage, and hope, in order to endure the trying ordeal of frontier life. Hundreds of unmarked graves of these lonely homemakers, who could not bear up under such trials, have yet to be found in the "Cross Timbers" belt and on the prairies; and in the same area are the final resting places of others who perished defending their homes and loved ones against the attacks of Indians, even giving their scalps to grace the spear or shield of their bloodthirsty murderers. In all the relations of border life, women played their roles superbly; in happiness, success, sickness, death, or toil they measured up well to a high standard of achievement, and because they did so, their deeds should be remembered by those who today reap the benefits of their early hopes and strivings.

From the time when immigrants first came to the southern plains until they had finally established themselves on their farms, they were subjected to ravaging attacks of Indians. Often, in crossing the plains, their wagons were burned, their teams were taken, the harness was destroyed, and women travelers were made captives, ravished, and carried off "to a life compared with which death would have been sweet. Men, women, and children were butchered and their bodies savagely mutilated." Albe B. Whiting, in an address before the Kansas State Historical Society, at Topeka, on December 6, 1910, recounts an incident which typifies the experiences of hundreds of prairie travelers during these Indian days. One of a rescue party which left a point near Fort Riley, on May 20, 1857, to seek out a fleeing party of emigrants who had been attacked by Indians, found the emigrants in the following condition when overtaken:

An hour later we met the last of the emigrant party, the mother and brother of its murdered captain. The larger number had slipped past our camp in the night, and while confident we were a relief party in search of them, the women were so terrorized they would not allow the men to show themselves to us. The scantily clad old lady of nearly seventy years, leaning heavily on her son, a man of forty, his head tied in a red cotton handkerchief, on his shoulder a couple of guns, and in his hand a firebrand, keeping a coal alive to light a fire at their next resting place, hardly able to drag their feet along, were a pitiful sight. . . . The old lady had dropped exhausted on the grass. Taking a handful of sorrel from her mouth she told me it had been her only food for five days."[1]

The experiences of such border heroines in the Indian country

1. Albe B. Whiting, "Some Western Border Conditions in the 50's and 60's," in *Kansas State Historical Collections*, XII (1911-1912), 5.

may best be treated in a chapter of this scope by selecting a few typical instances. There are accounts of hundreds of characters which might be included in a longer discussion, most of which are as interesting as the ones that follow.

II

During the days of the Texas revolution an Englishwoman was captured by the wild Comanches of the southern plains. The account of her captivity is one of the most amazing stories of hardship, suffering, and horror ever told by a prisoner of the American Indians. Mrs. Sarah Ann Horn was the wife of John Horn, an English emigrant and member of the ill-fated Beales Colony of Texas. Dr. John Charles Beales was granted permission by the Mexican state of Coahuila and Texas to plant a colony between the Rio Grande and Nueces River, and in 1834 he organized at New York "The Rio Grande and Texas Land Company" to carry out his project.[2] On November 11 of that year he sailed on board the *Amos Wright*, bound for the Texas coast, with his first and only colony. After a toilsome journey, both by sea and by land, the colonists established themselves on Las Moras Creek, within their grant, on March 16, 1835. Many things, however, conspired to make their experiences trying in the extreme. The Comanches were turbulent and warlike; invading Mexican soldiers, attempting to crush the rebellion of the Texans, were not friendly to foreign colonists; the lonely and isolated position of the site was not to the liking of many of the first comers; and the semi-arid country could promise little in the way of a livelihood. After almost a year's precarious existence the colony was abandoned and the survivors started for Matamoras, on the Mexican coast. After they had journeyed on their way several days, they stopped at a large lake on the San Patricio trail, and here, on April 4, 1836, they were attacked by a band of forty or fifty Comanche Indians. All the colonists were killed except Mrs. Horn, her two small sons, John and Joseph, aged four and five, and a Mrs. Harris and her infant child.

2. For Mrs. Horn's account of this ill-fated enterprise, see E. House, *A Narrative of the Captivity of Mrs. Horn, and Her Two Children, with that of Mrs. Harris, by the Commanche Indians.*

From this point the narrative of Mrs. Horn reads like the story of a horrible nightmare. The grief-stricken women and their helpless babes were forced to ride long hours on rough-traveling mules, without food and water, until they were exhausted; they were led by their captors on extended marches, sometimes on foot and sometimes astride a mule or horse, over gullies and ravines, across swollen streams, through brush-covered terrain, and up steep hills or mountainsides. Even the end of the day would bring them little relief, for they would be shackled and staked out, like the animals ridden by the warriors, and forced to submit to the ravages of swarms of mosquitoes. Until Mrs. Horn was ransomed at San Miguel, New Mexico, on September 19, 1837, both women lived a life of terror.

Mrs. Horn thus describes her plight at the end of the first day:

Before they laid down for the night, Mrs. Harris and myself were bound by passing a cord about our ancles [sic] and arms, so as to bring the latter close to our sides. In this condition we were placed upon the naked ground, with a blanket thrown over us, and the whole of that dreadful night, my agonized heart seemed ready to burst, as I listened to the cries of my orphan babes, as they called for their murdered father, and for water to quench their thirst; and as though my cup of anguish was not otherwise complete, the mosquitoes, of enormous size, were annoying me at every point, without the use of a single limb with which to defend myself. It is infinitely beyond the power of language to express the horrors of this painfully memorable night. The babe lay quiet till near day-light, when it began to cry with cold and hunger, as its mother's breasts were in such condition that she had not been able to give it suck, and it had been brought thus far upon food by hand. I had bestowed a mother's care upon it, but had no chance to prepare it any food since the day previous. As soon as we were permitted to rise, I asked the Indians for some flour with which to make the babe something to eat. They said, "yes, it shall have something to eat;" a smile accompanied the reply, and a tall, muscular Indian came to me and taking hold of it, swung it by its arms, and threw it up as high as he could, and let it fall upon the ground at its feet. This barbarous act having been repeated three times, its sufferings were at an end.[3]

3. *Ibid.*, 18-19.

The heroism of Mrs. Horn is best seen in her solicitude for her children and for Mrs. Harris and her child. Several times she was punished for her self-denial in caring for her loved ones. The savages seemed to take a great delight in cruelly abusing her babes, in order to see her own anguish. When she was captured, she held in her arms Mrs. Harris' infant, and for that reason they came to believe that it belonged to her. The morning after it had been slain, a string was tied about its neck and it was hung to the horn of a saddle on one of the mules. A warrior then told Mrs. Horn to mount, but she refused; he then demanded of Mrs. Harris that she mount, but she likewise refused. Finally, one of the warriors approached the mule, threw the child to the ground, and again commanded Mrs. Horn to mount; and she obeyed.

In the course of the second day's journey Joseph was thrown from the mule which he was riding, and his shoulder was seriously bruised. His mother was not allowed to dress his wound, which, after the passing of a few days, became blown by flies so that "the maggots were crawling about in the sore." The sorrowing mother writes thus of his suffering: "As though these savages would prove by actual experiment how much a mother's heart could endure, and not die within her, they would let this piece of suffering humanity lie all night, after a hard day's travel, with his body burned to a blister and his shoulder being devoured by worms, pleading as for life for a drop of water, as unmoved as the earth on which they reposed." Partly as a result of his weakened condition, a day or so later the little lad fell from his mount into a running stream. He attempted to scramble up its muddy bank, and had almost succeeded in doing so when one of the enraged warriors stabbed him in the face with his spear, and hurled him back into the water; "but," the mother writes, "the poor suffering little creature made another effort, and with blood streaming down his naked body from his wounded face, gained the shore." Then still later, both he and his brother were ducked in a stream until their "emaciated bodies were enormously distended," while the anguished mother was forced to look on without rendering them any aid, although she later states that she attacked her tormentors so vigorously that they did not repeat their act of cruelty.

After wandering from place to place, the Comanches finally came to the New Mexican town of San Miguel for the purpose of trading with its inhabitants. Here Mrs. Horn was ransomed by a kindly disposed Mexican, who paid for her a horse, four bridles, two blankets, two looking-glasses, two knives, some tobacco, and some powder and balls. Some time later Mrs. Harris was also purchased, but the two unfortunate children remained in captivity despite frantic efforts of the mother to redeem them. Missouri traders worked in her behalf, but the Indians refused to part with the boys. Mrs. Horn later heard that John had died a short time after she had left him. He contracted pneumonia when, insufficiently clothed, he was forced by his captors to guard a horse herd one bitterly cold night. The other lad was never heard from after Mrs. Horn returned to "the states." The traders were kind enough to escort her back to Independence, Missouri, and later she returned to England.

III

One who examines early manuscripts, newspapers, magazines, and other contemporary materials will find here and there brief statements which reveal the fortitude and courage of frontier women of the southern plains, but since nothing else is known about these characters, no trustworthy account of their deeds can be written. Such an instance is given by Touissante L. Cox of Kansas. Writing to an Indian agent in his territory, on March 7, 1857, he states that during his absence two Sac and Fox Indians had come to his home to obtain a chicken to cook for a sick child. His wife gave them the fowl, and the Indians were about to leave when they noticed a young brown horse standing near the front gate. They offered her sixty-five dollars for the animal, but she refused. The following night the horse was stolen, while Cox was still absent. Knowing that if she waited for her husband to return, the thieves might succeed in getting away, the determined woman decided upon a surprising course. "My wife missed the horse by breakfast time and went in pursuit but did not get their trail until next day. She followed them two days and one night. . . . ." Cox makes this statement as if the act was an ordinary one; yet the country through which she rode was only partially settled, and was frequented by hostile bands of Indians and outlaws. And although she did not succeed in recovering the horse, her act was an example of the rare courage and determination of border women.

Another brief glimpse of a border heroine is found in an article contributed to the *New York Herald* by W. L. Ormsby, its special correspondent, on October 31, 1858. Ormsby was a passenger on a stagecoach traveling on the Butterfield trail, and had arrived at Fort Phantom Hill, a station beyond the line of border settlements in western Texas. At one time this post had been occupied by federal troops but it was abandoned in 1854 and was now used for a stage station only. Concerning the keeper of the post and his wife, he writes: "Mr. Burlington and his wife we found here all alone, hundreds of miles from any settlement, bravely stopping at their post, on Phantom Hill, fearless of the attacks of bloodthirsty Indians—as brave a man as ever settled on the frontier. . . . ." And the writer might have added that the wife of the keeper, too, was as brave a soul as ever lived on the frontier, for the post was located well within the favorite hunting region of the fierce Comanches, and only a woman could understand the horrors attending a life of captivity in their camps.

Many brave women lived on the southern plains during the period when settlers began to establish themselves on this dangerous frontier. One of these is well described by Randolph B. Marcy in *Harper's Monthly Magazine* in 1870.[4] Shortly before, an enterprising pioneer by the name of Babb had established a home beyond the frontier of Texas, near the headwaters of the Colorado River. The household consisted of a wife and three small children, with the addition of "a female friend by the name of L—— (Mary Jane Luster), who having previously lost her husband, was passing the summer with the family. Marcy pictured the woman as a "graceful feminine person," about twenty-five years of age, "with an erect and commanding presence." She had, however, been born and reared on the frontier, and had inherited a robust constitution.

At an early age Mrs. Luster had been taught to ride, and in after life it had been one of her chief sources of pleasures. In this connection, Marcy writes: "In the saddle she felt perfectly self-confident; and while dashing at full speed over the gentle undulatings of the prairie upon her favorite horse, her long locks streaming in unconfined luxuriance in the breeze, and her lithe, supple person yielding in centaur-like unison with every movement, pulsation, and breath

4. Randolph B. Marcy, "Border Reminiscences," in *Harper's Monthly Magazine*, XLI (June-November, 1870), 120 *et sqq.*; and T. A. Babb, *In the Bosom of the Comanches*, 20-38.

of the generous animal that shared her enthusiasm, she presented an equestrian model of bewitching beauty and grace."

One morning in June, 1867, Mr. Babb set out for a distant market with some cattle, leaving the family without a male protector. Since Indians had not lately been seen in that vicinity, he decided that it was safe to leave the ranch. On this particular morning the women were busily engaged at their tasks within the house. The two oldest children, who were playing in the yard, called to their mother that horseback riders were approaching. When Mrs. Babb looked out of the door, to her horror she perceived that the advancing strangers were hostile Indians. She shouted to her children to come into the house, but thinking that the riders were white men, they remained at play. Before the distressed mother could make them see their peril, they were captured by the warriors, who soon surrounded the house. Mrs. Luster had climbed a ladder to the loft of the cabin for safety, but before Mrs. Babb and her remaining child could escape, the warriors had entered the home. Marcy describes the dreadful scene that followed. Some warriors "rushed toward the young child, which the terror-stricken mother struggled frantically to rescue from their clutches; but they were too much for her, and tearing the infant from her arms, they dashed it upon the floor; then seizing her by the hair they wrenched back her head and cut her throat from ear to ear, putting her to death instantaneously."

At this point, Mrs. Luster, who was watching the scene below from the loft, screamed, and revealed her hiding place. The savages soon dragged her down the ladder and overpowered her. She was then placed on a horse, the children were placed on another, and her captors hurriedly rode with them toward their prairie rendezvous. For several days and nights the Indians traveled as rapidly as their mounts could carry them, making only short halts to graze and rest their animals and to renew their own strength. Unaccustomed to such strenuous exertions, the captives suffered greatly from their forced travel. Finally, however, when the Indians believed that all chance of being overtaken by white pursuers was gone, they slackened their speed, and likewise relaxed their vigilance in guarding their prisoners.

During the long hours of their flight, Mrs. Luster had much time to think about the terrible plight she and the two children were in. Although she knew that she could not escape with them, she resolved to attempt to make her own escape at the first favorable opportunity, and to seek their rescue later. One dark night, while the weary warriors were fast asleep, she determined to make her venture. Quietly she crawled away from her pallet, caught one of the best horses which the Indians had, mounted his bare back, and started him off toward the north at a slow walk. As soon as she got out of hearing of the camp, she increased his speed, and fled through the night, looking back now and then to see if she were pursued. For thirty-six hours or more she urged him on relentlessly, denying herself the sleep which threatened to overcome her again and again, and trying to forget her extreme want for food and water. Just when she had come to the conclusion that she must halt and rest, she found that she was being pursued by a ravenous pack of wolves, which soon were snapping at the heels of her mount. Her only alternative was to continue urging on her tired horse until the coming of day, at which time she believed the cowardly wolves would slink away. At last, with the coming of dawn, the horse was so exhausted that "he was barely able to reel and stagger along at a slow walk"; but the light of the new day caused the wolves to leave. So at last she "tied one end of a long lariat to the neck of her horse, and with the other end around her waist dropped down upon the ground into a deep sleep."

After hours of profound slumber, she was awakened by "the pattering sound of horses' feet beating the earth on every side." To her dismay, she found herself again a prisoner, but of another band of Indians, in all probability Kiowas, who carried her to their camp a short distance away. But she was not to be balked in her efforts for freedom; once more she began to watch for an opportunity to escape. One day a foraying party of warriors, who had left camp six days prior to that time, brought back some green corn. She reasoned that, since the nomadic tribes did not cultivate the soil, the corn must have been grown in the field of a white settler, not more than three days' journey distant. On a subsequent night she again escaped astride an excellent horse. Guiding her course by the stars, she rode in the direction from which she had seen the raiding party come, and after three days of rapid riding, fatigued and hungry, she came upon the banks of a large river, flowing directly across her path. Its waters were swollen and swift; but she knew that if she tarried long, waiting for a more opportune time to cross, there was danger of her recapture by the Indians. So, mustering all the courage at her command, the dauntless woman forced her tired horse to plunge into the turgid stream and to swim to the opposite side.

She then continued on her way until she met some wagons in charge of Robert Bent, from whom she begged food. Bent, of course, was greatly perturbed at meeting a woman in this remote place, for she was then on the Santa Fe trail and the river she had just crossed was the Arkansas. He gave her food and water, and as she ate he inquired of her where she lived. "Texas," she replied. To the incredulous trader she then related her experiences from the day she was captured on the ranch. After she had eaten and satisfied her thirst, she again mounted her horse, thanked her benefactor, and rode away toward the nearest settlement, as directed by him.

When Bent arrived at Fort Zarah, Kansas, he called on the federal Indian agent located there and told him of meeting the lone woman rider. It so happened that at that time the agent was holding a council with the same band of warriors from whom she had last escaped and who had just told him of the whole affair. The agent at once dispatched a rider to follow the woman and conduct her to Council Grove. Here she was kindly received, and remained for some time, hoping that she could hear from the two captured children, but in this she was disappointed. Later, however, the children were ransomed by the agent. In the meantime, at Council Grove Mrs. Luster formed the acquaintance of a man whom she later married.

Concerning the exploits of this unusual woman, Marcy writes: "It will readily be seen, by reference to a map of the country over which Mrs. L— passed, that the distance from the place of her capture to the point where she struck the Arkansas River could not have been short of about five hundred miles, and the greater part of this immense expanse of desert plain she traversed alone, without seeing a single civilized human habitation."

IV

Another instance of fortitude and suffering on the part of women captives in the hands of southern plains Indians is recounted by

General Nelson A. Miles. In the early fall of 1874, the German (sometimes given as Germaine) family was traveling from western Missouri to Colorado in a small family caravan.[5] While crossing the Kansas plains, on September 11, they were suddenly attacked by a band of Cheyenne warriors; father, mother, son, and eldest daughter were killed and scalped; and the four younger sisters, ages 15, 13, 9, and 7, were taken prisoners.

For many weeks the girls were forced to suffer all the privations and hardships of their captors during this stressful time, for this was the year when the federal troops, under Colonel Miles, Davidson, Buel, and others, were trying to force the wild tribes to accept their reservations. Because of the relentless warfare the soldiers were waging against them, the Indians were given little peace; those who refused to settle down on their reservations were driven from one desert retreat to another until in a half-famished condition, their horses gone, and their war paraphernalia destroyed, they at last begged for terms. One of the girl prisoners later stated that on one occasion during this period her captor broiled a skunk and ate it, offering her a part of it also. Although she could not bring herself to the point where she could eat it, ravenously hungry as she was, she did partake of its liver. In the course of their travels from one place to another, in order to keep out of the way of pursuing troops, one band of warriors, under Chief Stone Calf, fled toward New Mexico, carrying with them the two older captives, Catherine and Sophia; while a second band, led by Chief Gray Beard, crossed the Red River, with the two younger girls, Julia and Adelaide, and established a camp on McClellan Creek, in what is now Hutchinson County, Texas.

It was this second band that Lieutenant Frank Baldwin with a detachment of troops from Colonel Miles' command attacked on November 4, 1874. The Indians were completely taken by surprise and fled, leaving their prisoners behind. According to Baldwin, the girls were found hiding under a buffalo robe.

Upon lifting the covering there were revealed two of the most deplorable and abject looking little girls ever seen, unkempt and ragged, their nether limbs sore, chafed and raw from riding. They

5. For three interesting accounts of this affair, see Nelson A. Miles, *Personal Recollections*, 159-60, 175-81; Grace E. Meredith, *Girl Captives of the Cheyennes*, chaps. ii-xii; and Alice Blackwood Baldwin, *Memoirs of the Late Frank D. Baldwin*, Part II, chap. iii.

were objects for commiseration. When the main command returned to the scene the girls were seated in an ambulance, and looking seriously at the observant throngs of soldiers, one of them said, "Be youns soldiers?" Upon being assured their captors were soldiers, the elder girl rejoined, "We-re so glad, we heard sisters praying all the time, that God would send the soldiers to deliver them."[6]

The girls then told their listeners of the many trying experiences through which they had passed, and said that the Cheyenne chief, Stone Calf, still held Catherine and Sophia captive. As to the effect of their story upon their listeners, Miles writes: "It was surprising to see the sympathy and emotion of the soldiers and trainmen as they listened to the story from the lips of these two little half-starved girls." Indeed, one of the teamsters remarked, as tears rolled down his cheeks: "I have driven my mules over these plains for three months, but I will stay forever or until we get them other girls." The children were then sent to Fort Leavenworth, Kansas, under the care of Dr. Powell, and were given the proper treatment and attention.

Colonel Miles also dispatched an Indian courier to the west in search of Stone Calf and his warriors, bearing a demand for their immediate return to the Darlington Agency, under the threat of extermination if they did not do so, and an order for the release of the two prisoners unharmed. The messenger also carried with him a photograph of Julia and Adelaide, which had been made at Fort Leavenworth after they had been properly attired, and upon the back of which was the following message:

> To the Misses Germaine: Your little sisters are well, and in the hands of friends. Do not be discouraged. Every effort is being made for your welfare.
>
> (Signed) Nelson A. Miles, Colonel, etc.[7]

Stone Calf and his starving followers were overtaken near the Texas-New Mexico boundary line, almost frozen to death in a blizzard which was sweeping the plains. Since most of his horses were dead from the cold or starvation, and his warriors were without food, disheartened, and grumbling, the chieftain was quite

6. *Ibid.*, p. 76.
7. Miles, *op. cit.*, p. 176.

willing to begin his journey toward his reservation, over the snow-covered plains. And heeding the warning of Colonel Miles, he now showed the two captives every consideration. Their teepee was pitched near his and he warned his young warriors that he would hold them responsible for their treatment of the prisoners. On March 1, 1875, the four orphans were happily reunited.

For a time the girls made their home at Fort Leavenworth; and Colonel Miles was appointed their guardian. From Congress he secured a provision in an appropriation bill diverting ten thousand dollars from the annuities of the Cheyennes for the benefit of the four girls. The interest was to go for their support until they came of age, and then the sum was to be divided equally among them. After the surrender of the warring bands, the Indians were formed in a long line in the presence of the troops. The two elder girls then slowly walked down the line pointing out to the officers seventy-five of those who had been responsible for the murder of their family and for other atrocities. Immediately the offenders were arrested and put under the charge of Captain R. H. Pratt who conducted them to Saint Augustine, Florida, for confinements; and it was largely by this treatment that the possibility of a future outbreak was averted.

V

In other frontier relations, women were often confronted with the peril of Indian raids. One instance is given in the life story of Mrs. Emily Haines Harrison, contributed to the *Kansas State Historical Collections*. This courageous woman migrated to the western frontier of Kansas in 1866, and settled on the Saline River. During the period of the Civil War she had served as a nurse, and she found her experience useful on the frontier. In September, 1867, a young man by the name of Schermerhorn came for her to go to the bedside of his brother's wife, an expectant mother. Since she had formerly agreed to perform this service, she went along without asking questions. Just before arriving at their destination, however, they heard firing in the distance. She asked for an explanation, and was told by her escort that the Indians were attacking a blockhouse above his brother's ranch, and that a courier had been dispatched to Fort Harker to ask for troops to drive the Indians away. When she arrived at the home of the sick woman, the thoroughly alarmed husband thus addressed her: "Mrs. Haines, my wife's life depends on you; I know you have no fear. I will put the bed in the wagon and take my wife away, if you say so." When the brave visitor looked at her prospective patient, however, she advised against such a move. He then said: "Well, if the Indians come down upon us and the worst comes, I will kill my wife." From the account given, there is little doubt that he would have carried out his promise, had it been necessary. As to what followed, Mrs. Harrison writes:

> Mr. Schermerhorn stood with his loaded gun at a four-paned window facing toward the besieged blockhouse, which was about a mile distant. The troops would come from the same direction. The young woman's mother was there also. I have no recollections of her saying anything. I have never been able to recall any incidents of the two hours before the troops came, except that when the child was born I tore a strip from the string of the white apron I wore, tied the cord and cut it with the bowie-knife. When the troops came like the wind from the direction of Fort Harker the Indians fled. The tension being over, I fainted away, there being nothing further for me to do. . . . .[8]

Concerning a later incident with which this border heroine was connected, the *Kansas State Record*, for October 17, 1868, states that "Mrs. Haines and Mrs. Doctor Greer, from the upper Saline river, came into town on Thursday, to ask our people for clothing and food to enable the settlers in that section of the state to live through the winter."[9] The crops made in that vicinity had been destroyed by the grasshoppers and Indians. "Not only did the Indians destroy what little crops were raised, but killed and drove off the stock of the settlers, leaving them entirely destitute of the means of living." The appeal of these two heroic souls met with a favorable response; sufficient supplies were dispatched "to make all comfortable for the winter."

During these turbulent days even the schoolroom was often shadowed with the fear of Indian depredations. Miss Rosella S. Honey, a Kansas teacher, writes that one day while her school was

8. Mrs. Emily Haines Harrison, "Reminiscences of Early Days in Ottawa County," in *Kansas State Historical Collections*, X (1907-1908), 629.
9. Quoted in *ibid.*

in session she noticed two of her girls shaking violently. "At first she thought that they were stricken with an ague, but upon looking around to see if she could find any other reason for their agitation, she discovered an Indian with arms resting on the window sill, grinning in a seemingly sarcastic way, enjoying the fright of the children." On another occasion her school was broken up for the day by the arrival of a large band of red men who were curious to inspect everything in the building. In each instance, however, the visitors were not hostile, and did little harm beyond frightening the children.

The oldest living settlers of Hamilton County, Texas, can still remember an incident of far graver consequence. On July 11, 1867, the Warlene Valley school, taught by Miss Ann Whitney, was attacked by a band of wild Comanches. At two o'clock on this fateful day one of the girl students chanced to see a band of horsemen approaching the schoolhouse, and called the attention of her teacher to it. Miss Whitney at first thought that the approaching visitors were cowboys from a nearby ranch, but when they had ridden into the school grounds, she discovered to her dismay that they were hostile Indians. She immediately barred the door and bade the children escape through the windows into the brush of the Leon River bottom, and most of them did so. But there were four children who had not suceeded in getting away from the building before it was surrounded by the Indian warriors. The leader of the band, reported to be a red-headed white man, cursed her and demanded that she open the door, but this she refused to do. They then fired through the cracks of the logs and wounded her several times, but she refused to listen to their demands and continued to plead for the lives of the children. Finally the Indians gathered at the door with the intention of forcing it. While they were thus engaged, Miss Whitney succeeded in helping two little girls out of a window on the opposite side of the house, and in this way they made their escape. She then used the last of her rapidly failing strength to lift a loose board of the flooring and temporarily hide two boys, the last of her pupils, under the house. After this she fell dead before the door. The warriors then broke down the door, and looking about, discovered the hiding place of the boys, whom they now made captives. One of them, however, Lewis Manning, made his escape by dashing into nearby underbrush.

In this same raid Miss Amanda Howard also distinguished herself by a wild ride past the schoolhouse while the Indians were there, in order to arouse the people across the river to their impending peril. As a result of her heroism, a posse was soon formed and the Indians were driven out of the country.

In view of these terrible experiences of frontier life, one often wonders why women living in well-developed settlements of the east, enjoying comparative security and material blessings, would consent to go with their husbands and fathers to a region where hardship, danger, and social isolation could be expected. The answer is a difficult one. Accounts of the horrors of Indian massacres and depredations, the drudgery an deprivations of frontier life, and numerous border handicaps were found in the newspapers and magazines of all the states; and, moreover, newcomers to the country often wrote to people living in the regions from which they came, describing to them their hardships and sorrows—and still they came. Some who came, evidently, were actuated by a desire to brave all dangers and tribulations in order to recover lost fortunes, or to establish homes for themselves and their children; but some, too, must have been led to make the sacrifice through a daring spirit of adventure—the same spirit which led their ancestors over the Alleghany Mountains to the "dark and bloody hunting grounds" of Kentucky, Tennessee, and the Old South.

10

LIFE OF THE RANGE RIDER

I

FROM the time when the rising tide of Texas pioneering first reached the cow country until the end of the period of Indian depredations, the ranchman played the role of the Anglo-American frontiersman, the advance guard of white civilization. White thieves and hostile Indians were his common foes; and from 1850 to 1885, he did more than hold his own against them, for he gradually took control of the best lands of the southern plains. By the end of the Civil War the "Cross Timbers" belt was pretty well grazed by his cattle, and soon after he was willing to contest with the redman the control of the hundreds of thousands of acres of grass-covered plains stretching west of this timbered barrier. In less than a decade after the Red River Indian War of 1874-75, he had well occupied this coveted grazing area.[1] In 1876, the Panhandle was partially stocked with cattle; and by November of the next year "Colonel" Charles Goodnight had driven a herd of 2000 cattle from southern Colorado to the headwaters of the Colorado, where he established a ranch. A short time later the Shad brothers located a ranch near the Wichita River in northwestern Texas, and Daniel Waggoner found a likely range for his herd a short distance below him. So rapid had been the advance of the ranch frontier that by 1880 more than 225,000 cattle ranged in this new region.

That the western cowboy was a unique personality cannot be doubted. His distinctive characteristics were the subject of comment by his early contemporaries as well as by the historians of today. Spanish manners, customs, and terms, his physical environment, the unusual features of his industry, and his limited social contacts

---

1. In writing on the Texas cattle industry in 1872, A. W. Lyman stated that the Texas grazing area comprised 152,000,000 acres; that in 1870 the state had a population of only 500,000; and that it had 3,000,000 beef cattle and 800,000 milch cows, and branded annually 750,000 calves. *Kansas Magazine*, I (April, 1872), No. 4, p. 318.

were undoubtedly four major factors which contributed to his uniqueness. Because of these influences the cowboy was as typically a westerner as the mountain man or the trader; and he was probably more of a westerner than the pathfinder. Since each of these factors played so important a part in shaping the life of the range rider, it will not be inappropriate to examine each of them in turn.

It is doubtful whether the language of the seaman or the mountaineer was more unusual than that of the cowboy. Many of the terms as well as some of the manners and customs of the range rider have been carried down from Spanish times, since the sons of "Old Spain" were the first American cowboys. The following is a list of representative words adapted or corrupted from the Spanish, together with their Spanish originals:

English	Spanish
hoosegow	*juzgado*
ranch	*rancho*
cinch	*cincha*
kin savvy	*Quien sabe?*
chaps	*chaparejos*
lariat	*la reata*
cavvieyard	*caballada*
mustang	*mesteno*
cayuse	*caballo*
wrangler	*caballerango*
dobie	*adobe*

Terms taken over directly include broncho, rodeo, corral, peon, sombrero, loco, and vaquero.[2] To these the cowboy added liberally his own words, such as buck, chuck, rustler, waddy, slow-elk, and maverick. His profanity, finally, was excelled only by that of the "bullwhacker."

The second factor, environment, was characterized chiefly by space. The southern plains country has sometimes been called "a land of magnificent distances"; its broad expanses and silent wastes never failed to impress greatly the traveler who crossed its bosom and must have influenced to a large degree its early occupants. Before the days of barbed-wire and the farmer the bounds of ranches in this area were not fixed; and the ranchers allowed

2. For an interesting discussion of Spanish terms used in the cow country, see J. L. Cowan, "Lingo of the Cow Country," in *Outing Magazine*, August, 1909, p. 623.

their cattle to graze on approximate ranges. Many ranches were as large as the properties of medieval princes. One of the earliest of these is described by a Texas immigrant guide book. The owner of the ranch was Thomas O'Connor. He was discharged from the Texan army in 1837, and his "entire earthly possessions then consisted of a Spanish pony, saddle and bridle, two old belt pistols, one of which was broken off at the breech, and one rifle gun, all of which were much the worse for having been in constant use in obtaining our independence." A short time later he established a ranch on a southern Texas stream, and began to raise cattle; his stock increased until they numbered 80,000 head of cattle and 500 horses, and his ranch had a river frontage of thirty-six miles. Captain Richard King was another poor man who came to southern Texas and developed a large property. In 1853 he acquired the Santa Gertrudes ranch and thereby laid the foundation of the famous King Ranch in the Corpus Christi country, consisting of over 60,000 acres of land, on which he grazed 50,000 cattle, 10,000 horses and mules, 20,000 sheep, and 8,000 goats.[3] A visitor facetiously writes that it was one hundred miles from King's front gate to the doorsteps of his ranch house.

These early ranches, however, were not so large as properties developed in the early eighties (with the aid, in most cases, of European capital). Among these later properties were the XIT, Matador, the Prairie Land and Cattle Company, the Turkey Track, LX, LIT, T anchor, 101, Cross L, LE, LS, Frying Pan, and several others. The XIT was the largest of all ranches established in the United States; it controlled 3,000,000 acres of land, and at one time grazed 160,000 cattle. In 1886, with the coming of barbed wire, 781¼ miles of fence were constructed about its properties. "It began at the northwest corner of the state and ran 150 miles without a turn," J. Evetts Haley, the cowboy historian, writes of the XIT.[4] Still another of these huge ranches was the Matador, with properties in Motley, Cottle, Dickens, and Floyd counties of Texas, consisting, by 1882, of 375,000 acres of land, on which grazed 75,000 head of cattle.

3. James L. Rock and W. I. Smith, *Southern and Western Texas Guide for 1878*, chap. vii. Other ranches were equally large. [The letterhead of rancher J. M. Daugherty as late as 1890, read : "Ranches in Jones, King, Presidio Counties, Texas. Eddy County, N. M., and the Indian Territory." Daugherty Papers, Archives, Library, University of Texas.

4. J. Evetts Haley, *The XIT Ranch of Texas*, p. 93.

The third and fourth factors which influenced the life of the cowboy—the unusual features of his industry and his limited social contacts—are so self-evident as not to require detailed consideration. During the period of the open range or even after the appearance of barbed wire, when the rancher could ride an entire day without completing a survey of his property, he spent much of his time in the saddle. He learned to be a line rider, "broncho buster," trail driver, and round-up hand, and became expert in the use of the lariat and branding iron. Generally in the course of these routine duties he did not have frequent social contact with others of his trade; at round-ups, however, in ranchhouse service, or on the trail he made the most of his opportunities. Otherwise he was busy at line riding, building fences, searching for cattle that had strayed from their accustomed range, pulling bogged-down animals from miry ponds and creeks, or doctoring cattle that had been cut on barbed wire fences, or infected with screwworms. About these numerous tasks, therefore, he rode his lonely way, for the frontier ranch was so far-flung and its herds were so numerous that the range rider seldom had opportunity to satisfy his yearnings for human comradeship.

II

A study of early records of the development of the cow country reveals two well-defined periods of the cattle industry; first, the years of the open range and "squatter" occupation, and second, the period following the coming of barbed wire and improved stock. An examination of the first of these periods further discloses three factors as a result of which the average cowboy was less likely to measure up to modern standards of right and wrong than his brother of the second period. First, it is not inappropriate to apply the term "wild" to all life on the southern plains at this time. The orderly process of civilization had not coordinated the organizing genius of man with the wild life of the plains. Indeed, nature itself—both plant and animal—was wild. The stern law of the frontier was self-preservation, and its harsh procedure was no respecter of life or things. Of necessity, the cattleman who was reared or who lived for many years in this kind of environment became a part of all he met, either to the detriment or the strengthening of his character. It was easier for him to merge his own personality with his surroundings than it was to struggle against the primeval rawness of the frontier; as a result, he unconsciously became thoroughly "westernized." He became the link which bound the civilized East to the savage West; he was the harbinger of western civilization, and not a major part of it. Second, the areas where law and order did not dominate were those to which the riffraff and desperado classes would naturally gravitate. On this particular point, an observer wrote in 1887 that Texas, during the early days of its frontier, "was almost a wilderness known to the outer world chiefly as a refuge for outlaws, who flying from justice and disguised by aliases, false beards, and quaint costumes, wandered hither and thither over the unsettled country."[5]

Third, as a result of these regrettable conditions it was necessary for the well-intentioned cowman to adjust himself to his environment. Frontier justice, now so often eulogized by enthusiastic speakers and writers, was at times crude, and even farcical. In this adjustment the rancher, pretty generally, became "a law unto himself," and was often driven to commit deeds outside the law. So, considering our modern standard of good citizenship, the average inhabitant of the ranch country during this first period would have found the restrictions of a well-ordered community irksome. A Quaker's opinion of Texas cowboys, unusually harsh by reason of his austere standard of sobriety, follows:

> The Texas herders were drinking and playing cards until late in the night, and as one small room serves as a kitchen, dining-room, sitting-room, bed-room, store, saloon, and corn-crib, there was not much space between my bed on the floor and the gambling-table where these degraded beings were keeping up their wild orgies—swearing, drinking, smoking, and shuffling their cards.[6]

Perhaps a more accurate appraisal of the cowboy is given by Joseph G. McCoy, who spent many years as a cattle buyer on the southern plains and who undoubtedly came in contact with as many cowboys as any other man of his time. In 1874, he wrote:

5. J. Ambulo, "The Cattle on a Thousand Hills," in *Overland Monthly*, March, 1887, p. 226.

6. Thomas C. Battey, *A Quaker Among the Indians*, p. 78.

LIFE OF THE RANGE RIDER

The life of the cowboy is one of considerable daily danger and excitement. It is hard and full of exposure, but is wild and free, and the young man who had long been a cowboy has but little taste for any other occupation. He lives hard, works hard, has but few comforts and fewer necessities. He has but little, if any taste for reading. He enjoys a coarse practical joke or a smutty story; loves danger but abhors labor of the common kind; never tires riding, never wants to walk, no matter how short the distance he desires to go. He would rather fight with pistols than pray; loves tobacco, liquor and women better than any other trinity. His life borders nearly upon that of an Indian. If he reads anything, it is in most cases a blood and thunder story of the sensation style.[7]

The emotional life of the cowboy played from one extreme to another. At best he was lonely in his daily routine, for the range might be many miles from the ranch house; and the occasional visits of the foreman or the owner of the property only accentuated his loneliness when he was left again to his herds, his horses, and his hut or half-buried dugout. His monotonous vigils in this squalid environment often made him as taciturn as an Indian; but when once he had an opportunity to open the floodgates of his pent-up emotions he did so with the enthusiasm of an irresponsible child. It may be said, therefore, that he was a creature of monkish abnegation during the days when he went about his ranch duties of riding the range and living in a line rider's camp; and a "roaring lion" when once his tongue was loosened with liquor and his eyes were dazzled with the glamor and show of the saloon, gambling hall, or ballroom. If on such a spree he shot out the lights of a brilliantly lighted saloon or gambling house, his act was generally not intended as a discourtesy to the proprietor; he was expressing, as best he could, his desire to "paint the town red" and have a good time. On this point, L. C. Bradford, a visitor to the southern plains in 1881, writes:

It was a wild, rough set of men that camp around the herds after they have been driven through the Nation and are resting on the grassy plains of Kansas. Clad in the soiled and dusty

7. Joseph G. McCoy, *Historic Sketches of the Cattle Trade of the West and Southwest*, p. 10.

jeans of the trail, for weeks in succession no water has touched their hands or faces, and unshaven and unshorn, they give free rein to their exuberant spirits, taking some quiet Kansas village by storm, setting the tame local laws at defiance and compelling the authorities to acknowledge the sovereignty of their native state.[8]

Even closer to the facts is the description of another observer of the period.

> With the loading of the cattle came the "paying-off" and the cowboy's brief vacation before returning to another year's round of hard work and coarse fare. It was not, perhaps, to be expected that after nearly a twelve-month of life on the prairies he should spend his outing in quiet and dignity. And seldom did he. The cattle towns catered to his worst passions, and saloons and dance-houses flourished with startling exuberance. During the height of the season might was the only law, and if occasionally a marshall was found, like William Hickok, the original Wild Bill, who could rule an Abilene in its rudest period, it was because he was quicker with the revolver and more daring than even the cowboys themselves.[9]

Outside of his lurid experiences in saloon, gambling halls, and disorderly houses, many of the contacts of the cowboy in other social relations were equally as bad. At the race track, a frontier dance, or a wedding, liquor generally flowed freely; and too often social entertainments came to an end amid wild orgies of drunkenness and gun play, with dire consequences. One such instance occurred at Fort Griffin, Texas, in January, 1877.

FORT GRIFFIN, January 18, 1877.
Life is uncertain and it is rendered more so by living in a frontier settlement, as will be shown by the following:
On the night of the 17th inst., the citizens of Fort Griffin witnessed a tragedy at Messrs. Donnelly and Carroll's varieties, which, when described, you will say must have satisfied the most sanguine lover of the horrible. It appears that two cowboys full of old rye and the devil, proceeded to what is called in frontier parlance, "to run the town." After firing several shots from their Colts to let people know they were in town, they

8. L. C. Bradford, "Among the Cowboys," in *Lippincott's Magazine*, June, 1881, p. 569.
9. C. M. Harger, "Cattle Trails on the Prairies," in *Scribner's Magazine*, June, 1892, p. 741.

entered Donnelly and Carroll's saloon for the purpose of breaking up what was then going on, a social dance. In spite of the intreaties of the proprietors, they persisted in drawing their revolvers and flourishing them to the danger and annoyance of the assembly. Their "racket," however, was suddenly stopped by the appearance of Mr. Crozier, the deputy sheriff, and Mr. Jeffries, the County Attorney, who, as officers of the law, ordered them to quiet. The order seemed to be the signal for the ball then closed to open in a different way. About ten shots were fired in succession, with unfortunately more injury to innocent bystanders than to the guilty parties. A gentleman by the name of Myers, a lawyer by profession, was shot through the back and died in about two hours—afterwards—esteemed and regretted by all who knew him. A young man named Barrow, who but lately had been married, was shot in the center of the forehead and died instantly. Mr. Jeffries, the County Attorney, was shot about three inches above the heart and now lies in a precarious state. One of the cowboys named Bland was shot about four inches above the naval, the ball passing out through the small of his back. Deputy Sheriff Cruger received a slight wound. He is entitled to praise for the cool manner in which he endeavored to uphold the majesty of the law, though directly in front of two cocked pistols. Altogether the affair was uncalled for and unlucky, rendered more so because of the fact that the other cowboy named Reed, after emptying his pistol, one shot of which, as was proved by his position, must have killed the young man Barrow, got away and is still at liberty. Though too late to witness the shooting, a fact by no means regretted, I was in time to see Mr. Jeffries led away; Barrow on the ground, with his brains oozing through the hole in his forehead; lawyer Myers dying, reclining on his side, and Bland rolling on his back in agony. All from the effects of a drunken spree and the useless habit of packing a six-shooter. Now that the law is touched in the person of Mr. Jeffries the wild and wooly cowboys no doubt will be compelled to lay aside their weapons on entering the township in order that the more peaceable and respectable members of the community may have a show for their lives. The excuse that Fort Griffin is a frontier town and that Indians are dangerous is now getting "too thin" to justify men necessarily carrying weapons, which, as a matter of consequence, they use, when frontier whiskey makes them feel like it.[10]

10. An article contributed by a citizen of Fort Griffin to the Dallas *Daily Herald*, January 26, 1876.

During the earlier period, the "six-shooter" was frequently employed to settle differences between the range riders. The etiquette of prairie life, which in most respects was not very exacting, absolutely forbade the use of a certain form of malediction, which, while calling down divine punishment on the person addressed, cast an unwarrantable imputation on the character of his mother. The utterance of the term was immediately followed by the drawing of weapons and death to one of the principals. An English visitor to the southern plains during these stormy days relates an incident of the kind:

> Two of our number, one of whom, a man of morose and surly disposition, had lately joined us from a strange outfit, disputed about some trivial matter. The quarrel waxed warm, and at last the forbidden expression was used against the stranger. Both men were on horseback and unarmed, but both immediately dashed towards the wagons in which they had left their respective weapons. The insulted man, as he passed, snatched out of its open scabbard the six-shooter of a looker-on, turned his horse, and rushed after his enemy. He came upon him as he was on the point of securing his cutter; and without another word, shot him dead. That afternoon he fled, and we buried the dead man where he fell. There were few to pity him. He had entered into the quarrel with his eyes open, had himself provoked the risk, and had paid the terrible penalty of his rashness. It was not for us to try the slayer. Vengeance might overtake him sooner or later if the dead man's friends or relations could lay their hands on him, but it would be difficult to find the scattered witnesses of a crime committed on the far-off prairies, after the long lapse of time which must of necessity ensue before a center of civilization and justice could be reached.[11]

According to another observer, ranchers, en route to market on cattle trains, would amuse themselves during the tedium of the journey by playing "draw-poker" and drinking frontier whiskey. "As a natural consequence there was a good deal of friendly riot, and occasionally an altercation, which was settled by the prompt weapons in every one's belt, and it more than once happened that a wounded cowboy, or even a dead one was taken out of the car at the next station."[12]

11. "The Cowboy at Home," in *Cornhill Magazine*, September, 1886, p. 302.
12. A. M. Williams, "An Indian Cattle Town," in *Lippincott's Magazine*, February, 1884, pp. 168-69.

*Upper, the "drag" of a cattle drive; lower, Dodge City, Kansas,
the end of the trail, 1878*

Not every one who started on the northern trail in the spring of the year lived to get back to his home; nameless mounds dotting the sides of the trails bore silent testimony to the danger that surrounded the range rider. Whether he fell by a shot from the gun of some hostile savage lurking in a ravine nearby, or was dropped by a six-shooter in the hands of a fellow rider, he was hastily buried and soon forgotten. Entirely released from the restraining power of the law while on the trail, men gave free reign to their passions, and the six-shooter or Winchester—the inseparable companions of the early cowboys—was often the arbiter of disputes. "It was common for two bosses having charge of different herds to jump down from their horses and proceed to crack away at each other until one had 'bitten the dust.'" Murders were so common on the southern plains that little was thought of them. On April 12, 1875, a citizen of Tom Green County, Texas, wrote ironically: "You will soon have to go west of this to find the frontier. We are becoming civilized. I do not think there were over half a dozen murders in this vicinity during the past year."[13]

A change for the better in the cow country is noticeable in the late seventies, and becomes unmistakable by 1885. Forces of law and order had naturally weeded out many of the outlaws and ne'er-do-wells, and the incoming settlers were as a rule sober and industrious folk. Concerning this second period, J. Nimmo writes in 1886: "A great improvement is also observable in the cowboys from Texas. Deeds of violence among them are now few. The morale of the entire range and ranch cattle business of the United States now compares favorably with that of other large enterprises." And by 1904 Arthur Chapman can assert: "In the main, the cowboy of today is much better behaved than the puncher of the days of the old cattle-trail. This is in a large measure due to the different environment. There is less drinking of bad whiskey, and less attention to the fascinations of the gaming-table. It is possible for a cowboy today to acquire a small ranch and start in business for himself with a small herd of cattle on an adjoining range. Consequently his eyes are always open to his opportunity."[14]

13. *Norton's Union Intelligencer*, Dallas, Texas, April 24, 1875.

14. For the two quotations, see J. Nimmo, "The American Cowboy," in *Harper's Magazine*, November, 1886, p. 884; and Arthur Chapman, "The Cowboy of Today," in *World's Work*, July, 1904, p. 5278.

As turbulent as was the first period, one should not conclude that there were not upright and honorable characters among the ranchmen of the time. For their number included many of the most substantial citizens of the frontier. One of these was J. M. Choate, whom McCoy characterized as a "true specimen, both in appearance and in manner of life," of the Texas cattleman, "a man whose sincere aim is to do right with his fellow man, one who suffers in heart when the people of his State are outraged or are made to endure unjust impositions."[15] "Clabe" Merchant of Abilene, Texas, was another rancher in this class. He never carried a pistol on the range. It was such honorable men as these who met at Graham, Texas, on February 15, 1877, to organize the "Stock Raisers' Association of Northwestern Texas," for the purpose of protecting themselves against "brand-burners" and thieves.[16] Nor, on the other hand, should one infer that all the ranchers of the second period were upright men, for among both ranch owners and cowboys of the time were hold-overs from the rough characters of early days. But contemporary records prove that on the whole the first period was turbulent, and the second was more amenable to law and order.

III

The dress, manners, and customs of the cowboy were virtually the same in both periods. In the selection of his clothes his main purpose was to provide against the rough wear of arduous ranch toil. Every cowboy owned a horse with saddle and bridle, for this was his only means of travel if he was thrown out of employment far from a settlement, or was hunting for work on the prairies. He usually wore boots, at times ornately designed, with the heels uncomfortably high, so that he could brace himself firmly on the ground while attempting to control an obstreperous steer or a bucking horse; or, with his feet planted well in the stirrups, could

15. *Op. cit.*, 17-18.
16. Some of the prominent cattlemen present were as follows: J. N. Simpson, C. L. Carter, J. C. Loving, Joseph Graham, Sam Glascon, Roland Johnson, A. B. Medlin, C. B. Brummett, J. T. Webb, George Wright, H. G. Bedford, Tom Merrill, John D. Smith, W. B. Slaughter, R. E. Mabry, D. B. Gardner, and J. C. Lindsey. These names are given in the *Proceedings* of the organization. The association later developed into the "Texas and Southwestern Cattle Raisers Association," one of the largest organizations of its kind in the United States.

better keep his place in the saddle in case his horse sought to unseat him. Jeans trousers tucked into his boottops were usually protected by chaps, or leather overalls, with fringes or metal mountings. Over his shirt of ordinary make, he sometimes wore a vest, unbuttoned, in the pockets of which he carried odds and ends, such as tobacco, paper, pencil, and matches; and about his neck he frequently wore a large handkerchief. Perhaps the most interesting part of his wearing apparel was his hat; it was made of heavy felt and was broad-brimmed, ornamented with a leather band or silver Mexican roll. It was used to protect his head from the fiery sun during the hot summers, to hold water when a drinking cup was not available, to flog a wild horse while he was bucking, and to cover his face while he was taking a midday siesta. Tied behind his saddle was the inevitable slicker, or water-proof coat, which did service during rainy weather or cold damp nights. On his boots he wore a pair of long-shanked, jingle-bobbed Mexican spurs, which were sometimes elegantly mounted and carved, and which clanked as he walked. And about his waist he generally belted a six-shooter, slung low in an open scabbard. Completing his equipment were a roll of bedding consisting of two blankets, a buffalo robe, or padded quilt, and tarpaulin covering; and, tied to his saddle a rawhide or hempen lariat. A visitor to the cattle range in 1902 thus sums up the attire of the cowboy:

> He is clad today as he was when he first appeared upon the plains. His character has been strong enough to be above prettinesses and uselessnesses. . . . The costume of the cowboy is appropriate because it is harmonious with its surroundings. It is correct because it is appropriate. It will remain as it is so long as the cowboy himself remains what he has been and still is—a strong character, a self-poised individual, leaning on no other soul.[17]

As a rule the cowboy was loyal to his employer, generous to his friends, affable to strangers, and chivalrous to women. If a large stack of stovewood, neatly arranged, was found near the kitchen of the ranch house, it was pretty generally concluded that the cook was a comely woman. When the pretty female school teacher in the ranch country turned out school for the day, one writer affirms,

17. Donald MacKay, "The Cow Puncher at Home," in *Munsey's Magazine*, August, 1902, p. 60.

she usually found seven or eight earnest-minded cowboys ready to saddle her pony, help her to mount; and, while on her way home, accompanied by her eager escort, "she would have unconditional offers of at least seven or eight good saddle ponies that could 'single-foot'." Indeed, the cowboy was stampeded at times into wearing his trouser legs drawn down over his boots, a stiff-bosomed shirt, a high collar and flaming colored necktie, a "store-bought" suit of tight-fitting clothes, and "a hard-boiled" derby, which rattled on the ground when some laughing comrade knocked it from his head. Yet, he was willing to suffer the embarrassment and the jibes of his friends if in the end he succeeded in winning the favor of his lady love.

It was on the northern drives that one encountered the singing cowboy—singing sometimes not from choice but as a part of his duties. It is difficult to understand how the nerve-frayed cattle, bedded down after a harrowing day's experience on the trail, could rest and be soothed by the high-pitched voices and tuneless melodies of some of their entertainers, but such seems to have been the case. In fairness to the obliging rider, however, it should be stated that many of the cowboys were excellent singers, and that they often entertained their comrades of the range with their songs as they sat about the campfires after a hard day's work. The effect of cowboy music on the herd at night may be judged from a comment in *Scribner's Magazine* for June, 1892. "The human voice seemed the most powerful influence that could be used to affect the brutes, force being entirely out of the question. As soon as the 'milling' began the cowboys began to sing. It mattered not what so long as there was music to it, and it was not uncommon to hear some profane and heartless bully doling out camp-meeting hymns to soothe the ruffled spirits of a herd of Texas steers."

On the trail there were times when the weary trail driver had no rest at night because of stampeding steers, storms, or attacks of Indians; but during the cool evenings he enjoyed sitting quietly about the glowing fire until it was time to turn in. One of these riders, writing for *Harper's New Monthly Magazine*, in July, 1884, thus describes the scene at an evening's camp:

At night we look out for wood and water as prime requisites for a camping ground. These are not readily at hand as may be

imagined in the region proverbially treeless, and where alkali is
the basis of most of the water deposits. They are found, however, and we pitch our tent, making it secure by banking against
the insidious draughts in the low temperature of summer nights
in this elevated region. Blankets are unrolled, and we proceed
to make our beds, having previously spread a canvass over the
damp or dusty earth, as the case may be. Others are cutting
wood, mixing bread, frying bacon, or making coffee, as called
upon by the chief cook. The welcome cry "To Supper!" soon
brings hungry men to their hams around the improvised table.
A smoke by the campfire concludes the day and exhausted
nature generally seeks repose ere twilight has fairly faded from
the western sky. A cowboy seldom indulges in the luxury of a
tent, but with his saddle for a pillow, and a soft hollow in the
ground for a cot, rolls himself up in a blanket, and takes the stars
for his canopy.[18]

Considering in general the social status of the cowboy during
the early days of the southern plains frontier, several important
factors should be noted. First, the cowboy should not be judged
by our modern standards of good citizenship, for he lived under
conditions vastly different from those of twentieth century America. Social life in the region during this period was in the beginning
of an evolutionary process, the development of which was slow and
disorganized. Second, handicaps and hardships encountered by the
range rider were infinitely greater than those which face the citizen
of the same country today, and the struggle to bring order and
symmetry out of chaos was correspondingly greater. Third, a
continuous struggle to overcome these handicaps, bred certain
virtues in the champions of law and order as bases for a new era
of development; honesty, hospitality, fair play, and respect for
womanhood stood the test of strenuous trial and emerged as the
most flattering virtues of our present civilization. At the same time,
enough of the objectionable elements of early society has remained
to our day to remind us of the crudeness and rawness of the early
frontier.

The cattle industry on the southern plains had its greatest
impetus after 1885; the Staked Plains of Texas, western Oklahoma,

18. J. P. Keese, "Beef from the Range to the Shambles," in *Harper's New Monthly Magazine*, July, 1884, p. 301.

the Cherokee Strip, southwestern Kansas, southern Colorado, and eastern New Mexico, were all largely developed since that time. The destruction of the vast herds of bisons which roamed the grassy plains opened up millions of acres of grazing land to the cattle industry, and as soon as the hostile Indian problem was solved, hundreds of cattlemen flocked into this virgin territory. Even highly capitalized organizations from the Old World bought up huge tracts of ranch properties on the southern plains, and soon the free range was no more.

As the advent of railways and the fencing of the open range made possible the introduction of improved stock raising, the buffalo, the wild Indian, and the wild cowboy had all alike seen their day, and the scientific stock raiser now came into prominence. The new cowboy became an enthusiastic apostle of schools, good roads, railway construction, and the building of boom towns with electric lights and paved streets. Yet, occasionally, there have been reminders of the old days, as sporadic renewals of drunken sprees, shooting affairs, and cattle thieving have created passing concern. But in general the range rider has settled down to the staid ways of those who had migrated from older communities and brought along with them the manners and customs of a humdrum life. Early traditions, however, are still perpetuated among the range riders.

11

THE SETTLER AT PLAY

I

HAD it not been for the few social contacts of border settlers during the days of drudgery and toil, it is doubtful that many would have remained in the country. They saw so much of danger, sickness, suffering, and death that they sorely needed an occasional opportunity to meet together and sing, dance, laugh, and join in social games, in order to brighten what otherwise might have been somber lives. They traveled by slow stages, roads were few and poor, and distances were great. As a result, when the settlers did get together, they did so in a hearty and enthusiastic manner; and loud laughter and talking, vigorous stamping of feet while dancing, and a buoyant good fellowship were pronounced characteristics of all social events along the frontier. Since settlers, living from twenty-five to fifty miles apart, for weeks at a time did not have an opportunity of seeing one of their kind, outside of their immediate family, they genuinely yearned for human companionship. Sometimes the sum total of community assemblies during the year would consist of a wedding, a picnic, a singing, and a party or dance and in some communities not more than one or two of these in that length of time.

The somber routine of frontier life was not always reflected in the home environment. Happy indeed was the early settler who brought with him to the raw frontier a never failing sense of humor. A prairie dweller with a generous measure of this quality is pictured in the Fort Smith, Arkansas, *Weekly New Era*, of April 27, 1882. On one of his tours of inspection General Forsythe, of General P. H. Sheridan's staff, had found the dwelling of a lonely station keeper which consisted of "four stalls for animals, and a combination parlor, kitchen, and sleeping apartment, six by ten feet in size." Outside, over the door was an inscription, reading: "Hotel de starvation; 1,000 miles from hay and grain, 70 miles from wood, and 15 miles from water." Inside, the walls of the small shack were decorated with pictures cut from police publications; and over the door, in large letters, was written in charcoal, "God Bless Our Home," and "Wanted a nice young girl for general housework. Apply within."

Even the dugouts and line rider's camps in the cow country were sometimes scenes of social contentment and good cheer, for the inmates could occasionally exchange pleasantries with strangers and enjoy a smoke or game of poker. Clarence E. Edwords cites an instance belonging to the time when western Oklahoma was first being occupied by white cattlemen. The scene was Thompson's ranch, which consisted of "a hole in a bank with a door in front, but no windows." On this occasion, the writer states, the dugout "was filled with cowboys who were very hospitable and helped to care for the ponies and get supper for the travellers." When the evening meal was finished, pipes were produced, "and the ill-ventilated room was soon so filled with smoke that Dyche and the professor, who were not smokers, were compelled to make frequent trips to the open air for a chance to breathe."[1]

II

One of the most popular forms of home entertainment on the southern plains frontier was the "breakdown," or square dance. Indeed, long before the southern plains was occupied by the white settlers, this form of entertainment was popular in the southwest, wherever Anglo-American immigrants had made their way. George S. Denison, a Vermont school teacher in San Antonio, Texas, wrote to his mother on May 13, 1855, that "dancing parties are frequent," and that he had become able to "trip the light fantastic toe with perfect looseness," although in a subsequent letter he stated that he had been appointed leader of the choir in a Presbyterian Church. That he saw no inconsistency in thus leading religious hymns in church and attending dances may be inferred from a statement in a letter to his family, on July 7, 1855. "I am going to a party tomorrow night, and I attended one night before last. I spent the evening very pleasantly in dancing,

1. Clarence E. Edwords, *Camp-fires of a Naturalist*, p. 99.

which I can now 'come with perfect looseness.' "[2] It is needless to add, however, that his attitude was not that of the average church member at that time; play-parties were tolerated, but "breakdowns" were frowned upon.

The one indispensable character at all frontier dances was the "fiddler." He was generally assigned a seat on a raised platform, at a place in the room where all could see, and through the long hours of the entertainment he would "saw out" on his violin, or "fiddle" as it was called, such tunes as "Arkansas Traveler," "Wagoner," "Turkey in the Straw," and other melodies of equal favor. The "fiddler" was sometimes accompanied by one or two others on the guitar or banjo. Occasionally the men were charged a small fee in order to pay the musicians, but if anyone was unable to pay he was given to understand that he was welcome. In fact, "it was necessary at times to corral the entire community to have a respectable party."

The next person in importance was a master of ceremonies known as the "prompter," or "caller" who sometimes danced while he called the figures, or sat beside the fiddler and directed those on the floor, in a nasal rhythmic voice. J. R. Craddock, in an article on the cowboy dance, gives the following examples of calls:

> Choose your partner, form a ring,
> Figure eight, and double L swing
>
> First swing six, then swing eight,
> Swing 'em like swinging on a gate.
>
> Ducks in the river, going to the ford,
> Coffee in a little rag, sugar in a gourd.
>
> Swing 'em once and let 'em go,
> All hands left and do-ce-do.
>
> You swing me, and I'll swing you,
> And we'll all go to heaven, in the same old shoe
>
> Chase the possum, chase the coon,

2. Denison Letters, MSS, in Division of Manuscripts, Library of Congress.

SOUTHERN PLAINSMEN

Chase that pretty girl 'round the room.

How will you swap, and how'll you trade
This pretty girl, for that old maid?

Wave the ocean, wave the sea,
Wave that pretty girl back to me.

Swing your partners, once in a while,
Swing them all in Indian style.

Rope the cow, and kill the calf,
Swing your partner, a round and a half,

Swing your partner before you trade,
Grab 'em back and promenade.

Grab your partner and sail away,
Hurry up, it's breaking day.

Swing 'em round, and round an' round,
Pockets full of rocks to weigh 'em down.

There comes a girl I used to know,
Swing her once and let her go.

When you meet your partner, pat her on the head,
If she don't like coffee, give her corn bread.

Three little sisters, all in a row.
Swing 'em once and let them go.

Old shoe sole is about wore out,
Grab a girl and walk about.

Swing 'em east and swing 'em west,
Swing the girl that you like best.[3]

3. John R. Craddock, "The Cowboy Dance," in *Publications* of the Texas Folk-Lore Society, II (1923), 34-35; for other calls see Roy S. Scott, "The Cowboy Dance of the Northwest," *ibid.*, IV (1925), 56-57; and Mary J. Jaques, *Texan Ranch Life*, p. 97.

THE SETTLER AT PLAY

In "swinging" the young man would grasp the hand of his partner or interlock elbows and make a complete turn, followed by a quick release. In the course of the long hours of the night it was not uncommon for the dancers to remain on their feet most of the time, resting only occasionally. And what with]the enthusiastic stamping of feet and the many whirls and turns, no wonder a young lady would often "dance her shoe through in one night's dancing," though the thick soles of the cowboy's boots were generally impervious to wear.

One of the most interesting accounts of an early dance on the southern plains is given by a visitor at a ranch south of Caldwell, Kansas, on Pond Creek. On his arrival at the ranch, he reports a dance had been in progress for twenty-four hours. A tall Arkansawyer, called "Short," on account of his size, was sawing away industriously at a fiddle, producing sounds, which, "by a good stretch of a vivid imagination, might be called music." Adds the writer naively: "The vigor of the dancers was evidence that his well-meant efforts were fully appreciated by the congregated cowboys and their partners. Visitors had come from miles way; and cowboys and Cherokee half-breeds were out in full force. However, there were more males than females, and in order to provide a female dancer for each man, as was more than once done in the prairie country, dresses were put on several cowboys present, who acted the feminine part to the satisfaction of all." The lady of the house is reported to have complimented fulsomely the ability of the fiddler and the willingness of the cowboys to play the part of the girl. She said:

> Short don't play music outen er book, ... but he plays real tunes. He don't know a note from a cow-track, but he gets everythin' outen er fiddle there is in it, he does. He's ther best fiddler in the hull country, he is, and he allers stops till ther dance is done, too, he does. This is nothin' now. You jest orter bin here las' night. There were over fifty here, and ther cowboys thet danced for girls was real good ones, too. It was ther best dance we ever had. Some er ther boys got a little too much licker, but everthin' went off real nice.[4]

"Short" continued his "fiddling," and the cowboys kept time to

4. Edwords, *op. cit.*, 97-98.

the rhythm of his fiddle by patting their feet and hands, making such a noise that the tired travelers could not sleep. During the evening, a deputy sheriff appeared on the scene bringing with him a prisoner whom he was escorting to a Caldwell jail. He became so interested in the proceedings, however, that he forgot his mission, and the prisoner coolly walked out of the door and disappeared in the darkness. When later his absence was made known, a desperate search was made for him but to no avail.

III

The church-going people of the southern plains generally held these early dances in disfavor. They had three objections: first, dances attracted the worst characters of the community; second, more liquor was drunk at these gatherings than at any other kind of entertainment, and dances were often broken up by drunken brawls; and third, they believed the "waist-swing" was indecent. To meet these objections, and at the same time gain the favor of the church element, young people introduced what was called the "play-party." In this form of entertainment they dispensed with the "fiddler" and "prompter," and substituted songs which all the participants would sing, and in the course of the singing they would play "games." During the evening's entertainment they would generally play seven or eight "games," which called for dancing with figures similar to those used in the square dance. Songs such as "Choose your Mate," "Old Joe Clark," and "Skip-to-my-Lou," generally known throughout the country, were employed at most parties.

When once the people from far and near had gathered at some favored home in a community the scene was one of riotous good cheer. The setting for the party was generally the front room, from which all furniture had been cleared away, except chairs and quilt-covered benches arranged conveniently along the four sides of the room. Sometimes, however, when the crowd could not be accommodated indoors, particularly if it were summertime and if a sandstorm were not blowing, the yard was used for the occasion, thus leaving the home for the "old folks" who had come along, and who could not subject themselves "to the night air." About seven-thirty or eight o'clock the party would begin rather tamely, but before it had been in progress an hour all timidity was dispensed with and the games were fully under way. There was such a wide variety of songs from which to select, each calling for different movements, that the young men present never lacked for a "game." A study made in 1926-27 at the University of Oklahoma "yielded, in addition to several hundred square dance calls, some one hundred and fifty play-party songs."[5] In them the players would walk, run, skip, march, swing, cross hands, circle, advance and retreat in rows, and bow and kneel. The words and lines of the songs were usually meaningless and idiotic, since frequently they were improvised by dancers whose poetic talents were not always recognized. It was chiefly the lilting rhythm for which they cared, and which they generally endorsed by extra gyrations and jigs in executing the figures.

Frequently, in the course of such vigorous exercise on a warm summer night, the players would become pretty well exhausted and would seek a brief rest, in which they would plan new games or make frequent trips to the water bucket to wet their throats made dry by much singing. The party generally ended about eleven or eleven-thirty o'clock when someone suggested that it was time to go home. It was not uncommon for parents to bring their children to these parties and sit in another room and carry on a conversation while the young people enjoyed their "games," and then drive home in the small hours of the morning.

IV

There were also other kinds of parties which came into the country, with or without energetic exercise. Popular among these were "candy-pullings" and "candy-breakings." When towns and villages were not accessible to rural settlements along the frontier, sorghum, or molasses, was used to make candy. This practice frequently offered an incentive for young men and women to assemble and "pull candy." After the syrup had been cooked for a short time it began to harden. Then, by moistening the fingers with water or butter fat, or by dusting the hands with flour, a couple would pull the candy back and forth until it solidified and

5. B. A. Botkin, "The Play-Party in Oklahoma," in *Publications* of the Texas Folk-Lore Society, VII (1928), 8-9.

could be broken into convenient sizes and eaten. Where towns were accessible, however, large boxes of stick candy were bought and what had been a "candy-pulling" now became a "candy-breaking." At both kinds of entertainments simple games were played, such as "snap," "clap-in-and-clap-out," and "spinning the plate."

Written invitations were seldom issued. Usually some socially favored "Bill" or "Jim" was responsible for the success or failure of the party. One or two weeks in advance he would ride over to a neighbor's house and ask for permission to hold the party there. Often he had to employ all his powers of eloquence and persuasion to gain the consent of the reluctant host and hostess, but once this had been gained he would joyfully ride from one home to another inviting the young people to the party. Sometimes he invited a select group which he thought would be congenial; at other times he would include all. But even in the former event, it was not uncommon for others to show up, including a rival for the hand of a community belle or a stranger who happened to be passing through the community. If the uninvited guest was not welcome, he sometimes had cause to regret his intrusion. In some instances he was warned to leave by the young men who did not care for his presence, and if he refused, physical force was employed to compel his departure. On the other hand, his presence might be ignored, particularly if he were known to be a "tough" or "rowdy."

V

But house parties were not so generally popular along the frontier as outdoor gatherings—tournaments, barbecues, fish frys, horse races, and basket picnics—in which persons of all ages could join with enthusiasm. Small children seldom favored the long tiresome rides to play-parties or "candy-pullings," and enjoyed still less the return in the small hours of the next morning after they had been "loaded into the family wagon" by their parents. At times their elders were averse to making such excursions, particularly in inclement weather.

One of the most popular of all outdoor sports during the early days of the cowboy was the tournament. One observer, Edgar

Rye, thus records his impressions of it: "This sport is peculiarly suited to frontier life and always appeals to the cowboy. To him it has all the charm of chivalry that induced the knights of old to break a lance in the arena, and he thinks nothing of riding hundreds of miles to be present on these occasions."[6] The rules of the game required a rider to race his horse at full speed over a 150-yard course, on which were spaced at regular intervals five upright posts, holding overhanging crossbeams. From each crossbeam was suspended a ring which the rider was supposed to take with a long tapering lance. A perfect score consisted of fifteen rings in three races, but a score of eight or ten rings was usually considered quite good.

Perhaps one of the most colorful tournaments ever staged in the cow country was at Albany, Shackleford County, Texas, during the seventies. As early as the day before the great event three hundred ranchmen with their wives, children, and friends, it was estimated, had pitched their camps about this little frontier town. When they arrived they found five or six negroes busily engaged in barbecuing five beeves over a long pit of glowing coals, and the savory smell permeating the atmosphere was a promise of the bountiful feast to come on the following day. To make music for those who cared to dance on the hastily constructed pavilion, an Italian string band had been secured at Fort Griffin.

The prize was a silver-mounted saddle, valued at one hundred dollars. For weeks in advance cowboys had heard of the coming tournament, and many, eager to try for the trophy, rode in from ranches more than a hundred miles away. The day of the tournament found the dusty streets of the town crowded with horses and vehicles which had brought an expectant throng. Here and there cowboys, "squatters," soldiers, buffalo hunters, and hide buyers gathered in groups to swap "yarns" and discuss probable winners of the day. To honor the occasion with their presence, Colonel George P. Buell and other officers, with their wives, had ridden over from Fort Griffin, on the Clear Fork of the Brazos

6. Edgar Rye, *The Quirt and the Spur*, p. 140. Professor J. Frank Dobie tells of a tournament held in Montgomery County, Texas, where the ring-posts were three in number, and the course was two hundred yards in length. On such a course a total of nine rings represented a perfect score of three trials. J. Frank Dobie, "The Tournament in Texas," in *Publications* of the Texas Folk-Lore Society, V (1926), 94.

River, fourteen miles away, and a bugler from the fort sounded the starting signal for each contest.

In the interesting contest described by Rye, Ed. Tucker, representing the "Flying Buzzard" ranch, led off, and took eleven rings. The other participants, the names of ranches represented, and the number of rings won by each are as follows: Tom Greer, "Circle G," thirteen; Luke McCabe, the "Bar M," ten; Mike Kegan, "Half Circle W," eight; Bill Johnson, "M. J.," nine; Glen Reynolds, "R. M.," thirteen; Zeno Hemphill, "101," twelve; Harvey Biggs, the "J. R.," eleven; Bill Lasser, "X," ten; Charley Jones, "D. C.," unhorsed after making six; Roe Lefflett, champion of the "Pitchfork" brand, bringing cheers from his followers when he scored fourteen; and the final contestant, known locally as "Texas," and not identified with any ranch, amazing the crowd by making a perfect score of fifteen rings in three dashes down the course, and thereby winning the prize. The attitude of the losers and the spectators was indeed sportsmanlike; they heartily shook the hand of the winner, slapped him on the back, and carried him from the field on their shoulders. The day was then given over to eating, drinking, and other amusements.

VI

The old-time informal basket picnics on the southern plains were also occasions of great enjoyment. Families, large and small, brought food in pails, baskets, boxes, and even tubs and spread it on the ground or on long wooden tables in the convenient shade of an oak or pecan tree. The merrymakers then flocked about and "helped themselves" to the abundant meats, sandwiches, pies, and cakes. Before this eagerly anticipated hour, however, they generally engaged in conversation, dancing, romping about the Maypole, and various sports. One of these picnics was held on the Red River, in the "Cross Timbers" belt, in May, 1874. For several days before the much anticipated event, the editor of the Denison *News* devoted a good deal of space to it. On May 17 he wrote enthusiastically of the features of the occasion which had been planned by the picnic committee. These included a cowboy tournament, a tub race across the Red River, in which the competitors, seated in number one wash tubs, propelled themselves with their hands only, and many other contests and attractions designed to make the occasion a continuous round of entertainment.

Interesting as the basket picnic was, it is doubtful if it approached, in sheer abandon of good fellowship and enjoyment, a Fourth of July barbecue. For this celebration beeves were solicited from ranchmen and they gave generously. Often ten or fifteen fat young animals were barbecued over the fire pits dug for the occasion by willing hands, and presided over by those skilled in the task, while others contributed fried chicken, pickles, cakes, pies, baked and boiled ham, and other foods. To generous applause, ambitious orators entertained the crowd with patriotic speeches, and a brass band played such stirring selections as "Hail Columbia," "Star-spangled Banner," "Yankee Doodle," "Tramp, Tramp, the Boys are Marching," the "Bonnie Blue Flag," and "Maryland, my Maryland." One of the first baseball games ever played in the southern plains country was held at a barbecue at Jacksboro, Texas, on July 4, 1876, and was described as a "spirited contest," which "afforded pleasure to the followers of both teams."

In the days when the streams were filled with fish, "fish frys" afforded settlers an opportunity to assemble. Usually they fished with hook and line, but they often employed nets and seines. Wading the stream, running the nets, and pulling the seine were pleasures sufficiently rewarding for those engaged in fishing, while other sports occupied those not so employed. The bountiful repast of fried fish and other foods made this informal outdoor gathering a popular summer pastime.

VII

The last two decades of the nineteenth century brought many innovations in the social life of the prairie country. Towns and villages springing up here and there hastened the appearance of new conveniences and customs. The young man who on Sunday afternoons had formely ridden horseback over the trackless prairie with the young lady of his choice could now take her for a buggy ride. Behind a spirited horse, or a pair of matched "bays," they could skim over the country in a newly polished buggy, its lacquered wheels shinning in the sunlight. With a slender rawhide whip, the driver would dexterously urge on his horse or team to maintain a comfortable speed; and with one patent-leather-covered foot jauntily swinging over the side of the buggy, and a derby perched precariously on the side of his head, he felt quite on a par with the citybred lad who was trained in the more sophisticated ways of the world. This means of transportation was considered so indispensable that the witty editor of the Guthrie (Oklahoma) *State Capital*, wrote on September 26, 1890: "The editor hereof has a horse, he has a friend that has a buggy, now if we could find a young lady that has a set of harness and likes to ride in the middle, oh! oh! oh!"

The importance of buggies, hacks, and surreys brought into prominence the livery stable, and the livery stable manager did a thriving business, especially when social events took place in his part of the country. A young man who could not afford to own a buggy and a horse could always hire an outfit from the liveryman. Rates for "rigs" were fairly reasonable, and in spite of the inconvenience, aspiring swains commonly took advantage of them. A cowboy who lived twelve miles from the home of his "lady friend" is a case in point.

To make arrangements with the girl, he rode twenty-four miles. To procure a buggy he rode sixteen miles to town and drove the same distance coming back, making thirty-two miles. Then he drove to the girl's home, covering the twelve miles, and thence to the dance, covering eight miles. After the dance Bill drove the girl eight miles back to the girl's house, the twelve miles to the ranch, and made the thirty-two miles round trip to return the buggy. In all, Bill covered a distance of one hundred and twenty-eight miles in order to take his "best girl" to the dance.[7]

Generally a one-horse rig could be hired at $1.50 an evening, and a two-horse outfit at twice that amount, the charge being increased proportionately for longer periods, and a favored, spirited horse bringing more. It was not uncommon for young men to contract for a rig weeks in advance, especially if their social obligations demanded weekly service.

During the period of urbanization, the formal ball became the elite social function of the large village or town, and local young

7. Craddock, *loc. cit.*, 31-32.

men and women would vie with visitors from neighboring towns in awkwardly observing the "new-fangled" formalities expected of them on such an occasion. Even though their own municipalities had only recently come into existence, they seemed to feel that they must measure up to the best manners and customs in vogue in older established cities. Shortly after Guthrie and Oklahoma City had been established, a legislative reception, held in the latter town, was thus glowingly described in the *State Capital*, on September 11, 1890:

OKLAHOMA GUESTS

Visitors from Every City in the Territory—How they Banqueted, Feasted, Danced. Gallant Men, Lovely Women.

Oklahoma City, September 10. — The legislative reception is a great success, two hundred strangers are in the city. Carriages met the visitors at the depot and drove them all over the city.

By nine o'clock the Overholtze house was filled with a gay throng of merry dancers, old and young, and in a few minutes the brilliant mass began to move to the music of the Grand March. Governor and Mrs. Steele led, and everywhere their stately steps were followed in a sinuous round. Soon, like the whispering night winds, the far away strains of a waltz breathed its inspiring spirit to the soul, and heart and feet were lost in revery, dreamily gliding, oblivious of the world.

At twelve o'clock a halt was called for the banquet that had been prepared in the Grand Avenue Hotel, where as rich a bill of fare was served as heart or palate could desire. The Governor and family held the place of honor at the tables. Between the smiles, jokes and laughter they fed, until wit o'erthrew the attractions of the board, and speeches were made, until everybody felt a neighbor to his next. . . .

Amazing as it may seem, this elaborate social function was held in a thriving young city which only two years before did not exist—when the ground upon which Oklahoma City stood was a part of a vast unoccupied prairie. Yet within this brief space of time the tall prairie grass had given way to fields of corn and cotton, and to flourishing cities such as Guthrie and Oklahoma City, which, springing up almost over night, with all the social and industrial characteristics of long-established cities, were soon to outgrow the old-time frontier amusements.

12

" 'CLODHOPPER' *vs.* GRASSHOPPER"

I

THE pioneering period of the southern plains farmer extended from about 1870 to 1905; it was the time when the homesteader was passing through the gruelling experiences of experimentation and adaptation. At the dawn of Anglo-American penetration, when traders like Josiah Gregg and Alexander Majors directed their caravans across the trackless wastes of the region, prairie travelers little thought that what to them was a desert would some day become a thriving center of civilization. Indeed, up to the beginning of the third quarter of the nineteenth century such men as W. T. Sherman, P. H. Sheridan, Richard I. Dodge, and R. B. Marcy, who had spent long years on the plains, looked upon the country as suitable only for the occupation of cattlemen. And the difficulties which confronted a prospective farmer seemed quite formidable: the aridity of the climate, the scarcity of timber, swarms of grasshoppers, and abundant predatory animals were only a few of his foes. But for the rancher's peculiar industry conditions seemed favorable. The region offered vast tracts of free land, fairly well watered by perennial streams; and the rolling landscape was carpeted with a luxuriant growth of bluestem, grama, and mesquite grasses. The Texas legislature came to the aid of the cowmen who occupied that part of the southern plains within the state by enacting a very liberal lease law whereby for a small fee they were allowed to have exclusive grazing rights for a period of several years on a large area of the public domain. Finally, the appearance of barbed wire on the southern plains in the early eighties enabled the rancher to fence his holdings and thus exclude all trespassers and "squatters."

But the cowman could not deny the homesteader the land he sought. After the conclusion of the Red River Indian Wars, immigration to the southern plains increased steadily, and the pioneer rancher was helpless to prevent it. He viewed with jealousy and deep concern this rising tide of homeseekers, and at the time he first became conscious that his free range was imperiled there was born in him a spirit of resentment which often found expression in open conflict.

During the early days of Texas a large amount of "school land" had been set aside for education, much of which, in western Texas, could be bought for a nominal sum. Before the Competitive Bid Law was enacted in 1905, "it was both the custom and the law to set a minimum price on all school and other lands coming on the market and the first bidder who complied with the law received the land."[1] Since the lease law mentioned above gave preference to the lessee in the sale of his state-contract property, the rancher had an advantage in his struggle with the farmer. Yet he was not always able to capitalize on this favorable feature of the land-sales act, for often he had previously bought his quota of four sections of land allowed him under its provisions. With his lease expiring, therefore, he was generally faced with ouster proceedings by his ambitious rival, the homeseeker. Sometimes, to save his ranch property from dismemberment, he would inveigle a close friend or kinsman to buy that part of his leased property offered for sale. Since the first bidder for an unoccupied or unsold tract who complied with the terms of the law received first consideration, it may well be seen how hard-fought contests would develop. The County Clerk's office was the scene of many a tug of war between rival factions, each seeking to file its application first. Early settlers at Lubbock, Stanton, Midland, and Big Spring can still remember the exciting experiences of the "land rushes," when cowboys and farmers fought for the right to buy lands offered for sale.

One of the most famous of all "rushes" on the southern plains occurred at Gail, the county seat of Borden County. On March 4, 1904, five sections of land came on the market, and seven days later an additional block of three sections was offered for sale. Prior to this time a friendly rivalry had been going on for several months, and both the cowmen and the homesteaders were ready for any action which would relieve the ever growing tension. The

1. J. A. Rickard, "South Plains Land Rushes," in *Panhandle Plains Historical Review* II (1929), 98.

editor of the *Borden Citizen* (Gail), on March 17, wrote an exciting account of what followed under the caption, "The War of the Ribbons. A Clash That Rivals the War of the Roses." During the first ten days of that month Gail had been the scene of a friendly but lively conflict between the "Red and Blue Ribbons," the cowboys wearing the blue, and the farmers the red. The land offered for sale had been occupied by farmers for some time before it was put on the market, and when they learned that it was to be offered for sale they took their position before the door of the County Clerk's office.

On February 29 a large band of cowboys rode into town for the sole purpose of expelling the waiting farmers. They looked over the situation and decided that the time was propitious for action, since the farmers were few in number. "Big Bob Odom, commander in chief of the Blue army, held a short council with his chiefs, and it was decided to make an attack at once. No sooner resolved than they filed into the courthouse yard and into the hall. The struggle was short. About ten minutes later they tossed the last red ribbon man out of the hall and then there went up a yell from the "Blues" that would have stampeded an army of Apaches." However, their celebration was a bit premature. The ousted homesteaders scoured the country for recruits for a hundred miles or more, and a short time later they appeared again with their numbers greatly augmented. Without any preliminary negotiations, they engaged the "Blues" in a twenty minute tug of war till they had sent the last of them rolling in the dust, victoriously resumed their siege of the Clerk's office—and finally were rewarded with the land. It was estimated that 225 men participated in this first brawl.

The cowboys abandoned the field to their worthy foes, but resolved that they would be on hand again when the second block was put on sale. Knowing, too, that they must expect formidable opposition, they brought in cowboys from as far away as Abilene, Colorado, and Big Springs, besides a large number of recruits from Garza and other counties to the north. Indeed, when the day of conflict came they had succeeded in marshaling 175 men, as compared with 125 on the side of the "Reds." The Sheriff of the County became apprehensive lest the rivalry of the factions would lead to bloodshed, and required that all leave behind their weapons before entering the courthouse grounds. A merchant of the town is said to have used a barrel to hold the discarded weapons of which he was made custodian. The contest which followed was as stubbornly fought as the previous one; "there was guying, grunting, and gnashing of teeth for a short time after which there was a Blue demonstration."

During these days of stress and conflict the range rider was not always tolerant toward the lowly farmer. He watched with growing hostility the destruction of his free range and the development of numerous farms; and in expressing his contempt for one who would "dig in the earth for a living, and break up the free range with his wire fences," he sometimes spoke of him as a "squatter," a "nester," or a "clodhopper." He warned that any attempt to cultivate the plains area would be met by the opposition of nature herself, in the form of grasshoppers, sandstorms, droughts, and predatory animals. Perhaps it was this linking of the name of the tiller of the soil with that of insect pests which caused an early plains lawyer to say that the agricultural conquest of the plains country resolved itself into a case of " 'Clodhopper' *vs*. Grasshopper." It is interesting to examine contemporary records in order to determine to what extent he was correct.

II

Early residents of the southern plains stoutly affirm that the grasshopper scourge during pioneer days was a far more formidable foe of the farmer than our present generation can conceive. A Kansas publication quotes Mrs. James Lewis, of Kinsley, as saying that the first people who came to Kansas to live were nearly crushed by the prairie. "They were smitten by the blizzard, they were parched by the drought, scorched by fiery winds, and scourged by grasshoppers. Their souls were tried by fierce experiences, and those who were not of the hardy type, gave up in despair and returned to more genial climes, leaving the desert and the unfriendly plain to those who were determined to dominate."[2] M. P. Gould, an early settler of this state, declares that during the early days of Kansas he had much "to do with vigilance committees, border ruffians, ma-

2. Mrs. James E. Lewis, Jr., "A Romance Century," in *Kansas State Historical Collections* (1907-8), 45.

laria, grasshoppers, schools, churches, and other things germane to that day."[3] That grasshopper scourges, too, were remembered by the average settler of the state may be inferred from such place names as "Grasshopper Creek," in Jefferson County, and "Grasshopper Falls," changed to Valley Falls in 1875. In fact, Easterners spoke of Kansas as the "Hot Wind and Grasshopper State."

Like the plague of locusts in ancient Egypt, in the days of Moses, grasshoppers swarmed over the hills and prairies of the southern plains in periodic invasions—and there was no Pharaoh to promise relief for the stricken people. Settlers along the frontier of Texas in 1848, 1853, 1856, and 1857 were subjected to the devastating forays of these pests. In the first year "clouds of grasshoppers came from the north, riding the winds of the first mild October northers." A recent Texas writer states that "in 1853 grasshoppers descended upon Navarro County in such numbers that they resembled a black cloud coming from the North and every living green sprig, grass, leaf or crop was destroyed by the hungry insects. The reddish green cloud of insects rolled over the country like a flood until there was a heavy coating of the insects upon the ground and after the third day Navarro County looked as though a fire had swept over it and singed every living plant."[4] Their breeding place seems to have been the foothills of the Rocky Mountains, and for this reason the southern plains area was more exposed to their inroads than the timber farther eastward. At any rate, both official and popular records indicate that they were more destructive to the plains country. The Kansas State Superintendent of Public Instruction, in his annual report of 1868, writes: "The periodic inundation of grasshoppers took place earlier this year than last, and consequently found vegetation young and tender. They ate and destroyed more than half the corn; also vegetables, including the potato crop. This, of course, had a tendency to retard the progress of education."

The grasshopper years more generally remembered in western Kansas and Nebraska are 1868-69 and 1874-75. In each instance the grasshoppers appeared in a great cloud, remained for several days, and destroyed all growing crops, even eating the leaves from the trees and all fruit in the orchards. Percy G. Ebbutt, an Eng-

3. Letter, *ibid.*, p. 176.
4. Annie Carpenter Love, *History of Navarro County*, 90-91.

lish immigrant in western Kansas during the scourge of 1874-75, thus describes the appalling swarm:

. . . .Some little idea of them may be formed when I say that there was a band at least two hundred and fifty miles wide, extending quite across the State, and about twenty miles deep from vanguard to rear, an ever-shifting mass, gradually moving on; and when I say that the majority of this belt of land—five thousand square miles—was so covered that each footstep killed dozens,—though of course they congregated mostly about the cultivated fields,—enough will have been said to show the utter impossibility of in any way destroying them.[5]

During the warm days of August, 1874, the Kansas and Texas farmers of the plains and "Cross Timbers" belt were in great need of rain for their crops, which were promising bountiful returns. According to the account of a settler in southwestern Kansas, one morning, while scanning the skies for a cloud which would bring the much-needed rain, he saw advancing from the northwest what he thought was the fulfillment of his hopes. The cloud seemed quite heavy and of threatening proportions; and members of the family, anticipating a heavy precipitation, were soon busily engaged in putting out pans, barrels, and tubs to catch the water from the roof, cooping the small chicks, and closing windows and doors on the threatened side of the house. He noticed, however, as the cloud approached, that it was of a silvery hue, glinting strangely in the morning sunlight. The sun was soon darkened and there was heard on the roof of the house the expected patter of supposed raindrops, which soon grew into a vibrant drumming. Then to his dismay, upon looking out of his window, he saw millions of grass-hoppers falling like hail. The ground was soon covered with them, and one who sought to walk through them found that they swarmed about his head at every step, striking him on his face and body. In the morning the fields were lovely with their growing wheat and corn; in the evening nothing was left but the blackened stalks; flowers, leaves, fruits, and even green corn had all disappeared as if by magic. Where one insect was killed by an irate farmer, a hundred flew down to take its place. They invaded homes, hopped into the water bucket, and pans of milk, and ate the bread and other

5. Percy G. Ebbutt, *Emigrant Life in Kansas*, p. 132.

food on the tables. Ebbutt states that for more than a week it was his daily task to go down into his well, forty-five feet in depth, and skim off the drowned and swimming hoppers.

After more than ten days the worst of the cloud had passed, but local swarms remained here and there to lay their eggs on the warm earth, from which were hatched millions of insects the following year. The bulk of the army traveled southward across the state and parts of Missouri, Arkansas, and Texas, carrying with it destruction for all growing crops, moving slowly "but making a thorough sweep of every region visited." Writing in 1892, Fannie McCormick tells of a surprising incident in connection with this particular grasshopper scourge in western Kansas: grasshoppers "called a halt several times" to trains operating over the Santa Fe railroad. "Heavy freight trains were delayed for hours by their gathering on the track in large numbers, the wheels crushing their bodies and forming an oily, soapy substance, which caused the wheels to spin around and around, with no power to go forward. The engineer would stand in the cab looking as humiliated as a dethroned monarch, and all hands would proceed to sand the track."[6]

To meet the emergency Governor Thomas A. Osborn called a special session of the legislature on September 15, 1874. In his call, he said that the state had been "invaded by an army of grasshoppers," and that it was the duty of the state to offer whatever relief it could. The lawmakers responded to his appeal by enacting a measure which provided for the issuance of $73,000 of state bonds, and also authorized the counties in the stricken belt to issue "special relief bonds." Local agencies over the state also contributed to what was called the "Grasshopper fund" to relieve the destitute people; and other states of the nation sent their contributions of money, clothing, planting seed, and food.

To the newly arrived immigrant the disaster wrought by the pests was a trying experience. Many had invested all their savings in purchasing a homestead, or in building a home and making improvements on a free government claim. In either case, they had expected their crops to yield them an income to meet their outstanding obligations as well as their needs for the coming year. But when they saw their maturing crops swept away by a swarm of grasshoppers, they were abruptly brought face to face with a

6. Fannie McCormick, *A Kansas Farm or the Promised Land*, p. 81.

desperate problem. How could they pay for groceries and drygoods they had already bought on credit from their local merchants? How could they meet the next mortgage payment on their homes? Or how could they raise sufficient funds to buy next year's supply of planting seed, groceries, and other things needed? According to one settler thus reviewing the devastation wrought, the grasshoppers had eaten everything about his farm, except the mortgage.

Many immigrants did not remain in the country to attempt a solution of their problem; they had tasted of the bitter fruits of drought, insects, and general adversity, and were now ready to turn their faces toward "God's country," meaning the land from whence they had come. The farmer, therefore, loaded his wife and children in a covered wagon, into which he had previously piled an assortment of worn furniture, faded quilts, blankets, sheets, pillows, a mattress or two, wearing apparel, and odds and ends. Over the bows of the wagon was usually stretched a dingy, patched wagonsheet, drawn up near the center by a worn rope or cord, in order that the passengers could peep from under the covering. The entire ensemble presented an appearance of destitution and adversity and unmistakable evidence that "Jordan is a hard road to travel." Often, as he drove through a small town on his way eastward, the farmer would stop to make purchases of bread and bacon, or at a secondhand store to exchange some prized piece of furniture for necessities, or sell it for money to defray the expenses of his journey. Occasionally, the travelers had the usual legends scrawled on their wagon sheets. One read, "In God we trusted, in Kansas we busted"; another, who had evidently left Kansas several times and wished to silence his critics, had inscribed the motto, "Wise men change their minds; fools, never." Still another legend was, "Hoppers et all but the wagon-sheet."

III

Those who remained on their prairie farms to face the uncertain future were confronted with numerous problems. Life to them was a constant battle against nature; insect confederates of the grasshoppers—fleas, ants, gnats, mosquitoes, spiders, worms, bugs, and centipedes—found entry to the settler's home through the screenless doors and windows, and plagued the members of the household. Moreover, predatory animals, such as prairie dogs, rabbits, wolves, and an occasional panther, destroyed either growing crops, or fowls and young calves and colts. Indeed, there was a common saying in the country that "we must get the Indian out of the country before we can grow trees," meaning, of course, that the wild life of the country must be destroyed before its development was possible.

In some parts of the country pure soft water could be had from wells, but in other areas ground tanks and cisterns must be constructed. In many such instances the larvae of the mosquito had to be strained from the water used during the summer months; and, if it came from the surface tanks—which were used by both man and beast—it was generally so filled with silt as to require settling before it could be drunk. To clear it, the settler would boil the water in kettles, or add a small quantity of alum. In any case, the water was often unfit for drinking, and much of the sickness of the frontier during this time may be charged to this source. Where water was used from ground tanks it was hauled to the home of the settler in barrels on a rudely constructed sled or a wagon. If he drew water from a well—in the days before windmills were introduced on the plains—it was necessary for him to take it from a depth of from forty to more than one hundred feet by means of a long cylindrical container with a water valve at the bottom. The task of drawing sufficient water for household purposes and for the livestock sometimes fell to the mother or a grown daughter, but more often to the younger sons. Many early settlers still living can remember the experience of drawing forty or fifty buckets of water, on a warm summer day, for thirsty horses and cattle.

The duties of the farmer were multifarious. He often arose at dawn—and sometimes in the fall of the year, before dawn—to begin his chores of making fires in the kitchen stove and fireplace, driving his work-horses from the pasture to the barn where they were to be fed, driving calves to the cowpen, feeding chickens, and many other routine tasks which he usually did before breakfast. Then after a breakfast of soda-biscuits, fat bacon, molasses, and occasionally stewed prunes or peaches, washed down with scalding black coffee, he hitched his team to a plow and started his more arduous labors of the day, often enveloped with a cloud of dust

A southern plains sandstorm. Upper, the approach;
lower, the results

for hours at a time during a hard-blowing sandstorm. He would come in at noon, or at the close of day, with red-rimmed eyes, irritated by pelting pebbles and sand and with his faded shirt and overalls so begrimed with sweat and dirt that he hardly resembled the man who went forth to plow in the morning.[7] All field work was hard; plowing, pulling suckers from growing corn, chopping cotton, following the row planter, cutting wheat or other grain, shocking the harvested wheat, corn, maize, cane, or kaffir—all required long hours of tiresome, back-breaking toil. The worker was forced to eat strong foods—meats, beans, potatoes, clabber, and butter-milk—in order to stand the strain of hard work. He wore coarse heavy shoes, cotton socks, heavy underwear, a hickory shirt, and duck overalls, for he found by experience that these were best adapted to his work; and if he could boast a "Sunday suit," hat, and shoes, in addition to his work clothes, he was indeed fortunate.

But strenuous as was the life of the farmer, his wife and daughter fared worse. Every day of her life the farm woman went through a dreary, monotonous round. Up at dawn, summer or winter, she prepared the same black coffee and fried bacon, day after day; and before she could clear away the dishes, she could hear the calves bleating for their morning meal and the milk cows stamping, both impatient to be served. After six or seven long-horned, gaunt cows had been milked, the wife's forenoon work began in earnest; straining the milk, churning, darning worn-out cotton socks or hose, mending garments, sweeping the accumulated deposits of dirt brought in by the heavy-footed farmer and other members of the family, or left by the previous day's sandstorm, drawing water from a deep well, bending for hours over the washtub, attempting to make fearfully soiled linen and foul socks and under-garments fit to wear—all these made up her routine of the day. And in addition she often helped in the field, coming home at eleven or eleven-thirty to prepare the noon meal. Of the southern plains as of farm country elsewhere it was true that "A man's

---

7. John H. Clarke, commissioner of a boundary survey between New Mexico and Texas in September, 1861, encountered a southern plains sandstorm, and wrote: ". . . .the opera-tions of the surveying party arrested by storm so violent as to turn over wagons, lift the instrument from the tripod, and fill the atmosphere with dust and gravel." He complained that the party was subjected to a varying temperature from mild weather to twenty or thirty-five degrees below freezing. Clarke to I. M. Edmons, report of September, 1861, MS, in Jacob Kuechler papers, 1804-72, Archives, Library, University of Texas.

work is from sun to sun, but a woman's work is never done."
John W. Bookwalter says of her:

To round up the duties and responsibilities of the day her
labors are carried far into the night and often, very often, they
continue long after those of the male portion of the family have
ended. She has long since ceased to think about her personal appearance. A tender kiss from her husband would almost surprise
her. Once she grieved that her little girls were so barely clad; now,
she scarcely thinks of it. That she should have a spare hour
every day to read never enters her head, and the bare suggestion
that on every Sunday she should "dress-up" and devote herself,
during the rest of the day, to social intercourse would cause a
stare of incredulity. For be it understood that Sunday for the
farmer's wife is a sort of clearance day to adjust the odds and
ends of the previous week's cares and labors to be in readiness
for the renewed labors of the coming week.

Of course, some one rises to remark, this is a fancy picture.
I would that it were so! But one has only to plunge into the
depths of a purely agricultural district, especially in the West,
remote from city or town, to find that it is a reality in thousands
of homes. Fortunately there are very many families in better
condition. There are farmers' wives who keep "help," and have
separate rooms and cool, airy bed-rooms, and leisure hours on
Sunday, and occasionally a comfortable carriage to go to church
in; but with the so-called lower middle classes it is as I have set
it down. They are frequently crowded together in small rooms as
unhealthy as the poor in the cities, and by day they are over-
worked, in summer they are chronically overheated, and in winter pinched by cold and roughened by exposure, while at all
seasons they have (worst of all evils) monotony and loneliness;
else why do the insane asylums hold such an enormous proportion of farmers' wives?[8]

Not only was the farmer's wife careless of her attire, but the
farmer, too, was conspicuous for his unkempt appearance. Seldom
would he shave more than once a week, and sometimes not that

8. John W. Bookwalter, "The Farmer's Isolation and the Remedy," in *The Forum*,
XII (September, 1891-February, 1892), 54-55. James W. Steele, writing two decades prior
to this time, gave about the same picture. Then he added: "There is no broad line drawn
between her and her thrifty and prosperous neighbors. For thousands of miles, there are no
better homes than hers, and with a patience which might have a touch of sublimity were
it not so unconscious, she waits for better things." "Women Under Difficulties," in the
Kansas Magazine, II (September, 1872), No. 3, 224-29.

often; his mouth and beard were frequently discolored by a mixture of dirt and tobacco juice; and he often allowed his hair to go unwashed for months at a time, with its accumulation of dirt, dandruff, and oil. His hands were gnarled and roughened from constant exposure and toil; his face was burned and tanned by the fiery sun of summer and the cold winds of winter; his steps were long and awkward because of long years of trudging behind the plow; and his shoulders were stooped from carrying heavy loads. Disappointment and failure were his companions; in defense of himself and family, he was driven to hopeful "drought philosophy" which enabled him to meet adversity after adversity with a stoicism which would have done credit to the ancient Spartan. On mornings after a blinding sandstorm or a grasshopper invasion, which had swept his field clean of all growing vegetation, he would whistle and sing as he replanted his crop; and when reminded of his misfortune, he would speak lightly of it and talk cheerfully of a better day. He finally came to accept adversity, hardship, sickness, and disappointment, with equanimity and worked hard to repair his fortunes. In short, he adapted himself to a plains civilization, unique among the people of the Western Hemisphere, and so claimed for habitation a region which had been denied the white race for more than three centuries. A clodhopper, indeed! Yet who can deny him the role of a border hero in his stupendous achievement of laying well the foundations of plains industry? He often lived in a sod house, he plowed up great clouds of earth which he "hopped" in following his gang-plow, he literally ate and breathed the elements as he went about his duties in a turbulent sandstorm, and earth covered his face and hands—but in undergoing hardships, misfortunes, and disappointments, and in working hopefully and steadily at his task, he has materially added to the prosperity of the nation and to the happiness of his family and neighbors.

13

HOME REMEDIES AND THE "PILL-BAG"

I

ISOLATION and poverty were the two most formidable enemies of the frontier home; together they conspired to deprive the settler and his family of their natural inheritance—health and comfort. Living on a remote frontier, and lacking means to purchase needed supplies, the pioneer suffered many inconveniences. In the absence of proper building materials he was compelled to use sod, adobe, or scrap lumber. These and faulty construction afforded little protection against the extremes of the weather. The frontier dwelling was invariably overheated in the summer, and underheated during the blustery periods of norther and blizzard. Isolation and poverty were likewise responsible for the poor quality of clothing, as little suited as the houses to the extremes of the weather. Often summer attire was worn in winter, and the settler suffered from cold; or, heavy winter garments in July and August made the heat almost unbearable. Finally, isolation and poverty dictated a restricted diet; salt pork, beans, molasses, cornbread, soda biscuits, and milk, occasionally varied with wild game. As a result of the scarcity of vegetables in the winter months and the difficulty of raising them during dry springs and summers, scurvy and dysentery were common.

Exposure and deprivation made sickness a dreaded visitor in the cabin of the settler. It was sometimes forty or fifty miles to the nearest town and twenty or thirty hours until the doctor's arrival; and in the case of a knife wound, a broken leg, acute indigestion, a snakebite, or other emergencies, the settler was thrown on his own or his neighbors' resources. Almost every frontier community was blessed with one or two elderly matrons proficient in administering home remedies. These women were often called to the bedside of an expectant mother, or a child stricken with fever, and though sometimes compelled to ride long distances, they seldom asked or expected pay for their unselfish services. Indeed, the homes visited were generally so poverty-stricken that little remuneration could be offered save gratitude and deep and abiding friendship.

In the ministering hands of these kindly creatures, many home remedies were effective, some of them, however, almost as disagreeable as the affliction. For the general toning-up of the body a tonic of whiskey, wild cherry bark, sarsaparilla, stilingia roots, and prickly-ash bark was prescribed; and sulphur and molasses or sassafras and sage teas were used to purify the blood, particularly if the patient was afflicted with boils.

In the winter months, when severe colds, grippe, and pneumonia were prevalent, hoarhound syrup, liberally mixed with whiskey was prescribed for a "hacking cough." To cure a deep-seated cold the patient was required to take a hot footbath, and go to bed, wearing over his chest a piece of red flannel soaked in turpentine and grease, or a plaster made of dry mustard and the whites of eggs spread on a cloth. A black sock or stocking about the neck or asafetida suspended from a string tied about the neck was good for sore throat.

Home remedies made use of the herbs growing on the plains, and the bark and roots of trees along the streams, besides many common products. Tobacco juice was good for stings and bites; a mixture of baking soda and molasses was applied to burns; mutton or beef tallow made an unguent for chapped hands, face, and lips; a mole's foot, tied about the neck of a teething infant, eased sore gums; the oil extracted from peach kernels relieved earache; and urine was used for sore eyes.

For mysterious ailments charm cures were required. The rabies, which was supposed to be transmitted by the bite of the small spotted skunk, known among the settlers as the "hydrophobia cat," could be detected and cured by a madstone. This mysterious and rare egg-shaped stone—sometimes there was only one in fifteen or twenty counties—was believed to have come from the stomach of a white deer or a cow. If the victim of the bite was infected with the virus, the stone would cling to the wound like a leech for several hours; and, when removed, it would change the color of milk to a bilious green. If, however, the patient was not infected, the stone would not cling to him, and he could return home in peace.[1]

Perhaps the most dreaded enemy of the settler was the rattlesnake, which frequently lurked in the shade of green corn, under the bundles of newly mown grain, in pathways through pastures and fields, and sometimes in cow and horse lots, barns, and homes of the immigrants. Its grayish-brown-and-black mottled body was so much like the color of the earth that often it had bitten its victim before its presence was made known; for, although the rattles on its tail generally kept buzzing, its actual position was sometimes hard to locate. Rattlesnakes were so numerous when the country was first occupied that it was not uncommon for a homesteader to kill forty or fifty of them in one year. With the approach of the warm days of spring, therefore, he must be on his guard.

To counteract the deadly poison of a snakebite, many remedies were used by the early comers. The most widely known remedy was liquor drunk in large quantities. Another method of treating snakebite was to bind a string or ligature firmly above the puncture, scarify the wound deeply, and suck out the poison. Colonel Marcy writes of a combination cure:

> I was present upon one occasion when an Indian child was struck in the fore-finger by a large rattle-snake. His mother, who was near at the time, seized him in her arms, and, placing the wounded finger in her mouth, sucked the poison from the puncture for some minutes, repeatedly spitting out the saliva; after which she chewed and mashed some plantain leaves and applied to the wound. Over this she sprinkled some finely-powdered tobacco, and wrapped the finger up in a rag. I did not observe that the child suffered afterward the least pain or inconvenience. The immediate application of the remedies probably saved his life.[2]

Hartshorn applied externally to the wound and drunk in small quantities diluted with water, pulverized indigo made into a poultice with water, gunpowder burned on the puncture, cauter-

1. It is altogether probable that the skunk was as harmless a hydrophobia carrier as the prairie dog, the coyote, or any other prairie animal, and that the supposed miraculous cure was only a figment of the imagination. The mad dog, too, was supposed to scatter this deadly malady, and on rare occasions did.
2. Randolph B. Marcy, *The Prairie Traveler*, 81-85; also see Reginald Aldridge, *Ranch Notes in Kansas, Colorado, the Indian Territory and Northern Texas*, 141-42.

izing widely around the bite with a strong solution of nitrate of
silver, cutting open a recently killed fowl and applying its warm
flesh to the wound, were other favorite remedies.

II

The earliest available records of medical practice on the southern
plains are those of the army posts scattered along the frontier.
To safeguard properly the health of the soldiers, medical officers
were stationed at each of the border forts. To the Indians in the
vicinity, the miracle-working wonders of medicine were a never
failing mystery. In 1850, soon after the peculiar properties of
chloroform became known, a quantity of it was sent to Colonel
Charles May, commanding a part of the Second Dragoons, stationed
at Fort Mason, on the Llano River in Texas. In order duly to impress some redskin visitors with the power of "the whiteman's
medicine," he told them that he could kill a man and restore him
to life at will, and offered to demonstrate his magic by experimenting
on one of them. They objected strenuously to this proposal, but
consented to allow him to try his skill on a small dog. The Colonel
then took the dog into an adjoining room to administer the chloroform, and soon returned with it apparently dead. To convince
the Indians that it was really dead, and that there was no trickery,
he cut off its tail, bit by bit. Each time he cut off a piece, the redskins watched closely to see if the dog showed evidence of pain,
and when it did not, they were convinced that it was dead. The
Colonel retired a second time to work the miracle of restoration.
He soon returned and threw down among the surprised savages
the tailless and equally frightened cur, which darted from the room
with whines and yelps. The dog, however, was not faster than the
alarmed savages.[3]

Assistant Surgeon Alexander B. Hasson, stationed at Fort
Phantom Hill, on the Clear Fork of the Brazos River, in what
is now Jones County, Texas, reported in 1852 that there were
eighteen cases of scurvy at the post when he arrived, and that one
of the patients had died. He attributed the malady to the lack
of vegetables in the soldiers' diet, adding: "Our gardens are yielding

3. Theodore F. Rodenbough (ed.), *From Everglade to Cañon with the Second Dragoons*,
167-68.

us little or nothing, and offer no prospect of vegetables for the winter. This is owing to the extreme drought, although persons from the country below us say that more rain has fallen this year than usual. Gardening operations in this country must always be precarious."[4] Dr. A. Taylor, who succeeded Hasson at the post in the same year, had pickles added to the rations, in the hope of remedying the condition.

At this post the total commitments to the hospital in 1852 were 293. In 1853, the number increased to 363, of which 91 were cases of chills and fever, contracted by men transferred from Fort Washita, where this ailment was prevalent. Diarrhoea and dysentery were the most common maladies, because soldiers on scout duty were often forced to drink brackish water from green-scummed ponds and sluggish streams, and to use it in cooking their own bread. Army officers soon learned that much of the water of the plains region was unfit for drinking, and in 1863 Colonel Marcy wrote:

> Water taken from stagnant pools, charged with putric vegetable matter and animalculae, would be very likely to generate fevers and dysenteries if taken into the stomach without purification. It should, therefore, be thoroughly boiled, and all the scum removed from the surface as it rises; this clarifies it, and by mixing powdered charcoal with it the disinfecting process is perfected. Water may also be purified by placing a piece of alum in the end of a stick that has been split, and stirring it around in a bucket of water. Charcoal and the leaves of the prickly pear are also used for the same purpose.[5]

The prickly pear mentioned by Colonel Marcy in this connection was a very valuable plant. Its apples were eaten as a fruit; its large fibrous and juicy leaves, when once their thorns were burned away, were food for cattle, and, when reduced to a poultice, were used for inflamed sores and swollen breasts of females. Even the juices extracted from it were used for medicinal purposes. Yet its sharp-pointed needles were a source of constant annoyance to the barefooted boy who roamed the prairies about the homestead.

4. Report of Brevet Lieutenant Colonel W. G. Freeman, Assistant Adjutant, of the Eighth Military District, April 22, 1853, MSS, in Old Records Division, Adjutant General's Office, War Department; and *Senate Executive Document.* Thirty-fourth Congress, first session, No. 961, 375-78.

5. Marcy, *op. cit.*, 27-28.

III

One of the most important persons in every frontier town was the physician. It was not uncommon for him to have almost exclusive jurisdiction over a region of four hundred or five hundred miles in diameter; and in order to minister to the needs of his patients he occasionally traveled both day and night, sometimes with his medicines and instruments packed in saddlebags, and sometimes—when he traveled in a buggy—in a small satchel which the frontiersman often called a "pill bag."

Moreover, during these early days, the physician was a "Jack-of-all-trades." Reginald Aldridge writes of an early southwestern Kansas doctor, established in a small village of only four houses, who, in addition to his busy life of waiting on the sick, was a station keeper on a stage line, a land agent, a coal merchant and a farmer.[6] Sometimes the frontier doctor maintained a general establishment in which he sold groceries, hardware, drugs, dispensed liquors over a bar, and provided for the wants of buffalo hunters and trappers operating in his trade territory. In some instances he taught the village school, helped to prepare the dead for burial, and gave legal advice pertaining to the filing of land claims, the drawing up of deeds, or the mortgaging of homesteads. Indeed the average doctor during frontier days was an indispensable figure, a person who generously and unselfishly gave of his means and services for the common welfare of his neighbors and friends.

He is seen in his most heroic role, when, mounted astride a fast-traveling horse, with his saddlebags thrown across its back, he makes his way to a distant dugout or sod house, through a raging storm or chilling blizzard, in order that he may help a pneumonia patient in his struggle for life, or assuage the pain of one stricken with the colic, "locked bowels," or the rheumatism. He was not only a general practitioner, but also a surgeon and dentist. With crude forceps he extracted teeth, with a hunting knife he performed operations, and from whatever materials he found available he made his splints and bandages to bind up broken bones. In his numerous duties, it was not uncommon for him to go for forty-eight hours or longer without sleep, and to sit up all night beside the bed of a desperately ill neighbor until the crisis was passed,

6. Aldridge, *op. cit.*, p. 19.

and he could announce to the deeply anxious wife or husband that the loved one would live.

When Dr. P. C. Coleman first came to Colorado, Texas, in January, 1883, his field of practice was as follows: "on the south it extended some forty miles, or about halfway to San Angelo, to the east it did not extend so far, since the doctors at Sweetwater had some of the practice, but to the west it extended more than a hundred miles." Most of his long trips were "to ranches to treat injuries to cattlemen—setting broken limbs, adjusting fractures (they were not all peaceful in those days), removing bullets"; and he "used ether and chloroform only; no local anaesthesia was known at that time."

From his experience he gives two unusual and interesting incidents. On one occasion a rider called for him to visit a sick woman who lived at a ranch a hundred miles away.[7] As he was making preparations to start on his journey, the sheriff of the town called him aside and told him that the man who had come for him and who was to ride back to the ranch with him, leading his horse behind the buggy, was a "bad man," wanted on a charge of murder. He and his deputy, he added, expected to arrest the man somewhere between Colorado and the ranch, and he warned the doctor to keep out of harm's way, in the event that it became necessary to use firearms in getting their man. Dr. Coleman pleaded with the officer to abandon his errand, and although the other would not agree to do so, no effort was made to arrest the man on the trip to the ranch. He was, however, arrested later by the rangers and tried, but was cleared of the charge. On another occasion he rode forty miles south of town, guided by a lad riding a horse over hills and valleys, through long hours of a dark night.

After we had made a long and tiresome journey with many turns the boy said, "this is the place." In the darkness it seemed to me that there was nothing whatever in the vicinity except a bank or bluff set back a short distance from the river [the Colo-

7. It was not uncommon for a doctor to travel a hundred miles or more during these early days. During the early seventies Doan's Store was established on the Red River at a crossing of the Western Cattle Trail. "In 1880 J. Doan took ill with fever, and, as the nearest doctor was no closer than Henrietta, a covered wagon was sent for him. Three days later the doctor arrived and found his patient so sick that he remained three weeks. The pioneer conscience is shown by the physician's charge of $25." After the sick man's recovery he was returned to Henrietta in the same wagon. Mrs. Bertha A. Ross (niece of J. Doan) to Ruby L. Smith, April, 1935, MS.

rado] bank proper. But I hitched my team, took my medicine and followed him down this bluff. Near the bottom of the steep incline we found a door opening into a dugout. After I had seen to the wants of the baby (suffering with some temporary trouble) the family gave me the choice bed. This was on the ground under the bed on which the sick baby lay. This dugout was about fifteen feet square, with low ceiling, but twelve persons occupied it that night![8]

On still another occasion, Dr. Coleman was the attending physician in a case in which a lad had become entangled with a runaway plow-team, and the sharp point of the plowshare had penetrated the abdomen. When the suffering boy was found, his intestines "were out of the body cavity covered with dirt and trash." The doctor "cleaned the parts and replaced them, closed the ugly cut with stitches, and the boy made rapid recovery." In another runaway accident in 1887, a woman was thrown from a cart into a wire fence, and her scalp was almost torn from her head; "she had been dragged through the sand, trash and grass burrs." When Dr. Coleman arrived he carefully cleaned the scalp, replaced it on the head, and she, too, soon recovered.[9]

Dr. Henry F. Hoyt, in his book, *A Frontier Doctor*, tells of his unusual experiences as a physician in the Panhandle of Texas. On one occasion he came to the bedside of the daughter of Don Casimiro Romero, wealthiest Mexican in the Panhandle. The girl, Piedad, was so badly stricken with smallpox that there was not a spot on her body without a pustule. In order to allay her sufferings from the intolerable itching which usually accompanies the disease in this stage, he experimented by mixing gunpowder with water and spreading it over the entire body. He reasoned that since gunpowder consisted of charcoal, saltpeter, and sulphur, it should be helpful in a case of this kind, and the experiment was such a decided success that Senorita Piedad, his first patient in the Panhandle, soon recovered. On this same trip he stopped at a shack near Tascosa, at the crossing of the Canadian River. Upon entering the room he found a Mexican on his back in great pain, which he found was caused from a dislocated shoulder sustained while chasing buffalo. Since he had no anaesthetic with him,

8. For a discussion of the various experiences of Dr. Coleman, see West Texas Historical Association *Year Book*, VII (June, 1931), 35-39.
9. *Ibid.*, p. 39.

he pulled off one of his boots, used his heel as a fulcrum, and by hard pulling reduced the dislocation. He then improvised a bandage and bound his patient's arm to his body, and left instructions for him to keep quiet and visit him the next day in Tascosa. The following morning, however, the Mexican tore the bandage from his arm to see whether or not it was ready for use, and again the dislocation occurred, necessitating painful repetition of the treatment.[10]

Similar experiences of heroic and resourceful pioneer physicians could be multiplied. The average physician was subject to call at all hours of the day and night; through fair and foul weather he traveled, and over roads rough and long. Remuneration for his services was seldom adequate, except in the satisfaction of knowing that he had eased the pain of a sufferer, or had aided him in his struggle with death.

During the period of the ranchmen the physician was generally paid his fee at the completion of his call. Later, however, with the arrival of the poor homesteader, or those who were able to pay but who had little sense of obligation, the doctor occasionally had a hard time in making his collections. Albert D. Richardson relates an amusing experience of a Denver dentist, which may or may not be true. The dentist had made repeated efforts to collect a debt from a female patient but without success. Resorting to artifice, one day he called on her and asked how a plate, which he had recently made for her, was working; and he also asked that he be allowed to examine it. When it was handed to him, he coolly pocketed it and returned to his office. "This," he said, "brought the money very promptly; for is not mastication as essential to dining as dining to existence?"[11] That collections were equally hard to make in Texas is evident from the following article in the Denison *News* of July 3, 1873:

A Texas doctor recently rode fifty miles to attend a patient. After he cured the patient he presented a bill for fifty dollars, and completed his preparations for the journey back to the post, thinking no more about the matter. As he was about to mount, the patient's husband put in an appearance, trusty rifle in hand. "Doctor," said he, "I reckon we'd better settle this matter right

10. Henry F. Hoyt, *A Frontier Doctor*, 54-55.
11. Albert D. Richardson, *Beyond the Mississippi*, p. 304.

now;" and taking him aside, "You wan't going off without a settlement, was you? I don't want to owe no man nothing. Here's a ten, which is about a square thing, I reckon. Now if you aint satisfied just git yer weppin and come behind the hill thar, so's the old woman wont be riled up, and we'll settle it. I don't want no man to go away from my house dissatisfied; especially you, Doc."

IV

If the settlers did not care to pay doctor's fees and if they lived at no great distance from a town or village, they depended for all ordinary maladies on patent medicines, in addition to their home remedies. In fact, the period of the homesteader was the heyday of the patent medicine seller. One who scans the issues of frontier newspapers and other local publications at this time will notice the unusual space given to patent remedy advertisements. *Peruna*, *Hostetter's Bitters*, and *Simmons Liver Regulator* were three of the popular ready-made prescriptions. Manufacturers of remedies advanced extravagant claims for their "cure-alls." An advertisement sponsored by J. H. Zeilen and Company, in a southern plains immigrant publication in 1876, offered *Simmons Liver Regulator* as a remedy for dyspepsia, diarrhoea, dropsy, sick headache, bilious fever, bilious cholic, costiveness, and jaundice; and in the same publication *Dr. Radway's Sarsaparillian Resolvent* was advertised as a remedy for twenty-two specified diseases, "etc."[12] Wheelock, Finlay, and Ball, importers and wholesale druggists of New Orleans advertised in the *Texas Almanac for 1867* that *Argyle Bitters* will strengthen and invigorate the entire system, and effectually cure "Dyspepsia, Liver Complaint, Nervous Debility, Disordered Stomach, Disgust for Food, Heartburn, Loss of Appetite, General Debility, and Prostration of the System."

That thousands of dollars were spent for patent medicines by every community of homesteaders was indicated by a varied assortment of discarded empty bottles about the premises of the average rural home. Yet by no means did the people abandon their home remedies for these new ready-made prescriptions; they mixed the two! Patent medicines were now used in their homemade poultices,

12. Albert Hansford, *Texas State Register for 1876*, pp. 109, 116.

ointments, salves, tonics, and teas. Often when a physician was called in, he was greatly chagrined and embarrassed by demands of the settler or his wife that one of these new prescriptions be substituted for the one which he offered. In some instances the substitute was harmless and was allowed, but in other cases it was harmful and was rejected, although by voicing his disapproval the physician would occasionally lose a patient.

Was the pioneer of the southern plains made of "sterner stuff" than the people of today? The question has frequently been asked by those who read of the trials and hardships of our early pioneers, and has been answered in the affirmative by pioneers still living. Perhaps the issue will never be settled to the satisfaction of all. Yet evidences are found which at least lend color to the claims of the pioneer. One of the favorite arguments of the early settler is that the frontier woman was a hardier type than her sister of today. On the southern plains there were no maternity hospitals, and it was not uncommon for a mother to give birth to a child and be up and about her household duties two or three days later. And this was true not only once but repeatedly during the rearing of a family of seven or eight children. Often a physician would never make a call at the home of the expectant mother until childbirth, and then one call would suffice. Records of early medical practice along the frontier are replete with instances of operations of a simple character performed without the use of anaesthesia, of sewing up gaping wounds requiring ten or more stitches, without even a sedative being administered. But these instances arose out of necessity because no better treatment could be given. It is entirely probable that our own generation could measure up to this rigorous standard of hardship and self-discipline in case of similar necessity.

14

"SOLDIERS OF THE CROSS"

I

THE southern plains preacher, whom the early settler dubbed "the parson," served the border settlements as unselfishly and as constructively as did the physician. He was a valuable asset to every community; in addition to his ministerial duties of preaching at isolated mission stations, and in churches, and homes scattered along the border, and performing marriages, he frequently rendered such services as teaching a community school and sponsoring spelling matches, literary societies, singing schools, and picnics. Sometimes, too, he helped to wait on the sick, and when he found that household remedies did not yield results he often suggested a new method of treatment; he labored in the field by the side of the farmer, helping to chop cotton, to pull suckers from growing corn, to shock the bundles of newly mown wheat or oats, to pick cotton, to gather the ripened corn or other grain from the fields, and to haul it to the barn; he acted as a cowboy on the open range, and handled a rope expertly, or rode a "bronc" as well as the average range rider; and when Indians raided the frontier he was sometimes a member of the posse which drove them from the country. The early circuit riders of the Methodists and the itinerant preachers of the Baptists and Presbyterians and other denominations which served the frontier during this period have often been called "Soldiers of the Cross"; and the name is not an inappropriate one, for it is doubtful if a greater measure of valor and fortitude was required of the federal soldier who was stationed at an army post on the frontier than was demanded of him who "with a gun in one hand and a Bible in the other" braved the uncertainties of the border wilds in order to carry the Gospel of Christ to remote settlements.

Long before Anglo-Americans had begun to occupy the southern plains area, the Catholics had been carrying on missionary activities among the Indians roaming over the country, but without any considerable success. Moreover, Protestant preachers and teachers had also entered the field two decades before the coming of settlers, and had established mission schools among the tribes and sought to christianize them. Since these missionaries were generally far removed from white settlements, they were often deprived of the common necessities of life, including adequate clothing, food, and medicines. The people among whom they worked were mainly un-tutored Indians, who in some instances were not only indifferent but hostile to the white man's religion, maintaining that it was in opposition to their own tribal teachings. The work of preachers often carried them on long rides from one Indian camp to another, and forced them to subordinate their civilized habits to primitive conditions existing in camps of the wild plains tribes. Teachers, however, were more generally stationed at mission schools located among the semi-sedentary tribes. Their work was directed toward instructing Indian children how to read and write, giving them an understanding of the rudiments of the white man's civilization, and bringing them to accept the Christian religion.

In 1830 the Missouri Conference of the Methodist Church appointed Reverend William Johnson as agent to introduce learn-ing and religion among the Kansas Indians. Shortly thereafter he departed for his mission field, and on June 26, 1831, after he had been at work for several months, wrote to the Corresponding Secretary of the Missionary Society, that "We have no converts among the Indians yet; though, I have thought some of them were under religious impressions."[1] At this time his school was composed of about ten Indian and six or seven white children, the latter probably from the families of white traders and government offi-cials who had settled about the Indian agency.

Although he met with many hardships and discouragements in his work, on August 30 he writes: "I intend to go on in the strength of the Lord of hosts. I feel no unwillingness to spend my life in this missionary cause."

In this field of missionary activity workers encountered malaria, dysentery, and contagious diseases. In the spring of 1819, the United Foreign Mission Society of the Presbyterian Church, of

1. "Letters from the Indian Missions in Kansas," in *Kansas State Historical Collections*, XVI (1923-25), 228.

New York City, sent Epaphras Chapman and Job Vinall to see about opening missionary work among the Osages. Of their experiences, Professor Morris L. Wardell writes: "Vinall met the fate of his many successors—not death at the hands of the Osages for they were never guilty of killing those who came to help them, but death as the result of fevers, malaria and exposure."[2] This was also the lot of the aforementioned Methodist missionary, William Johnson. As to his desperate plight in a remote mission station where he could not secure the service of a physician when serious illness afflicted his family, he writes: "Several cases of fever, and other diseases, continued to resist every effort we were able to make." A physician was finally sent for, "but being ninety miles out of the United States, it took four days and nights to obtain a physician, at which time it was too late to do anything in one of the cases and the unfortunate sufferer, Mrs. Bensley, died the next night, leaving a husband and five little children all sick." He adds, however, that "she died in peace, professing resignation to the will of God." Then, turning to his own afflicting:

> For about three weeks after this Mrs. Johnson and our two little children lay very sick. We were uneasy for every one of them. In another room lay Mr. Greene and wife, and none to administer to them but two of us and neither of us well, with ten sick, and two of us to do all that was done. We had no time to rest day or night. We were next called to part with our dear little daughter, Mary Frances. We had now to bear trials new to us. We knew we loved our little children, but never knew how tender the ties of affection were before. But the breach was made in our little family, and we committed her to the grave, praying God to give us grace to bear it.

One of the most remarkable experiences ever recorded by a missionary teacher working among the southern plains Indians is from the pen of Thomas C. Battey. As a representative of the Society of Friends (Quakers), Battey first established a school among the Caddoes, on the False Washita River; and later, at the request of Kicking Bird, worked among the fierce Kiowas, in what is now western Oklahoma and the Panhandle of Texas. It is worthy of note that during the war of 1874-75 between the federal troops

2. Morris L. Wardell, "Early Protestant Missions Among the Osages," in *Chronicles of Oklahoma*, II (September, 1924), No. 3, 287.

and the Red River tribes, Kicking Bird's band of Kiowas remained at peace with the whites. Cyrus Beede, Chief Clerk of the Central Superintendency, at Lawrence, Kansas, in a statement prefaced to Battey's *A Quaker Among the Indians*, observes that the chieftain's peaceful attitude could be attributed to Battey's influence over him. The strenuous life lived by this Quaker in the course of moving about from place to place, subjecting himself to constant dangers of bodily harm and eating the unwholesome food of the redmen—in the hopeless task of teaching his charges how "to walk in the white man's road,"—all combined to make a burden greater than he could bear. After a stay of little more than eighteen months among them, he was forced to withdraw from the field, defeated in his purpose and broken in health.

His experiences among the Caddoes were trying enough. Tribal superstitions, irresponsibility of parents, truculence and intolerance of discipline on the part of the boys and girls in school, and a general lack of appreciation of the white man's civilization, were only a few of the unconquerable influences which worked against him. It is not surprising, therefore, that he was willing to accept the invitations and urgent request of the Kiowa chieftain to become a teacher among his people, though Battey was soon to learn that he had "jumped from the frying-pan into the fire!" As an example of his trials in teaching the untamed children of the Kiowas and of his courage and faith in meeting these trials, the initial entry may be cited:

1st Month, 23d.—I this day record the opening of a school in the Kiowa camp, on the Washita River.

Having got my tent, blackboard, maps, charts, &c., in readiness, I left the Agency [the Wichita Agency, near Fort Sill, Indian Territory] last 2d day; a son of the agent and two of the employees accompanied me, to assist in setting up my tent. But not getting the right directions as to the road, we were two days in reaching camp and setting up the tent. They left me yesterday, and having some other preparations to make, I could not open school until this morning, when, with twenty-two scholars, it was opened in the presence of most of the chiefs, several women, and a number of young men. It being the first attempt at anything of the kind ever undertaken among the Kiowas, it is regarded as a novelty by them. After the withdrawal of the chiefs and old people, several young men remaining in my tent, a middle-aged man came in with an uplifted hand-axe, his face hideously painted with black lines, expressive of intense anger, advanced towards me with a most horrid oath in broken English, and suiting his action to his words, was, in appearance, in the attitude of striking me with the edge of his weapon. Putting on as bold a front as I could command, I stepped up to him, seized him by his uplifted arm, and forcibly put him out of my tent, telling him I should permit no such talk or action in my lodge.[3]

When the Caddoes heard that Battey had left them for Kicking Bird's tribe, certain disgruntled leaders came to the Kiowa camp and sought to persuade the chieftains to expel him. The Kiowas then held a council to ponder the advice of their Caddo visitors. Battey's anxiety as to the outcome is revealed in another entry in his diary: "What the result of their deliberations may be I know not. Their children are kept away from my tent, and a couple of young men, armed with bows, arrows, and revolvers, are remaining in and about it, watching me while I am writing these lines." A short time later, while several children were quietly sitting around, attentively engaged in their several tasks, an elderly warrior came in, and, with great violence, took the slates and pencils from their hands and drove them out of the tent; and school was over for the morning. In the afternoon, when the children had again assembled, young men came to the tent to repeat the performance, and then demanded the slates and pencils which the pupils had been using. Battey writes: "I refused to let them have them, telling them, if they wanted to use slates and pencils, to come in quietly, and sit down, and they could have them." This the young warriors refused to do, and though they later sought to break up the school, the attitude of the school master was so unyielding that they gave up in defeat. Battey felt deeply grieved at this reception, but he was able thus to confide to his diary:

. . . .I have no reason to complain, if in the wisdom of Him whom I desire to serve, He sees it to be best for me to keep in the low places, neither abounding in fullness, nor yet wholly destitute of Divine favor, so that His will concerning me be perfected, whether I see the desire of my eyes as regards this people, yea

3. P. 115.

or nay. I know that they are equally with their more favored
. brothers the objects of Divine regard and compassion; that "his
arm is not shortened that it cannot save" even to the uttermost;
that His grace is sufficient even for their redemption, by which
they must be changed, if changed they ever are, from this savage,
heathen life to that of Christian civilization.[4]

Battey's work among the Kiowas resulted in failure, but it should
be pointed out that general conditions militated against success.
From the time that he opened his school among them, on January
23, 1873, until his withdrawal eighteen months later, life among
the Kiowas was in a state of constant turmoil and confusion. By
aggressive campaigns against the rebellious elements of the southern plains tribes, the federal troops were seeking to bring to an end,
once and for all, depredations on the frontier. Thus driven from
"pillar to post" the Indians had little time to think of religion,
education, or anything else pertaining to ways of peace. Moreover,
warfare of this kind naturally caused them to be prejudiced towards
the work of white missionaries. Finally, the Caddoes sought to
make the Kiowas believe that the sickness which prevailed among
the children of the camp was to be attributed to the fact that
Battey was "a bad medicine man." Kicking Bird and other influen-
tial leaders refused to believe this, but undoubtedly the charge had
considerable weight with the more superstitious members of the
tribe; and, until the end of his stay among the Indians, Battey
was forced to combat it. It was while he was engaged in this
stupendous struggle that his health became seriously impaired
and he was forced to withdraw from his work.

II

The work of Baptists, Methodists, and Presbyterians among
the Five Civilized Tribes had met with more success, but even
here the final results wrere disappointing. Tribal superstition and
tradition were formidable weapons used by Indian leaders who
wished to oppose the influence of Christianity. When white settlers
finally came into the territory, therefore, they found the results of
missionary work among the Indians far short of what had originally

4. As cited, p. 124.

been planned. Where hundreds of the tribesmen had nominally accepted the white man's God, thousands had steadfastly refused to do so.

Even missionary work among white people settled in parts of the southern plains area fell short of anticipated results. By the time the Mexican War came to a close, Protestant missionaries were found in New Mexico. A government official in this newly acquired area, writing on July 29, 1851, states that a "Mr. Nicholson from the Pittsburg Conference" was stationed at Santa Fe; "he is a glorious fellow. . . . and if any individual missionary could do any good to this population he would be the man. But with all his labors, he has not only not got a single convert, but he cannot get a dozen hearers out of the whole population, Mexican and American." Yet in the face of this discouragement, "he continues to preach, sometimes to ten hearers—sometimes to five. Reverend Mr. Kephart, whom you know, is my room-mate. He hitches teams with Nicholson and I think has about abandoned the field in dispair, although he continues to do all in his power. . . . . There are besides these two, two Baptist preachers whose success is just equal to their co-laborers. We made an effort to raise a temperance meeting on Sunday night last, but 'nobody didn't come.' "[5] It is quite probable that the primary reason for the failure of the Protestant missionaries was that the field had largely been preempted by the Catholics. Concerning the influence of a newly arrived dignitary of this church, the writer says: "A new Bishop has arrived in the territory from Cincinnati, and is said to be a Christian and a gentleman. He will make the cock-fighting and gambling priests of New Mexico either move their boots or discard their evil practices." When the Bishop arrived at one of the Rio Grande towns the inhabitants got on their knees about his carriage, but he commanded them, "Get off your knees. Don't kneel to me. Worship God."[6]

5. T. B. Galloway, "Private Letters of a Government Official in the Southwest," in *Journal of American History*, III (1909), No. 4, 545.

6. Other visitors to this area made similar charges against the New Mexico priests. Captain O. M. Knapp, stationed at Fort Bliss, Texas, near El Paso, wrote thus to "My Dear Friend," on January 12, 1867: "People all go to mass and then come out and run horses and fight cocks for the rest of the day, and the priests always make the biggest bets and have the finest fighting cocks." MS, in O. M. Knapp papers, Archives, Library, University of Texas. Also see James W. Steele, "Among the New Mexicans," in the *Kansas Magazine*, I (February, 1872), No. 2, 105-12.

Up until well past the period of the Civil War there were many settlers along the southern plains frontier who seldom had the privilege of listening to a religious discourse. During the struggle, settlers occasionally "forted up" for protection; or they grouped themselves together in small temporary villages about which would be built defensive earthen works. Sam Newcomb, an early school teacher, was located at such a station, called Fort Davis, in Shackleford County, Texas, during 1865 and a part of 1866. A diary which he kept during his stay at this isolated post reveals the many inconveniences and tribulations endured by the settlers. On January 29, 1865, he writes that the "men, women, and children all met at J. M. Frans' residence at 6 o'clock this evening and organized a Sunday school." On July 8, a "couple of the fort's leading ladies indulged in a fist fight this morning, the result of differences among the children." On August 26, "There will be no preaching here tomorrow, as the people had expected." And then, apparently as an afterthought he adds the surprising statement: "There are several persons here, grown, married and raising children, who have never heard a sermon." The preacher finally came, however, for in an entry of December 24, we read: "The first sermon ever preached in Fort Davis was preached here today by Parson Slaughter, and it was the first sermon many of our people ever heard." Still later, he writes of the "parson" engaged in "preaching at the school house," performing wedding ceremonies, and baptizing new additions to the church; and in other entries he tells of sickness among the settlers, Indian raids, the return of buffalo hunters with their wagons loaded with meat and tallow, and the departure of trail herds for Kansas.[7]

The inference to be drawn from Newcomb's diary, that the life of the frontier minister was as hazardous as that of the average settler in an exposed frontier settlement during this early period, is borne out by numerous statements in early records and reliable secondary accounts. Reverend Hiram Stone, who was a preacher in Kansas during the stressful days of the Civil War, writes that frequently he had "ridden out on horseback in the night to meet an engagement or answer a call, holding the reins in one hand and a drawn pistol in the other, peering into the darkness," not knowing what

7. Don H. Biggers, *Shackleford County Sketches* (A day-by-day diary kept by Sam Newcomb, a pioneer school teacher), p. 14 *et sqq.*

was before him. As late as December 18, 1878, the Fort Smith
Weekly New Era carried an article contributed by a visitor to
Caddo, Oklahoma, in what is now Bryan County, thus picturing
the difficulties of preaching the Gospel at that place:

This little town is very quiet at the present time, and everything seems to be moving as calmly as the most peace-loving
citizen could desire. But this is not the usual state of the burg,
I understand, and indeed it was conclusively proven to me a few
days ago, when the Reverend Mr. Morris, pastor of the Con-
gregational Church, called my attention to a hole in the door of
the edifice made by a bullet, which was intended for the reverend gentleman himself, and to further convince me, that
neither life nor property are safe in this locality, I see almost
daily on the street a man who murdered in cold-blood a Sunday
School Teacher for no cause whatever, and yet this red handed
assassin walks the earth as free as the most law-abiding citizen.
Why? Because his victim (a white man) had become a "citizen"
and was under the protection(?) of the high and mighty Choctaw
Nation.

It was rumored here a few days ago that Deputy United
States Marshals Ayers brothers were killed in an engagement
with Wiley Stewart and "Texas Dick" the murderers of Doctor
Jones of this place, but as the rumor has not been substantiated
by any proof the story has gained very little credence.

The introduction of Christianity to the early settlers of Texas
was beset with many dangers and difficulties. Reverend Z. N.
Morrell, a Baptist minister, has contributed to Western Amer-
icana an interesting narrative of his work during the time of the
Texas revolution and after. Having come to Texas in the early part
of 1836, and arrived at Nacogdoches, he writes the following account
of his first sermon in the West.

Several Sundays had come and gone while we were in the wilderness and only one sermon had been preached, and that on an
evening during the week. This was by no means the course I had
pursued for fourteen years in Tennessee. My very soul burned
within me to preach Jesus. An election was in progress when we
reached the town. This was the law and custom in the country
in that day. Here was a large crowd of Americans, Mexicans
and Indians of several different tribes. My mule was soon tied

and after consultation with my great Master—for I had no one else to consult with—I decided to preach, and began looking around for a suitable place. Near by the vast crowd I saw the foundation timbers of a large framed building laid. No floor had been laid no upright pieces raised. No sooner discovered than I selected one corner of this for a pulpit. The sills and sleepers, already laid and well adjusted, would answer for seats. I held up my watch in my hand, and cried at the top of my voice.

"O yes! O yes! O yes! Everybody that wants to buy, without money and without price, come this way!" and commenced singing the old battle song—

"Am I a soldier of the Cross."

Before I had finished my song, there was around me a large crowd of all sorts and sizes and colors. A brief prayer was offered and the two verses sung—

"'Tis religion that can give," etc.

Amidst profound silence, astonishment rather than reverence was stamped upon their features. Across the street was a large upper gallery and by this time it was full of ladies and gentlemen. Just at this point some wagons and a carriage, evidently belonging to movers, drove up close to where I was standing, and I recognized Bro. William Whitaker and family, from Hardeman County, Tennessee, three of whose daughters I had baptized in the old state. The preacher who reads this will understand the effect this produced on the speaker. My text was announced from Isa.35:1: "The wilderness and the solitary place shall be glad for them; and the desert shall rejoice and blossom as the rose." Never did the canebrake preacher receive better attention. God blessed me with great liberty for one hour amid many tears shed around me. The congregation was dismissed in due form and there were many hearty shakes given the strange preacher's hand. My soul was full to overflowing, and that moment I believed the text. God has not disappointed me.[8]

As the settlements of the state spread westward and south-westward, this bold preacher along with many others extended his own sphere of influence. He braved the dangers of Indian massacre,

8. J. M. Carroll, *A History of Texas Baptists*, p. 86.

capture by the Mexicans, and rough treatment at the hands of outlaws in order to carry out his chosen work. That there were dangers incidental to preaching in a lawless environment is proved by many available sources. According to Mrs. Viele, in her book, *Following the Drum: A Glimpse of Frontier Life*, published in 1858, "there was current, and generally believed report, that the post-master of Rio Grande City was a good Baptist, the only man in the settlement who owned a Bible, in consequence of which he had acquired the familiar cognomen of 'Bible-back,' a name that he stoutly resented!" It seems, however, that he defended himself by affirming that the Bible belonged to his wife; but that he had a brother in northern Texas who had "got religion and done well," and that "he thought *some* of 'getting it' himself!"

To southwestern Texas came the Reverend John McCullock, a Presbyterian, during the period of "outlaw days." W. G. Blaikie, editor of *The Catholic Presbyterian* (London), writing in 1879, tells of McCullock's reception of an outlaw. One day the leader of a band of desperadoes rode his horse into the building in which McCullock was conducting religious services, and finding the "parson" within, began shooting at him. To escape the shots, the latter dodged about behind his books, which were piled in heaps around him. "He pointed out to me," writes Blaikie, "the bullet holes in many of the volumes."[9] A Methodist preacher, Reverend H. D. Fisher, while conducting services at Olathe, Kansas, a short time later, tells of a similar experience in which a border "tough" sought to kill him while he was in his pulpit.[10] While he was preaching earnestly, "Whang!" went a gun, and a window was broken by a bullet which flattened against the opposite wall and fell into a lady's lap. When members of the congregation hastened outside to apprehend the would-be assassin, he was gone, astride a horse.

Working on a turbulent frontier, the successful "parson" was of necessity a bold resourceful person. He had to accept conditions as he found them, and make the most of them. If he manifested an aversion for frontier people, or their way of living, he was not greatly respected; but if he were adaptable, resourceful, and brave,

9. *The Catholic Presbyterian. An International Journal—Ecclesiastical and Religious* (ed. by Professor W. G. Blaikie, D.D., L.L.D., F.R.S.E., London), I (January-June, 1879), 283 *et sqq.*

10. Rev. H. D. Fisher, *The Gun and Gospel*, p. 212.

he was heartily welcome to the average frontier home, and did not
have to pay the usual "fare" of the transient boarder. Many a
frontier preacher gained the sobriquet of "fighting parson." The
Galveston *Tri-Weekly News* of May 16, 1897, carried an account of
the death of one such preacher, Reverend E. A. Briggs. He was an
honored citizen of his state who had run the usual gamut of frontier experiences, having been at various times a school teacher, a
frontiersman, and a ranger. The *Tri-Weekly News* cites an instance
in which he was presiding over a frontier school at Richmond, in
Fort Bend County, during a Mexican invasion of Texas in 1842.
Nearly all of his students were young men who joined a company
of rangers for service against the invaders. When Briggs learned
that his pupils were about to leave him, he is reported to have
said: "Well, boys, if you are all going to the war I had as well go
too," and he also joined the volunteer company. Later Governor
J. H. Bell commissioned him to raise a company of rangers to
protect an exposed German settlement west of San Antonio, and
for some time he remained in frontier service.

Reverend William Allen, a Methodist circuit rider, was another
"fighting parson," who was assigned the task "to go all up and
down the border of the settlements from Red River a hundred
miles south." When he went into the field, he was at a loss as to
how to proceed, since there were few places along the frontier
where public worship could be held. His first sermon was in the
home of a Baptist settler. When he asked this frontiersman for
permission to hold services in his home, the latter expressed regret
that Allen was not a Baptist, but, said he, "we must have preaching
anyhow. We don't get much of it in this Western country. Methodist preaching is better than none. I suppose you are willing to
preach for us." When Sunday came, the preacher was greatly surprised to find so many people assembling. He said: "For miles
around they came—from Hickory Creek, Clear Creek, and Denton
Creek, and from other places wherever a frontiersman had dom-
iciled himself anywhere in reach. Then came men, women, and
children, with their dogs and a few cats, to hear one of their number—a pioneer, now turned preacher—proclaim the tidings of
salvation."[11]

11. Rev. William Allen, *Five Years in the West*, p. 62 *et sqq.*

Often on his long tiresome rides, when night overtook him, he was forced to ask a settler for accommodations for himself and his horse. Generally he was received hospitably, but occasionally he was given a grudging welcome. On one unusually cool reception, after being rudely questioned by his host as to his reasons for being in that part of the country, he was shown to his bed for the night. As to his trepidations, he said: "The cabin had two rooms, and I was shown to the other. In it there was a place cut out for a chimney which had never been built. The head of my bed was immediately by that. I blew out the sort of burning wick which I had been supplied—taking care first, however, to reconnoiter the room, and to evade as far as possible any uneasiness should any one in any conceivable way be watching me." No harm came to him, however, and he proceeded on his way the following morning.

A short time later, Allen traveled to a distant schoolhouse to deliver a sermon, as he was accustomed to do at infrequent intervals. Upon arriving he found the men of his congregation forming a posse for the purpose of driving marauding Comanche and Kiowa raiders from the country. Being a practical man, he thus concluded: "I saw no use in trying to preach that day, and therefore joined in with them, to take a lesson in an Indian hunt. In following the trail, we passed within a few hundred yards of the house in which I had an appointment for the day."

III

As a result of the efforts of these bold and courageous preachers churches soon sprang up along the frontier. As a rule the settlers were eager to establish schools and churches, even though they had to give of their time and slender means in building houses in which services and classes could be held. In a publication sponsored by the Bureau of Immigration of Texas and authorized by the legislature of that state, entitled *Texas the Home for the Emigrant from Everywhere* (Austin, 1873), appears the following statement, relative to religious conditions in western Texas:

. . . .Whenever a party of settlers assembled they at once took the necessary steps to organize churches, and build houses of worship and schools. Ministers of the various religious denominations were to be found in nearly every settlement, however small they were, and many of them traveled over the country as missionaries, organizing communities, and schools, and attending to the spiritual comforts of their co-religionists.

One of the principal agencies of the Protestant church for the increase of its membership was the revival meeting. A "revival" was generally held in the summer season of the year after "the crops were laid by." For weeks after a congregation had agreed to hold such a series of meetings, the services of the church would be pointed toward the coming revival. A convenient meeting place would be provided, and usually a brush arbor would be constructed, under which straw was liberally scattered and benches were provided for all who came. An ideal site for such a series of services was a grove of trees near a running stream or spring, for shade and water were prime necessities. The duration of a revival was ten days or two weeks, and longer; and the order of procedure consisted of a ten or eleven o'clock service in the morning, "dinner on the ground," a period of relaxation and visiting in the early part of the afternoon, a four or five o'clock prayer service, and an evening service "at early candle light," which sometimes lasted until midnight.

The revival was one of the most remarkable developments ever sponsored by Protestant churches. In the southern plains area it served both as a spiritual uplift for the community and as an occasion for social contact. To these assemblies would come settlers from every part of the community, and sometimes from homes twenty-five or fifty miles away. In the early morning the pioneer would load his entire family into a wagon and drive to the assembly grounds. On arriving he would help to unload the children, unhitch his team of mules or horses and tie them to a tree, feed them, then take the basket of food they had brought along and carry it to where the noon meal was to be served, or leave it in the wagon until after the morning service. When he was not listening to a religious service, or occupied with his duties as a member of the church, he was usually engaged in conversation with a neighbor, and each member of the family likewise visited with friends. The camp meeting period was one generally enjoyed by all members of the family, for it meant a period of freedom from work, a chance to enjoy the comradeship of neighbors, and an opportunity for spiritual development.

It was not always expected of children that they should sit through a lengthy service without going to sleep—although there were some parents who exacted this punishment. More tolerant parents brought quilts along to spread on the straw under the arbor for the younger members of their "brood" to stretch out on when they became sleepy. It happened more than once that mischief-making young men would change sleeping babes from one pallet to another, causing great confusion when the time came to go home.

The extraordinary emotional expressions of those attending these pioneer religious gatherings may perhaps be accounted for in part by environment. The frontier was sternly exacting of those who came to it; loneliness, sickness, sorrow, hardship, and severe toil constituted the common lot of the average family. The stark realities of life made the settler conscious of a need which he could not supply and which caused him to seek strength for his ordeals from a higher power. It was in services like these, therefore, that he believed he found the strength and comfort "to carry on" with his daily routine. As a rule, he was intensely sincere in his religious manifestations, even when in the midst of the preacher's sermon he gave vent to his pent-up emotions with a loud "Amen!" And in justice to the average church member of this period, it should be added that he sought earnestly to live the kind of life which the "parson" pointed out to him.

All pioneer churches maintained strict discipline; such activities as card playing or other gambling, dancing, tattling (or "back-biting," in frontier parlance), horse racing, liquor drinking, and falsifying were generally frowned upon. Members of the church were supposed to be spiritually minded and "to walk circumspectly before the world." If they did not, they faced the embarrassment of expulsion. In some of the churches they were visited (or "waited on") by a committee from the church and admonished of their "worldly ways"; and if the warning was not heeded, they were then called upon to "make acknowledgments" to the church. If this was not done, the recalcitrant member was "churched." The manuscript records of early southern plains churches are curiously interesting in this connection. The minutes of the Crystal Falls, Texas, Missionary Baptist Church of November 14, 1881, reveals the following pledge at the time of its organization: "1st. That we will exercise Christian care and watchfulness over each other; and faithfully warn and exhort each other as occasion may arise, 2nd, That we will not forsake the assembling of ourselves together. . . .; 3rd, That we will not omit closet and family religion at home, nor neglect the great duty of religiously training our children and those under our care, for the service of Christ, and the enjoyment of heaven." Other resolutions relate to seeking Divine aid when tempted by "worldly lusts," to contributions of property as "God has prospered us," and to striving "unto death" to live to the glory of "Him who hath called us out of darkness into his marvelous light," as well as to the growth of the church, the "opening of the doors of the church," the ordination of deacons, and the sending of delegates to the "Red Fork Association." But the minutes of March 2, 1887, records a motion that the "Church Clerk was ordered to write a letter to Bro. L.——— stating to him that the Church could not grant him a letter of dismission [sic] until he had either proven the assertion that he had made about a Bro. & Deacon of our Church (to wit) that he had lied, or make an acknowledgment to the Church that he had done wrong in so saying." Other entries are records of committees "waiting" on an offending "Brother" or "Sister" and of acknowledgments or expulsions.[12]

Undoubtedly one reason for the general "ministerial humility" of frontier days was the attitude of the settler toward "paying the parson." Often "missionary boxes" were considered as part payment of the teacher or preacher. Missionary societies in Georgia, North Carolina, or other eastern states would set apart a day "to make up a box" for some needy preacher's family on the frontier. When it arrived and was opened, what a motley array of clothing and sundry articles it contained! Coats and pants of ancient style, made shiny by much use, black derbies, brown derbies (often frayed about the border), feminine wearing apparel of ridiculous style and design, little suited to frontier use, shoes with pointed toes, patent-leather shoes, shoes with buttons on the sides or with elastic sides, boots, leggings of all shapes and sizes. Some of the articles were useful but many would have made the missionary and his family objects of curiosity to frontier folk.

12. Manuscript Record Book of the Crystal Falls, Texas, Baptist Church, in Crane Collection, Hardin-Simmons University, Abilene, Texas.

The "pay of the parson" was never munificent. For preaching at a fourth-time or half-time church the average salary was one hundred or two hundred dollars a year. Thus, for a year's work his salary sometimes ran as high as four hundred and fifty or five hundred dollars. This did not mean, of course, that he received all his salary in cash. Produce—such as chickens, pork, corn, potatoes, buffalo robes, and sorghum molasses—was often offered as part pay; and the average minister was too respectful of his generous church member's feelings to refuse the gift. Thus after an absence of four or five days at an appointment forty or fifty miles away, the pastor might return home with a sack of worm-eaten meal, a tainted ham, or some other commodity which the giver could not use in his own home. Yet the average church member was generous. He gave unstintedly of his money, even though his income was small, and divided with the preacher the best products he derived from his farm or ranch. His home was always open to "the parson," and he seldom demanded pay for a night's lodging. At best, however, the average preacher was poor, and his family was reduced to a kind of poverty not known by the best class of people among whom he worked. The preacher was a man who was supposed to be subject to call at all hours of the day or night, to go to the bedside of the dying, to visit the sick, to perform marriage ceremonies, or to give council to the distressed; and his unselfish devotion to duty was taken as matter of course. Should he have demanded pay commensurate with his services, as did the professional man, he would have been regarded as a presumptuous beggar, too "worldly minded" for his calling.

There is no doubt that the services rendered the border settlements by "Soldiers of the Cross" were of inestimable value.[13] They helped to make cheery a drab existence, to ease the sufferings of the sick and dying, to give the settler a deeper faith in his ultimate victory over hostile forces, to point toward a more wholesome moral atmosphere for the frontier, and to deepen his faith in a great friendly God who ministered to him in sorrow and tribulation. Church discipline was severe and religious practices were

13. The opinion of General James F. Rusling, relative to the influence of Christianity on the development of Kansas, as expressed in *The Great West and the Pacific Coast*, p. 28, is as follows: "Kansas, of course, abounds in enterprise and thrift. Saved to freedom by Sharpe's rifles and the Bible, she invested largely in school-house and the church, and already reaps her fit reward."

often circumspect, but frontier conditions demanded a radical faith. The general level of society was appreciably lifted by the rigorous requirements of those who sought "the higher life." Indeed Christianity was a powerful leavening influence which tended to make a more wholesome frontier society.

15

FRONTIER JUSTICE

I

FOR more than seventy-five years after the first Anglo-American squatters had built their homes beyond the Mississippi River, the West was known as a lawless region. To the extent that a larger element of desperadoes were found here than in any other area of the nation, this reputation was justified. Indeed, so many outlaws had gravitated westward that by the middle of the nineteenth century thousands were found in the vast unorganized stretches between the Canadian boundary and the Rio Grande. As a consequence, the settler faced an ever present problem of organized crime. It threatened not only his economic tenure but also his home. By new methods of cultivation and conservation he could in some measure withstand the devastating effects of the drought; in the absence of lumber he could construct his dugout or adobe home; and when he did not have available imported subsistence, or that provided by his own labor, he could kill wild game for food; and, also, when he lived far beyond the reach of organized law, when he was the sole defender of his home, and when he found himself surrounded by outlaws and subject to their exactions, he was equally resourceful. It is not surprising that he became in a measure a part of his turbulent environment. As a last resort he came to depend on his revolver or rifle—the only authority respected by outlaws—in defending his home and rights. "In the absence of law," writes Professor Webb, "and in the social conditions that obtained, men worked out an extra-legal code or custom by which they guided their actions."[1] It was as natural for the frontiersman to go armed when he moved among his fellows as it was for him to ride a horse in crossing the fenceless and roadless prairies. And in many instances when he could not protect his interest

1. *The Great Plains*, p. 497.

single handed, he and others similarly situated organized a vigilance committee, or resorted to the more violent means of mob action.

Texas was the first of the southern plains states to feel the blight of outlawry. Many absconders, thieves, and murderers had sought an asylum there and operated in large bands by the end of its war for independence. "Gone to Texas" ("G. T. T."), was an expression often heard both in America and Europe when referring to persons running away from obligations or from justice. Rev. H. Newell, who came to Texas a short time after the revolution, wrote at some length about its society. As to the reputation of the young republic, he asked: "But why this prejudice against Texas?" Then he answered his own question. "Because it has been represented to be the resort of criminals, of insolvent and fraudulent debtors, of outlaws, and bad characters of every description. . . . ."[2] This notoriety had not changed after the lapse of forty years, as is seen from the statement by Edward King who visited Texas in the seventies. "The Texan has been paraded on the English and French stage as a maudlin ruffian, sober only in savagery; and the vulgar gossipings of insincere scribes have been allowed to prejudice hundreds of thousands of people."[3] Both writers stoutly maintained that this reputation was undeserved; that a majority of the people were as substantial as could be found in part of the nation.

As ready as were these two writers, as well as other contemporaries, to defend Texas against outside critics, there is little doubt, as previously stated, that outlawry had assumed large proportions. Many observers bore witness to this fact. For example, on September 28, 1859, Albert D. Richardson, while resting at a frontier station in western Texas on the Overland stage line, wrote:

. . . . All of which I learned [referring to the characteristics of the country] from our landlord who nervously paced his porch, ravenously chewing tobacco, and casting uneasy glances at the navy revolver by his side. Three weeks before, he had killed an employee of the stage company in a sudden quarrel, upon the very spot where we now conversed. He was under three thousand dollars bail to appear for trial; but in this lawless region men were seldom convicted of homicide, and never punished. Within

2. *History of the Revolution in Texas*, 188-89.
3. *The Great South*, p. 138.

a month there had been three other fatal shooting affrays near by; and our driver enjoined us:

"If you want to obtain distinction in this country, kill somebody!"[4]

Conditions in Texas after the Civil War were even worse than they were when Richardson visited the frontier. Restless and questionable characters freed from the restraints of military discipline sought excitement and employment in the unsettled wilds of the West, contiguous to well settled areas. A federal revenue officer who came to Texas during this period was authorized to call for a military escort in the discharge of his duties because he had "to deal with a lawless set of white men, chiefly renegades from the American army and the off-scourings of all the disreputable classes set adrift after the Mexican War."[5] The messages of the governors and the annual reports of the adjutant generals frequently gave considerable space to the activities of criminals, in large and small bands, throughout the state. The report of the latter for 1872 is a fair example. The Adjutant General pointed out that "lawless bands of armed men depredated continually throughout the state, ...local authorities, in many cases, through fear and intimidation, under the control of the desperadoes themselves. Sheriffs, who would, otherwise, dare make arrests, having no means of securely holding prisoners when arrested." Then indicating why the situation could not be easily remedied, he said:

In such an immense territory, with a population not exceeding four (4) persons to the square mile, with very limited railway facilities . . . .telegraph communication equally limited, fugitives from justice could defy the law, or if too closely pressed, found a secure and convenient harbor of refuge by simply crossing the Rio Grande, or passing into the Indian Territory, where their recapture was almost impossible. Thus these desperate characters found Texas a very El Dorado for their operations, and rendered the name of "Texan," a byword and reproach.

Conditions in New Mexico were quite as bad. Since there were few officers of the law, criminals boldly plied their trades. After visiting the area, Albert Hyde pretty well described conditions when he said that outlawry was such that cowboys, mule drivers,

4. *Beyond the Mississippi*, p. 226.
5. "A Ride on the Texas Frontier," in the *Overland Monthly*, July, 1868, p. 157.

tye-cutters, miners, ranchmen, gamblers, and all men generally wore their revolvers openly on their hips, and "those who rode about over the country added the winchester, carrying it in a leather holster fastened to the saddle under the rider's left leg."[6] More than one deadly ranch war resulted from horse and cattle stealing, and brand burning, the worst of which, perhaps, was that between the J. H. Tunstall and Company and the L. G. Murphy and Company, in which many were slain, including "Billy the Kid," Charles Bowdre, Tom O'Folliard, and Dave Rudabaugh.

Outlawry in Colorado was largely premised on the discovery of gold. The lure of an El Dorado brought thousands of adventurers and ne'er-do-wells, who, when they found that "all that glitters is not gold," turned their attention to other things. Denver soon became the center of the boom area and its wild turbulent society was the subject of more than one writer who visited the gold fields. According to Samuel Bowles, it was so lawless that "gamblers reigned, and 'to be or not to be' was the everlasting question that fretted everybody."[7] William Hepworth Dixon, an English visitor, was impressed in the same manner. "According to the code in fashion, here in Denver," said he, "murder is a comparatively slight offense. Until two or three years ago, assassination—incidental not deliberate assassination—was a crime of every day. At the door of some gambling-house. . . . it was a common thing to find a dead man in the streets each day-break."[8]

But Denver was not the only lawless town in this area. Leadville, Pueblo, and Central City were equally as bad. In regard to the latter, and in commenting on the border ruffian's regard for life, Dixon continued:

Unless a ruffian is known to have killed half-a-dozen people, and to have got, as it were, murder on the brain, he is almost safe from trouble in these western plains. A notorious murderer lived near Central City; it was known that he had shot six or seven men; but no one thought of interfering with him on account of his crimes until he was taken red-handed in the very act. Some persons fancied he was heartily sorry for what he had

6. "The Old Regime in the Southwest," in the *Century Magazine*, XLIII (1902), 692. An American army officer would not enter a gambling den of Santa Fe because, he said, "it looked like entering the door of hell." O. M. Knapp's diary, MS, in O. M. Knapp papers, Archives, Library, University of Texas.
7. *Our New West*, p. 88.
8. *New America*, p. 139.

TO THE PUBLIC!

ON Saturday, September 19th, 1863, the Judge of this District caused the arrest of a client of mine, on a Bench Warrant, and ordered the Sheriff to commit him to Jail. I, as attorney, called on the Judge and offered to give any bail that he could in reason ask, for the appearance of the party accused, at the next Term of the Court.

He refused to recieve a bond,—refused to name the amount of bail,—and stated to me that an application for a WRIT OF HABEAS CORPUS would be of no avail, as he "WOULD NOT GRANT IT!".

Knowing his conduct to be INFAMOUSLY tyranical and in violation of all law, I determined, on Sunday morning that the scoundrel's Fears SHOULD grant what justice demanded on the previous day, AND ON SUNDAY MY CLIENT WAS LIBERATED.

Knowing that the rights of my client had been most grossly outraged by the Judicial vagabond who pretends to be a JUDGE, and feeling that I had been insulted, I addressed to him the following note, to which, up to this date he has made no reply:

"Central City, C. T., Sept. 20th, 1863.
Sir:—I demand from you an apology by the hands of the bearers of this note, Joseph A. Thatcher and Thomas R. Sanders, Esqrs.—or by some other friend whom you may select, for the ungentlemanly manner in which you treated me yesterday, and I also demand from you assurances of professional and gentlemanly courtesy for the future.
I am &c.,
JAMES M. CAVANAUGH.

To Hon. Charles Lee Armour.

Believing myself to be entirely justified in my course, I do hereby PRONOUNCE and POST Charles Lee Armour, Judge of the 2nd Judicial District, Colorado Territory,

A LIAR AND A COWARD

JAMES M. CAVANAUGH.

Dated at Central City, Sept. 22nd, 1863.

A challenge to the authority of an early pioneer judge

done, and he himself, when tossing cocktails with his rough companions, used to say he was sick of shedding blood.

One day, on riding into Central City, he met a friend whom he invited to take a drink. The friend, not wishing to be seen any more in such bad company, declined the offer, on which the ruffian drew his pistol in the public street, in open day, and saying, with a comic swagger of reluctance, "Good God, can I never come into town without killing some one?" shot his friend through the heart. Seized by the indignant crowd, the callous ruffian had a stern trial, a short thrift, and a midnight escape upon the famous cotton-tree in the city ditch.[9]

Perhaps the railways building across the Southwest and the great cattle ranches were as strong attractions for criminals as were the gold fields of the West. In connection with the former, the termini towns—Abilene, Dodge City, and Ellsworth in Kansas, and Denison, Fort Worth, and El Paso in Texas—were fair examples. R. M. Wright, an early citizen of Dodge City, thus described outlawry there: "We were entirely without law and order, and our nearest point of justice was Hays City, ninety-five miles northeast of Dodge City. Here we had to go to settle our differences, but take it from me most of those differences were settled by rifle or six-shooter on the spot."[10] Denison, Texas, in 1873, was at the southern terminus of the Missouri, Kansas and Texas railway. "Every third building in the place," said Edward King, "was a drinking saloon with gambling appurtenances, filled after nightfall with a depraved adventurous crowd, whose profanity was appalling, whose aspects were hideous. . . . . Robberies were, of course, of frequent occurrence in the gambling hells. . . ."[11] A still more striking example of the lawless terminus town was El Paso. Before the Southern Pacific reached it, its reputation for lawlessness was little worse than other Rio Grande towns; but by 1880 it had gained considerable notoriety. Adjutant General John B. Jones of Texas thus summarized the new situation:

Recently complaint has been made by the mayor and board of aldermen of the town of El Paso, that their community is overrrun and over-awed by gamblers, rowdies, thieves and murderers, who are congregating at that place in anticipation

9. *Ibid.,* p. 141.
10. *Dodge City, the Cowboy Capital,* p. 10.
11. *The Southern States of North America,* p. 178.

of a rich field for operations as soon as the Texas Pacific and Southern Pacific roads reach there; and they ask that troops be sent there to protect them against these lawless characters.[12]

II

Under such conditions as portrayed by these early writers and observers it is not difficult to understand why the West was lawless. Its extent was so vast and settlements so few that peace officers and law courts could have no jurisdiction. Therefore, under the circumstances, a new procedure was inevitable. Of course it was harsh and generally individualistic but it helped to hold outlawry in check until better means could be employed. To adopt the ways of older communities, new attitudes must be cultivated, and this was not easy. Individualism must give way to group action and community responsibility.

The first indication of a change is found in the work of vigilance committees. Although these unique tribunals were without legal foundation, they were generally sanctioned and participated in by substantial citizens. Desperate situations necessitated their organization; threatening outlaw problems demanded solution, if the last vestiges of civilization were to be saved. How could a San Francisco, a Denver, or an Ellsworth have been saved without such an organization? Unquestionably such procedure temporarily encouraged mob action, and resulted in the death of more than one innocent victim, but in the large the vigilantes helped to bring order to a turbulent frontier when no other agency was available, and in this their claim for recognition deserves thoughtful consideration.

The first evidences of vigilance committees, and the extent of their activity, are difficult to establish, for often early writers used the term "vigilantes" when they should have employed "mob." Conversely, others referred to mob actions when such deeds were carried out by vigilance committees. Then, too, the self-imposed jurisdiction of a committee would sometimes extend for a hundred or more miles from the community in which it was organized.

As early as 1844, an English visitor, a Mrs. Houston, wrote that the Texan was allowed to take the law into his own hands, but that should it afterwards be pronounced by his neighbors, that either

12. *Annual Report of the Adjutant General of the State of Texas*, December 31, 1880.

the punishment of his enemy was undeserved, or not warranted
by the first duty of self-preservation, he became himself amenable
to punishment by his fellows. "At present, however," said she,
"the Texan people go on remarkably well with their primitive
system of administering justice."[13]

Vigilance committees were formed in Kansas as soon as it was
given its territorial status. Missourians, in June, 1854, on the Kansas side of the boundary, three miles from Leavenworth, organized
the Squatters' Claim Association, the members of which agreed to
the creation of a vigilance committee of thirteen members. This
organization, however, was to promote the interests of the slave-
holders by driving out free state agitators. Soon other organizations sprang up, such as the "Self Protective Association of Linn
County and the Council City Committee.

Early Denver presents the vigilance committee in its most striking role. Like San Francisco, after the discovery of gold on the
American River in 1848, gold-crazed Denver was swamped by an
unruly element. Their murderous and thieving activities were not
halted until the better class of citizens organized a vigilance committee. An observer who visited the town during these turbulent
days thus described its summary work:

> The Denver people were a law unto themselves. Whenever a
> grave crime had been committed, an informal court was organ-
> ized, some leading citizen placed upon the bench, and a jury
> made up of substantial merchants and mechanics. The prisoner
> was tried, allowed counsel, and if guilty, sentenced to be hanged
> within one or two days.
>
> These courts were as alert as the pioneer circuit judge in the
> early days of Iowa. His honor, accompanied by sheriff and clerk,
> meeting a horse-thief on a public road, held his court upon the
> spot, tried and convicted the criminal, and sent him to the
> penitentiary for five years.
>
> The week after our arrival, a murderer was thus condemned
> and executed. A few days later, another was tried. The jury
> found him guilty. The judge asked the prisoner, if he had
> any reason to offer why sentence of death should not be passed
> upon him. He replied: "I have nothing to say."

13. *Texas and the Gulf of Mexico; or Yachting in the New World*, II, 102-3.

Then the judge submitted the question to the four or five hundred spectators:

"Gentlemen, you who believe this verdict is just will say Aye."

The answer was an overwhelming roar of affirmatives.

"Contrary-minded will say No."

One solitary negative came up from the crowd. With immovable serenity, the prisoner heard the question of his life and death submitted to the assembly, like a resolution or a point of order. He was sentenced to die on the following morning; and remanded to the custody of the volunteer officers. But that night he eluded the guards and decamped, stealing a wagon and a pair of mules to facilitate his traveling. He was never caught; but the indignant people came very near hanging the officers on bare suspicion that they connived at his escape.[14]

The work of the vigilance committee was not always so openly done. While riding along the Texas frontier shortly after the Civil War, A. B. Greenleaf found a man who had been hanged by a vigilance committee. To his back was pinned a piece of paper on which was written: "Hung for horse-stealing. He said his name was William McBride, but he was a liar as well as a thief."[15] At Fort Griffin, from the limbs of pecan trees growing along the banks of the Clear Fork of the Brazos River, was found more than one lifeless body, swinging at the end of a rope, as mute evidence of the work of a vigilance committee. A correspondent of the Dallas *Herald*, writing from Fort Griffin, on April 23, 1876, said: "A vigilance committee is now astonishing the authorities, both military and civil, by the off-hand way it does business. Already several suspicious characters have been ordered to leave or fare worse. The characters aforesaid have taken the hint from their unknown admonishers and cleared out. So far, so good, and as long as the committee cleans out and strings up the right party or parties, it has the well wishes of every lover of tranquility."

The vigilantes were equally active in Kansas. The editor of the Topeka *Commonwealth*, on July 14, 1875, wrote: "A vigilance committee has been organized at Dodge City, and it would not be surprising if some of the telegraph poles were found ornamented some

14. Richardson, *op. cit.*, 290-91.
15. *Ten Years in Texas*, 35, *passim.*

of these days." J. H. Beadle succinctly indicates how this prophecy was fulfilled. " 'Dad Smith' was hanged by the vigilantes. 'Long Steve' met a similar fate at Laramie. . . . 'Rake Jake' made his exit from a tragedy more dramatic than any ever shown upon the stage. With two companions he took refuge in his cabin on the prairie, and maintained a desperate fight against the vigilantes. The infuriated Kansans set the dry grass on fire; the cabin was soon in flames, and issuing therefrom with a revolver in each hand, scattering leaden death on all sides, the three died as became their lives, brave men to the last."[16]

III

As previously mentioned, frontier settlers took advantage of every occasion where assemblies were held to meet their need for social intercourse. Even the sessions of the court were not altogether looked upon as being the mediums through which frontier justice was dispensed. They also furnished an opportunity for social gatherings, and were looked forward to by most settlers with pleasant anticipations. Often the farmer and rancher with their entire families came prepared to stay for a week or more, depending on the length of the session. An instance of this kind is given by the Tascosa *Pioneer* (Texas), for May 4, 1889, which announced to its readers: "District Court meets a week from Monday, and we look for music and fun then. Lawbreakers will need to look wary on that day, and so will the state because we look to see the bar represented by nearly all the illustrious lights of the Panhandle— her Wallaces and Matlocks, her Plemonses and her Turners and her Hendersons and her Vivians, and her Gowans and her Brownings and her Woodmans and her Houstons and Grigsbys and Bakers." Then in the column dealing with personalities, this additional item was offered: "W. H. Woodman and his lady arrived here Wednesday and will remain through court and race week."

Among the frontier lawyers were men of rare ability, and others who knew little law but who were quite resourceful in using that which they knew. Judge Thomas F. Turner, of Amarillo, knew most of the prairie lawyers during the formative period of his section of Texas. In an article captioned, "Prairie Dog Lawyers," he

16. *Western Wilds*, p. 213.

gives brief sketches of some of them. He stated that on one occasion, District Attorney L. D. Miller became outraged by the fluency by which the witness for the defense seemed to have purjured himself, and let fly this withering blast, which soon became known throughout the Panhandle: "Gentlemen of the jury, I could take that witness and prove that Jesus Christ had a hog ranch on the North Fork—Yessir, a hog ranch on the North Fork." On another occasion, according to Judge Turner, he was thus able to escape a legal entanglement:

> Again, before a Justice of the Peace, his opponent undertook to read, or quote some law to his Honor, but L. D. was impatient. He was indignant that such foreign substance should be dragged into a court of justice, but he had either to admit or deny the correctness of the proposition asserted, and so he boldly attacks, but in his original way. Confidently he said to the court;
> "Your Honor, that is not the law."
> The other lawyer stoutly maintained his position. Then the redoubtable L. D. made the startling proposal:
> "I'll bet you Ten Dollars it's not the law," and made good his offer by producing the ten-spot and laying it banteringly on the table. His opponent sought to ignore this innovation in settling law questions, but L. D. was persistent. He said:
> "Now cover it. Money talks. Put up or shut up."
> Not having the ten, the other lawyer looked imploringly at the court, but got scant sympathy there. Instead, his Honor said coldly and deliberately:
> "Yes, Mr. H., money talks. If you haint got the nerve to kiver his ten I guess you are wrong, and the court rules agin you."[17]

Another instance of resourcefulness related to a Kansas lawyer. Before the panhandle of Oklahoma became a part of the territory created by the organic act of 1890, a German settler had taken up a claim south of Beaver. On one occasion he took into his bachelor home a stranger who chanced to be passing through the country. Shortly, however, he had to go to Dodge City for supplies and leave his guest. Upon his return he found his house deserted and twelve hundred dollars missing, which had been hidden in the

17. For these two quotations, see "Prairie Dog Lawyers," in *Panhandle Plains Historical Review*, II (1929), 117-18.

bottom of his trunk. He reported his loss to the provisional sheriff who immediately took up the thief's trail and overtook him at Ashland, Kansas. At this time, district court was in session at this town, and the sheriff did not care to trouble the authorities with his case, for fear they would challenge his authority. He therefore waited until night to make the arrest. All went well until he reached the street with his prisoner, where he ran into a crowd of men and women returning from a social function. The thief, seeing his advantage, and believing that the panhandle sheriff had no jurisdiction, shouted, "murder"! The county attorney chanced to be in the crowd and immediately refused to accept the authority of the officer. He informed him that the "peace and dignity of the great State of Kansas was involved in the transaction," and that he was guilty of kidnapping. The thief then began to taunt the sheriff, freely acknowledging that he had taken the money. But the county attorney, seeing his mistake, was quick to correct it; he held the thief for bringing stolen property into the state. A short time later he was tried and sent to the penitentiary, and $1050 was restored to the German homesteader.[18]

Many times peace officers were handicapped in the administration of their duties because they had no jails in which to hold their prisoners. On this point Judge R. C. Crane, of Sweetwater, Texas, is authority for the statement that the commissioners court of Fisher County, in its first planning did not consider that a jail was needed or would be for some time so it made arrangements to board its prisoners, whenever it had any, with Nolan County and did without a jail for several years.[19] *Texas Pioneer Magazine*, published in 1880, gives another instance in which Sheriff J. P. Simpson of Fannin County was forced to board a prisoner in his own home while his case was pending. But to forestall another similar embarrassment, he built his own jail without contract or pay. Its size was four by eight feet, and it was built of logs pinned together and made secure.[20]

In the early development of the Territory of Oklahoma the lack of courthouses and jails was also a problem. A Kingfisher lawyer

18. R. L. Williams, "The Judicial History of Oklahoma," in Oklahoma Bar Association *Report*, V (1911), 154-55.
19. "Early Days in Fisher County," in West Texas Historical Association *Year Book*, VI (June, 1930), 145.
20. P. 215.

commenced an action for a client, involving the title of a town lot, before the provisional court at that point, and finally won his case. Whereupon the defendant immediately erected a tent upon the lot, and, with several of his friends, all armed with Winchesters, sought to defend it. The attorney for the plaintiff called upon the court to enforce his judgment, and was met by the excuse that there was no jail in which to imprison the offenders. The attorney was not to be outdone; he immediately began to look about for a structure which would serve the purpose of a prison. At last he found a log stockade in the course of construction which could be used. This he fitted up as a jail by putting locks on the doors and bars on the windows. When all was complete, he again presented himself before the court and asked that his dignity be upheld, offering at the same time his improvised prison for his use. Since there was no other pretext available, the court commenced to swear in deputy marshals to uphold the majesty of the law. When the defendant saw that further opposition was useless, he quietly withdrew from the lot and left it to the plaintiff.[21]

At best, much of the court procedure of frontier days was little better than that of the vigilance committees. Decisions of both judge and jury were at times unique, and even comical. Perhaps the best known of all early legal characters was Judge Roy Bean who "held forth" with his "Law West of the Pecos," at Langtry, Texas, on the Pecos River. During his earlier years Bean had been a bullwhacker, Indian fighter, saloon keeper, transcontinental emigrant guide, and owner of freight wagons plying between Chihuahua and San Antonio. In the late seventies, with Bart Gobble as partner, with all his belongings loaded into a wagon, including a copy of the *Revised Statutes of Texas*, he established a saloon near a Southern Pacific railway crossing over the Pecos River. Here, too, he set up his remarkable jusrisdiction, "Law West of the Pecos," over a region of more than forty thousand square miles, largely a waterless waste covered with gray sage, greasewood, mesquite, chaparral, and cactus. This region was sparsely occupied by cattlemen with their herds, and by a large number of renegade

21. After the opening of the "Oklahoma Lands" to settlement by the "run" of April 22, 1889, and before the federal government had made provisions for the government of the territory, temporary courts and governments were set up by the people. O. H. Violet was elected as the first police judge of Oklahoma City on May 1, 1889; Frank P. Cease at Guthrie, on June 4, 1889; and C. J. Keeney at Kingfisher on April 24, 1889.

Americans, Mexicans, Indians, Negroes, and breeds of every hue.

In his "rough and ready" interpretation of the *Revised Statutes* and administration of justice, Bean's only authority were the two heavy revolvers he wore on his hips and those of his tall, lean constable, Bart Gobble. He knew little or no law but he was ever ready to quote astonishing passages from his favorite and only law book. Yet, in justice to his decisions, it may be said that he was a source of terror to the many evildoers who operated in the Pecos region. At times he resorted to jury trial, at others he dispensed the law, but in either case court was held in his saloon and all participants were expected to patronize his bar. On one occasion, when one of his customers killed a Chinaman, the obliging Judge disposed of the case by ruling, "There ain't nothin' in the *Revised Statutes* that says it's a crime to kill a Chinaman." On another, he was called upon to hold an inquest over the body of a dead man found on the railway. After a brief examination, he found on the body a revolver and forty-eight dollars in money. He then ruled that the man had met his death by accident, but he fined him forty-eight dollars for carrying a concealed weapon!

As extralegal as were many of Judge Bean's decisions, they were hardly more unique than those rendered by judges in other parts of the southern plains. The *Intelligencer Echo* (Austin, Texas), for March 29, 1875, cites an interesting case, under its caption, "Cross Timber Justice." A citizen of Grayson County was accused by a settler of Cooke County of stealing a cow. When arraigned before a local judge, the defendant produced a bona fide bill of sale, attested by two reputable witnesses. But the judge bound the accused over for appearance at the next term of court in Gainesville on a bond of six hundred dollars with the statement that though he was satisfied that the accused had bought the cow and paid for her, still as there had been considerable cow stealing going on in his county, which had gone unpunished, he was forced to take this action. Moreover, he refused to take any one outside of Cooke County on the bond, on the ground that it was not permissible on a criminal offense.

In establishing the northern boundary of Texas and the southern boundary of Colorado and Kansas, the federal government left an area one-half degree wide and three degrees in length outside the jurisdiction of any state or territory. The region was known as the

Public Land Strip, or No Man's Land, and was subsequently attached to the Territory of Oklahoma as Beaver County. Prior to March 1, 1889, when it was attached to the Eastern District of the State of Texas at Paris for judicial purposes, the settlers of No Man's Land had their own provisional government and courts. Concerning the extraordinary character of the courts thus set up, R. L. Williams wrote:

> But occasionally trouble, infractions against the rights of the community, arose. In such instances courts were organized for each specific case, and when the case was settled that court went out of existence. Such courts were rather a board of arbitration, to seek concessions from both sides. In other words, they were peace committees. But occasionally a human life was the penalty of a quarrel, and then the court had to determine whether human life should atone.[22]

One of the most unusual instances of the latter type was a trial over the killing of a saloon keeper. Against the wishes of the settlers a man of questionable reputation came to Beaver to establish a saloon; and after getting well located in a sod house, with thick walls, and having imbibed generously of his own refreshments, he proceeded to express his displeasure because of his neighbors' opposition by shooting into their sod houses. The settlers returned the fire and the saloon was left without a proprietor. Although the bully well deserved his fate, a jury assembled to try his slayer; a settler admitted firing the fatal shot and was acquitted.

More unusual still was a trial incident to an accidental shooting, given by Williams, as follows:

> In another case, three men, two of whom were named Clark and Eugene Brusher (the name of the other not being available), came into Beaver from Kansas and proceeded to get drunk. About that time the community, as usual in frontier life, was grotesquely apparelled. Funds were exhausted and most men

22. Williams, *op. cit.*, 137-38. O. S. Chase was president of the provisional government of Beaver. Citizens were assembled at his home, at Lane's store, or elsewhere. Minute entries of March 2, 1887, reveal the unique character of the undertakings of this body. "Coroner jury inquest report in death of Thompson and Bennett endorsed. Rev. J. A. Overstreet authorized to conduct funeral. . . . . Moved that a committee of three be appointed to consider matter of issuing marriage license in Cimarron Territory. Carried and M. MaGann, H. S. Smith, and Lafayette Wells were appointed." MS, *Record Book of Beaver Neutral Strip, Indian Territory*, No. 1, 53, Oklahoma Historical Library, Oklahoma City.

were compelled to bring out their wedding suits for every-day use. It was not uncommon to see a man dressed in broadcloth, with a dollar hat and coarse cowhide shoes on. A doctor by the name of Lindley was the proud possessor of a complete dress suit, including a silk hat. Incongruous as it may seem, the doctor was obliged to wear the suit every day. He never missed an opportunity to accept an invitation to drink, and soon he fell in with the three Kansans, who seemed to be amply provided with funds. While ranged along the bar in one of those low-celinged sod saloons, the property of Sam Mills, one of the three spied the doctor's head-piece, and grabbing it remarked, as he placed it on his own head. "Let's see how I would look with a gentleman's hat on." The act started the brain of the next man to working. It struck him that it would be capital fun to shoot the hat, but his aim was unsteady. He missed the hat and hit his companion's head just back of the ear. A coroner's jury was empaneled by A. Mundell, the town marshal, and all the parties were arrested. The jury, consisting of Merritt Magan, John Garvey, E. E. Brown and T. P. Braidwood, took charge of all of the effects of the three strangers, and from the money found on the dead man and the two live ones, a man was hired to haul the dead body to Dodge City, eighty miles away, and there notify the dead man's people by wire. As soon as the body of the deceased was disposed of, the jury after a hearing acquitted the defendant. About a week later, William Brusher, a brother of the deceased, appeared upon the scene and on the night after his appearance, he killed the slayer of his brother and escaped into the darkness.[23]

Generally, the lawyers and judges of frontier days were fearless in the performance of their duties. Sometimes the courtroom was filled with armed men—including the judge and attorneys. On one occasion, in a small western Texas cow town, a thief was being tried for murdering a citizen who had turned informer. When the day of trial came he and his gang stalked into the courtroom heavily armed. "Indeed," said an eyewitness to this well-known trial, "the judge and lawyers were also fully armed." The jury was duly impressed with these evidences of hostility, and, although witnesses to the shooting established beyond a doubt that the defendant had committed murder, it brought in a decision of "not

23. Williams, *op. cit.*, p. 152.

guilty!" The judge was enraged; in a fiery lecture he reprimanded the jurymen for their lack of courage and responsibility, and ended his tirade by fining each "twenty dollars and cost!"[24]

Although many of the decisions of the frontier courts were irregular, as is seen from the foregoing examples, law and order rapidly supplanted chaotic conditions. As soon as the settlers came in and organized counties, they also elected their judges, attorneys, and sheriffs. Some of these were good and some were bad, but in the course of time the general level of their efficiency in weeding out criminals from frontier society was appreciably raised. Much credit for this constructive work is due such famous peace officers as "Wild Bill" Hickock, Bill Tilghman, Chris Madsen, Frank Canton, Pat Garrett, "Red" Hall, Captain Bill McDonald, George W. Arrington, and many others who could be named. Their arduous and unremitting services often carried them on long journeys of hundreds of miles in efforts to bring outlaws to justice.

Unquestionably the most famous group of peace officers on the southern plains were the Texas rangers. Their long years of service prior to the Civil War gave them a background of tradition and of experience which materially aided them in breaking up the large bands of outlaws who infested the border during the period, 1865-90. J. H. Beadle, a visitor to Texas during this period, was greatly impressed with their work. He stated that when the "militia" was organized, "eight hundred robbers and desperadoes fled the state in a body." Adjutant General John B. Jones, in his annual report of December 31, 1880, is more detailed in pointing out the services rendered by this organization.

The three companies stationed on the border of the settlements, under Captain Roberts, Marsh and Arrington, have been constantly engaged in scouting after Indians and outlaws, except when attending the courts at the request of the civil authorities, or guarding prisoners, or escorting them to the interior counties to lodge them in secure jails. The field of their operations has been the whole line of the frontier extending from Demmit county, on the Nueces river to Fort Elliott, in the Panhandle, a distance of five hundred miles, and as far west as Fort Stockton and the line of New Mexico. There were several raids into this region during 1879 by small thieving bands of Indians from

24. *Ibid.*, 153-54.

the Fort Sill and Fort Stanton reservations, and these raids were more frequent last winter than for several years before, especially during the months of January and February, when severe snow storms prevented the troops from following their trails successfully. The rangers had several engagements with these bands, in one of which private W. B. Anglin, of Company B, was killed.

These companies have arrested many fugitives from justice and sent them to the interior counties from whence they had fled. The sparse population of the unorganized counties have no other protection against the thieves and outlaws who infest the border than afforded by the rangers. Company E, Lieutenant Nevill, while stationed near Austin, was kept constantly employed hunting fugitives from justice, guarding prisoners and jails, escorting prisoners and attending the courts to assist the civil officers in enforcing the law. Detachments from this company by request of the civil officers, attended court as far east as Hempstead, and as far north as Brown county. They made scouts in pursuit of fugitives from justice and to execute processes of the courts, as far south as Houston, and as far north and northwest as Denison, Jacksboro and Taylor counties.[25]

In summarizing the work of the "Frontier Battalion," covering the two preceding years, the Adjutant General listed the following: 1001 scouts, 7 fights with Indians; 31 Indian trails followed; 5 fights with outlaw bands; 12 outlaws killed and 4 wounded; 685 fugitives from justice arrested; 67 courts attended by the request of civil authorities; 67 jail and other guards furnished; 180 scouts; 152 occasions of other assistance rendered civil authorities; 1917 horses and cattle recovered; and 1 Mexican child recovered.

25. An early minister to western Texas, in writing of these critical times, said: "In the region I went first to preach in Texas, when the Circuit Court met, the judge had to be surrounded by about twenty-five Texas rangers with loaded guns, while the horse thieves and murderers of the place were being tried. I remember well how glad the judge was on first meeting with me. He said: 'The very presence of a gospel minister out here means even safety for the judge on the bench.' So it turned out to be, in his case at least, for not long after the rangers were dispensed with in his court." Parson Ralph Riley, *Twenty-five Years a Parson in the Wild West*, p. 163.

16

SPANIARDS AND TEUTONS

I

THE Anglo-American culture developed on the southern plains after 1845 was modified to some extent by Spanish and German influences. Long before the coming of the immigrant from areas east of the Mississippi, or from parts of the Transmississippi West settled by Anglo-Americans, Spanish *conquistadores* had crossed and recrossed this part of the Great Plains. Indeed, their settlements constituted radiating centers of Spanish culture for more than two hundred and fifty years. Although they were not planted within the heart of the southern plains, the southern half of the area particularly was constantly under their influence. Oñate established the first settlement on the borderland of the southern plains, at San Juan, New Mexico, on the Rio Grande, in 1598. About 1610, Santa Fe was founded, and by the close of the century the Rio Grande Valley was pretty well occupied.[1] The first settlement in Texas was at El Paso, about 1659, and in 1718, San Antonio was established as the most important settlement in this province. By the middle of the nineteenth century the strategic points along the borderlands of the southern plains, beginning in southern Colorado and running thence in a wide semi-circular range including New Mexico and southern and eastern Texas, were fairly well occupied by the Spaniards. These plantations represent the period of Spanish control up to 1821 and the few years of Mexican control from 1821 to 1848.

Anglo-American visitors to such towns as Santa Fe and Albuquerque, New Mexico, and El Paso and San Antonio, Texas, were generally much impressed with the Spanish manners and customs.

---

1. For interesting treatment of Spanish explorations and colonization in the Southwest, see H. E. Bolton and T. M. Marshall, *The Colonization of North America, 1492-1783* (New York, 1920); and H. E. Bolton, *The Spanish Borderlands* (New Haven, 1921, in *Chronicles of America* Series, XXIII); and I. B. Richman, *The Spanish Conquerors* (in *ibid.*, II).

In dress, language, architecture, literature, and the nomenclature of the region, the Anglo-American settlers appropriated that part of the culture of their predecessors which best served their needs. Indeed, long before the southern plains had passed under the control of the United States, such Spanish names as Llano Estacado, Santa Fe, and Rio Grande were spoken glibly by Anglo-American invaders and traders, who were not always careful, however, to give the correct Spanish pronunciation.[2]

Perhaps the most characteristic element of Spanish influence along the borderland of the southern plains—or at least the most noticeable one is to be seen in dress. With the passing of time the New Mexican *caballero* accepted more and more the habiliments of the invader, but during the same period the Anglo-American was also adapting himself to Spanish costume. By 1870, the *serape*, which for centuries had been regarded by the swarthy son of old Spain as indispensable, was being replaced by overcoats and cloaks; and the *reboso*[3] of the woman was giving way to the American black shawl.

In both New Mexico and Texas during early days the attire of the *caballero* was most picturesque. It consisted of a *sombrero*— a low-crowned hat with a band of tinsel cord nearly an inch in diameter; a *chaqueta*, or jacket, "gaudily embroidered with braid and fancy barrel-buttons;" and bell-shaped *calzoneras*, or pantaloons, handsomely slashed or ornamented up the outer seam with silver buttons or some richly colored cloth or velvet. About his waist he wore a tightly drawn silk or satin sash. But perhaps the most colorful garment was the *serape saltillero*, or fancy blanket carelessly hung from the shoulders, or in bad weather used as a cloak. These clothes were generally worn by the *rico*, or wealthy *caballero;* the garments of the poorer man were of cheaper quality. According to Josiah Gregg, "common velveteens, fustians, blue drillings and similar stuffs" were very much in fashion among such *rancheros* and *vecinos* as were able "to wear anything above the ordinary woolen manufactures of the country."[4] Coarse wool or

2. J. L. Cowan, "Lingo of the Cow Country," in *Outing Magazine*, August, 1909, p. 623 *et sqq.*

3. It is entirely probable that the *serape* and *reboso* were of Mexican and not Spanish origin.

4. *Commerce of the Prairies*, p. 342. A comprehensive article on New Mexican life is James W. Steele, "Among the New Mexicans," in *Kansas Magazine*, I (February, 1872), No. 2, 105-12.

palm-leaf hats (*sombreros de petate*), all with low crowns, were worn by the common people.

An army officer who visited Santa Fe in 1866 writes that "the universal dress of the women was first, the essential, or the indispensable; second, a petticoat, more or less worked or ornamented, according to the means and condition of the wearer; third, the *reboso*, a sort of scarf, worn to cover the head and greater part of the face, the ends falling in front, with one of them thrown gracefully back over the shoulder."[5] If a headdress was used, the *reboso* was worn around the shoulders. Gregg was interested in this peculiar Spanish shawl; it was sometimes seven or eight feet long and nearly a yard wide, made of silk, linen, or cotton, and usually variegated and figured in the warp by symmetrically disposed threads waved in the dying. The finest rebosos were valued at fifty to two hundred dollars, but those of poorer quality seldom sold for more than five.

The ordinary garment of the poorer women and *rancheras* was the *enaguas*, or petticoat, of homemade flannel, or coarse blue or scarlet cloth, "connected to a wide list of some contrasting colored stuff, bound around the waist over a loose white chemise, which is the only covering for the body, except the rebozo." Women were also fond of rouge and other cosmetics. When nothing else was available, red berry juice was used to paint their faces. Necklaces, pendants, earrings, brooches, bracelets, and rings were held in great favor, and were generally regarded as marks of distinction.

Generosity, politeness, and hospitality were three well-known characteristics of the Southwestern Mexican or Spaniard. From the *jacal* hut of the peon to the palatial home of the *caballero* an unmistakable atmosphere of courtesy, formality, and generosity prevailed. Almost all Anglo-American travelers in the Spanish-inhabited area of the Southwest were much impressed by the hospitable treatment accorded them in the homes of the people. An army officer's wife who came to New Mexico a short time after the close of the Mexican war writes that on one occasion she and her husband were invited "by a mannerly Spaniard to alight and rest in his house." She was greatly pleased with the courtly grace with which she was received by the wife of the Mexican, who entertained her in the "pleasantest manner," although the home

5. James F. Meline, *Two Thousand Miles on Horseback*, p. 169.

consisted of only one room, which was a store, sitting-room, and kitchen. Their host, a Señor Rodriguez, was accustomed to weigh the gold the miners from a nearby camp brought to his store. While the travelers were being entertained, the miners came in. The visitor thus describes the polite and generous recognition given her by these rough men: "A bearded Mexican stepped up to the little counter, now, and emptying his leather bag of its shining contents, selected the largest piece—the size of a hazel nut—and presented it to me, with an air of such genuine honesty, such chivalric grace, that I felt I could not refuse the gift without wounding the man's feelings."[6] Others followed his example and presented to her the largest piece they had found that day. Charles F. Lummis was also impressed by the spirit of generosity and hospitality in New Mexico: "A stranger be he poor or princely, is master of the house to which he shall come. It may be the veriest hut of a *jacal* amid the farther ranges, it may contain but a single crust of bread and a sheepskin upon the clay floor; but house and crust and couch are his, though his hosts sleep supperless upon the bare adobe—and all with a high, gentle courtesy that palaces might study."[7]

George F. Ruxton, an Englishman who traveled through New Mexico during the Mexican War, gives another example of hospitality. At the close of a cold wintry day, as he was journeying from Santa Fe toward Taos, he came to the small village of Ohuaqui. He spent the night in the home of a Mexican villager where he was royally entertained. His horses were comfortably housed in a barn and given all the corn they could eat, which "was a luxury they had long been unaccustomed to." The humble *patrona* prepared for her guest a supper of *frijoles* (brown beans) and *atole* (Indian meal, mixed with water into a thick gruel).[8] As to the crowded conditions in the home, Ruxton writes:

> After supper the women of the family spread the floor with blankets, and every one, myself included, cigar in mouth, lay down—to the number of fifteen—in a space of less than that

6. "An Officer's Wife in New Mexico," in *Overland Monthly*, January-June, 1870, p. 158.
7. Charles F. Lummis, "The Land of Poco Tiempo," in *Scribner's Magazine*, X (July-December, 1891), 767-69.
8. Another food similar to *atole* but far more agreeable was *piñole*, which consisted of parched maize, mixed with sugar and spices, and two tablespoons full in a pint of water made a refreshing drink.

number of square feet; men, women, and children, all smoking and chattering. Just over my head were roosting several fowls; and one venerable cock every five minutes saluted us with a shrill crow, to the infinite satisfaction of the Old Indian, who at every fresh one exclaimed, "Ay, como canta mi gallo, tan claro!"—how clear sings my cock, the fine fellow!

The *caballero* was fond of horse racing, cock fighting, and gambling, but the social occasion which gave him an opportunity to meet his favored *señorita* was the *baile* or *fandango*. Some writers and observers of the early days of Anglo-American occupation, made a distinction between the *baile* and the *fandango*. The former was said to be a formal ball attended by the elite; the latter was sponsored by the *vecinos* and common people in general. There were occasions, however, when both the poor and the rich met on the same plane. The *Daily New Mexican* (Santa Fe) of January 2, 1872, gives an account of "The baile of the 'Arcade' on New Year's eve" which was "largely attended, and everything passed off pleasantly. The supper was served in a room adjoining the ball room, and the tables were loaded with substantials and delicacies. The dancing was kept up to a late hour, when the guests dispersed well pleased with their entertainment." Fourteen days later, the same paper published a still more interesting account of such a function.

THE BALL OF THE SEASON

The ball given by Don Antonio Lerma at his residence in Alameda, on the evening of the 6th inst, in honor of the marriage of his daughter Angelina to Don Jose Mondred, was all that could be anticipated. Two hundred and forty-seven persons were present by actual count, filling the apartments to an almost uncomfortable degree. One of the best suppers that New Mexico could supply, was furnished for the occasion, and notwithstanding the large number of guests, hundreds of pounds of roast meats, game, poultry, cake, pastry remained to be distributed among the poor. . . . As to drinkables, the best champagne and other wines flowed freely; and those who preferred a stronger liquor had their choice. The music was good and the dancing was kept up until daylight, or as Jenkins would say "till the blushing physiognomy of Miss Aurora appeared in the east, a herald of rosy morn." The wealth, fashion, beauty, wit and talent of Bernalillo county graced the festive scene, and all present, either enjoyed themselves hugely, or else their appearance was really deceptive. Taking it altogether, it was the most brilliant affair of its kind this county has witnessed for many years. It is a pity Don Antonio has not another daughter to marry, for then we might expect to be remembered. Another remarkable feature, and one worthy to commendation, connected with this affair was: no invidious comparison, or odious selections, but invited all of his acquaintances who bore the semblance of respectability. The terms of satisfaction in which he is spoken of for this sensible trait, are proof positive that he did just right.

The *fandango* meant to the Spanish of New Mexico and Texas very much what the country or village dance (breakdown) meant to the Anglo-American settler. It was the common man's dance. During the days of the Santa Fe trade, according to Gregg, as soon as wagoners of the caravan were freed from their responsibilities following their arrival at Santa Fe, they "flocked to the numerous fandangoes, which are regularly kept up after the arrival of the caravan."[9] They were held in private residences, in town halls, or in any public place available.

In the summer of 1866, James F. Meline made a tour of the Rocky Mountains and New Mexico. On his arrival at Mora, some eighteen miles from Fort Union, he writes on July 16, that a *baile*— which from his description of it was in all probability a *fandango*— was given in his honor. Meline admits that at one time such a function was called a *fandango*.[10] He describes the dance hall as a rough-looking room, scarcely recovered from its astonishment at the hasty washing it had just received. The halls had been

9. *Op. cit.*, p. 254. Captain O. M. Knapp was in Albuquerque for forty-two days while detailed on court-martial service in 1867, and attended thirty *bailes* and other social functions. Knapp to "Friend," May 18, 1867, MS, Knapp Papers, Archives, Library, University of Texas.

10. Meline classifies these social functions as follows: (1) *baile*; (2) *gente baile*; (3) *gente fino baile*; and (4) *baile gente fino decente*. In explaining his classifications, he says: "The sex attending No. 1 is, simply, not 'on the street.' Those of No. 2 are exclusive 'for a term of months or years,' as the case may be. Those of No. 3 are all American attachments, and are pointed out as Judge A's, Mr. B's, Captain C's woman, etc., as the case may be. The Mexicans, with a dash of sarcasm, sometimes designate them as '*Las wayfas Americanas.*' No. 4 are, as the designation eloquently expresses it, not only exclusive, but what is more and better, decent. Newly arrived Americans look upon the *baile* as a Mexican institution; but I am assured by Mexicans that it exists only by, through, and for 'Los Americanos.'" *Op. cit.*, 184-85.

whitewashed for the occasion and a few dim lights of oil and candle were fastened to the walls. The *senoritas* were meekly sitting on benches and chairs along one side of the room, "occasionally refreshing themselves with a *cigarito*." The *caballeros* were grouped about, with hats on or off, and smoking or not smoking, as best suited them. Both men and women were modestly attired and conducted themselves with propriety.

"The gentleman's invitation to the dance (which were quadrilles and Spanish waltz, neither gallop nor polka)—no introduction needed—being the merest intimation, as going up, and without parley, leading off the damsel, or possibly, standing in the middle of the floor, and beckoning her to come to him." After each dance, the *caballero* was expected to lead his *señorita* out to what was equivalent to a bar, for refreshments. The young lady was "usually moderate, *vino* or *dulces* being her stereotyped answer to 'What will the Señorita have?' "[11]

The home of the poor Mexican was generally a very humble one. It was sometimes made of poles daubed with mud (*jacal*), with earth covering the roof and with an earthen floor. Screens were unknown, doors were usually left open to all comers, including pigs, chickens, cats, and dogs. Under these circumstances the cool interior of the hut was often infested with fleas, lice, ticks, and bugs. The furnishings were usually meager; a straw mat on the floor, a bench, two or three plain chairs, pallets of straw covered with buffalo robes, sheepskins, or patched quilts made up the *tout ensemble*. *Tortillas* (a simple bread pone), beans, peppers, and occasionally mutton or beef, were the simple fare. The entire life of the peon was spent in squalor and misery. Yet he seemed contented with his lot, satisfied to raise a small patch of beans, pepper, and melons, and tend his small flock. Indolent, carefree, and hospitable, he knew little of the outside world, and cared little. So long as he was undisturbed in the even tenor of his ways he did not trouble himself to attempt to understand the hurly-burly life of his Anglo-Saxon neighbor, or to better his own station.

Conditions were different with the Spanish *rico*.[12] Often he was of noble lineage, or of a family which had become known for its

11. *Ibid.*, p. 106.
12. George F. Ruxton, who traveled through New Mexico in 1847 stated that the "families of Armijo, Chaves, Perea, and Ortiz are *par excellence* the *ricos* of New Mexico." See *Adventures in Mexico and the Rocky Mountains*, p. 186.

social, financial, or political leadership in Spanish North America. His home was seldom pretentious on the outside, since it was usually constructed on the Moorish fortress style—low, adobe, flat-topped, with thick walls and one or two outside openings. But the interior was much more prepossessing. From the front entrance one was admitted to a *patio* about which the home was constructed, and in which grew flowers, ferns, shrubs, and even trees. On either side of this inner garden were the spacious apartments of the family, generally well furnished with beautiful rugs, tapestries, and furniture. On every hand were evidences of elegance and ease.

Etiquette and decorum were scrupulously observed by the *rico* and his family. Reverence for paternal rights and authority were strikingly maintained; one writer asserts that even young men who had reached the age of maturity would still maintain that kindly respect for their parents which they had shown as children. To strangers who might be guests in their home, each member of the family was accustomed to demonstrate the utmost degree of cordiality, civility, and generosity. Anglo-Americans who visited in the homes of the *caballeros* of New Mexico and Texas during the first part of the nineteenth century were generally impressed with this unusual refinement and wrote in glowing terms of it.

There is little doubt that much of the misunderstanding that arose between the two peoples was due to the wide differences in culture. The *caballero* stressed social amenities, strict formality, and decorum; the Anglo-American was socially careless, gruff, and brutally frank. What the former often took to be lack of civility on the part of the latter was ignorance of Spanish observances, or the use of unvarnished expressions; and what the latter often thought to be evasion or deceitfulness was the Spanish-American's inherent tendency to clothe his actions and speech with courtesy and politeness. The Anglo-American generally ascribed to his Spanish-American neighbor an "inferiority complex," which he believed to be revealed in the Spanish-American's actions and speech. To the quick-tempered and easily offended *caballero* this was the grossest kind of insult; consequently, there was often "bad blood" between them. This condition was gradually improved, however, as representatives of the two cultures came to understand each other.

For several decades, the southern plains area was the twilight zone between these two cultures, and settlers, whether Anglo-American or Spanish-American, who came to establish homes there during the last half of the nineteenth century, were exposed to both influences. The Texas cowboy's rope, bridle and bit, saddle, hat band, boots, and quirt often bore unmistakable evidence of Mexican manufacture. Likewise the *vaquero* from south of the Rio Grande often wore clothes manufactured in the United States. Curiously enough, the jargon employed by the cowboy was often little like either English or Spanish, yet it had something in common with both languages. There were other striking instances of cultural contacts. Newspapers in towns inhabited by the two people would publish one column in English, and the adjacent column in Spanish. Court interpreters were employed to translate for the English part of the jury the speech of a Spanish-speaking attorney, or to the Mexican jurors the words of the Anglo-American lawyer. Even in the construction of homes the Anglo-American often used Mexican architecture and materials, or the Spanish-American chose the style of the "Gringo." The blending of the two cultures, therefore, gave to the region a distinctiveness not found east of the Mississippi.

II

Shortly after the establishment of the Stephen F. Austin colony in Texas, German immigrants began to arrive, and with the passing of time, contributed much to the culture of the Southwest. On April 16, 1831, Friedrich Ernst was given a grant of a league of land at Mill Creek, near San Felipe de Austin. This became a nucleus about which was shortly established a thriving German settlement, but by no means the most important one in this area. No part of the United States has had a more interesting experience with foreign colonists than the southern plains with its three unique German settlements, which will be described briefly.

During the first half of the nineteenth century thousands of Germans left their native land and came to America. Adverse economic conditions in central Europe due largely to over population, social discriminations, political unrest, and a desire to build new homes in the western part of the United States were four important factors which led to this ever increasing migration. Becoming alarmed lest this movement would materially harm the fatherland, and apparently desirous of maintaining intact the transplanted German culture, as well as of receiving some economic benefits from this movement, a large group of German noblemen founded an immigrant aid society, in 1842, known as the *Verein zum Schutze deutscher Einwanderer in Texas*. The movement was chartered by the Duke of Nassau, but was sponsored primarily by his adjutant, Count von Castell. The *Mainzer Aldelsverein*, as the organization was called (also styled *Adelsverein*, and *Verein*), was headed by the Prince of Leiningen, as president; Count Castell, as commissioner-general; and Prince Frederick of Prussia, the Duke of Coburg-Gotha, and some thirty other princes and nobles as associated members.[13] Each nobleman deposited with the *Verein* a considerable sum of money which was to be used as capital for the promotion of the organization. At Mayence, on April 9, 1844, a prospectus was issued for the benefit of immigrants, which thus set forth the purposes of the association:

. . . .It wishes to regulate and guide emigration, that a chance may be afforded the Germans of finding, in America, a German home, and that by maintaining an unbroken connexion between themselves and the old country, an industrial and commercial intercourse may arise, morally and materially beneficial to both. It is after this manner that the association wishes to contribute their mite towards Germany's glory and prosperity, and perhaps, at some future period, to afford the German poor a field for rewarded labor, to open to German industry new markets, and extend German trade over the seas.[14]

About the time that the *Verein* was organized, Henry Francis Fisher and Burchard Miller had received two colonization contracts from the Republic of Texas, granting more than 3,000,000 acres of land between the Llano and the Colorado rivers. Fortune favored

13. Important princes and noblemen who were members of the organization were as follows: the Duke of Nassau, Duke of Meiningen, Duke of Coburg-Gotha, the Prince of Prussia, the Landgrave of Hessen-Homburg, the Prince of Schwarzburg-Rudolstat, Prince Moritz of Nassau, the princes of Leiningen, Neuweid, Solms-Braunfels, Colloredo-Mansfeld, and Schonburg-Waldenburg, the princes Alexander and Carl of Solms-Braunfels, the counts of New-Leiningen, Westerburg and Alt-Leiningen, Westerburg, and counts Ysenburg-Meorholz Hatzfeld, Knyphausen, Colloredo-Mansfeld, and Carl von Castell. A. B. Faust, *The German Element in the United States*, p. 493 (footnote 1).

14. John Wilmer, "The German Colony in Texas," in *Tait's Edinburg Magazine*, New Series, XV (March, 1848), 219 *et sqq.*

Fisher when President Sam Houston appointed him as consul to the free city of Bremen, on December 20, 1843. Shortly after his arrival in Germany he interviewed members of the *Verein* and interested them in his grant.[15] In glowing terms he pictured to them the possibilities of a German colony. Streams which flowed through the country were spring-fed and clear as a crystal; the region abounded in wild game—deer, turkey, bear, buffalo, and antelope; and the entire area was naturally adapted to farming, the soil being rich, rainfall adequate, and the climate excellent. The *Verein* accepted Fisher's recommendations without further inquiries, thus showing themselves to be wholly unfitted for the task of colonization. Moreover, had they sought a grant from the Texas government it is entirely probable that it would have been given. Fisher was paid $8,000 for his rights, and was promised a share in the future profits of the society.

It is probable that the British government was interested in the movement. According to Frederick Law Olmsted, Prince Leiningen, the first emissary sent to Texas by the *Verein*, was a half-brother to the Queen of England, and Prince Solms-Braunfels, commissioner-general of the society, was an intimate friend of Prince Albert, with whom he was educated at Bonn. During this period England had become much interested in Texas as a potential market, and probably for this reason was interested in the German colonization movement. Indeed, Olmsted affirmed that an agreement was effected between the British government and officials of the *Verein* whereby the former was to give adequate protection to a German colony planted in Texas and the latter was to furnish 10,000 families for the project.[16]

From the very beginning the *Verein* promised much to the immigrants and gave little. For a modest sum they were promised passage across the Atlantic to the Texas coast, conveyance from the port of debarkation to the colonial site, storehouses from which they could purchase supplies when once they had begun the work of developing their new homes, apothecaries, physicians, tools and implements for tilling the soil, and live stock. But the capital of the organization was far too small to carry out all these promises.

15. R. L. Biesele, "The Relations Between the German Settlers and the Indians in Texas, 1844-1860," in *Southwestern Historical Quarterly*, XXXI (1927-1928), 118 (footnote 6).
16. Frederick Law Olmsted, *A Journey Through Texas*, p. 173 (footnote).

In May, 1844, Prince Carl von Solms-Braunfels, as commissioner-general, started for Texas and was soon followed by about one hundred and fifty families, who sailed from Bremen in three ships. Upon arrival at Lavaca Bay they were transferred to ox-carts and began their long trek to the San Saba River, in the heart of the Fisher grant. They were soon to learn the difficulties which would attend the carrying out of their project. Mile after mile of country over which they traveled was barren and desolate; Indian attacks warned them of the perils which awaited them at their new homes; and, worst of all, they were told that their grant was more than a hundred miles beyond the settlements on the hunting grounds of the fierce Comanches. Upon arrival at the junction of the Comal and Guadalupe rivers, Prince Solms bought two leagues of land and established on the Comal, on March 21, 1845, the settlement of Neu-Braunfels. Each settler was given a town lot upon which to construct his residence, and ten acres of land to cultivate, independent of the land he was later to receive when the Fisher grant was ready for occupation.

In an address at Clinton Hall, New York City, on January 18, 1855, Frederick Knapp stated that Prince Solms was so unqualified for leadership in the new country to which he came as to gain the "nickname of the Texan Don Quixote." He inaugurated the ridiculous pomp and ceremony which were in vogue in Europe during medieval times. He held his "levees," he was followed about by his "Squire" bearing a sword, "and a bodyguard which would have done the greatest honor to Sir John Falstaff." Olmsted says that the Prince appeared to have been "an amiable fool, aping, among the log-cabins, the nonsense of mediaeval courts"; and adds that "in the course of a year he was laughed out of the country."[17] In 1845 he was succeeded by C. von Meusebach.

Although the new leader seemed to be better able to adapt himself to frontier conditions than his predecessor, he was soon to cope with problems far beyond his ability to solve. The European members of the *Verein* were entirely ignorant of conditions in Texas during this period; mismanagement and blunders in methods of procedure soon brought the organization to grief. What followed is thus described by Knapp:

17. *Ibid.*

But the most horrible catastrophe in the enterprise in question occurred in the spring of the year 1846. The second grand expedition of emigrants had arrived between the fall of 1845, and April, 1846. More than 5,200 persons were landed in Galveston and Indianola, and left to shift for themselves. The war against Mexico had broken out; Indianola consisted at that time but of a few huts, and even those were not for the immigrants, but for the soldiers on the march. The transportation of baggage and provisions had raised the cost of conveyance immoderately, and there was not enough money among them to buy teams. Thus the unfortunate ones had to camp longer than six months under tents, exposed to the obnoxious change of weather on the low, unhealthy shore. They had neither shelter against the burning sun, nor fire when drenched by the rain or chilled by the bleak wind. Rum-holes increased their misery, and changed men into beasts; an epidemic broke out among them, and more than two-thirds of the number fell a prey to it. A few of them formed into a company of rangers, and went to Mexico. The survivors resolved to leave the place for New Braunfels; but it is impossible to give even a faint idea of the misery which befell them on the road. It was lined by corpses and dying men. Wolves and vultures followed the groups, and devoured their prey while still warm. Husbands left their wives behind them to perish by hunger and thirst, and were left to the same fate themselves when their turn of sickness came. But few, in proportion, reached New Braunfels, which consisted of but a few poor huts and several tents, where the starving infected wretches were received, and communicated the epidemic to the whole community. The Association, bound to furnish the provisions, had nothing on hand but beef—the cheapest, and, in that state of things, certainly the most unwholesome food—the very cause of the epidemic. Death stared all in the face. They tried to forget their horrible situation, and to enjoy the few moments they had to live. They drank, sang, and danced day and night, although touched by the poisoned dart and having the dying or the dead before and beside them. The miserable hut used for a hospital was but a few rods distant from the bar-room, where, to the sound of an ear-rending clarinet, drunken men waltzed with women, crazy with excitement and fever. All the ties of society or family were loosened, and the most horrible crimes were perpetrated without even being heeded. Similar scenes of misery and atrocity happened likewise at Fredericksburg. There, even men were torn from their families and buried before being dead, only to get rid of them at once. There is no exaggeration in all this. Much that is still more cruel and execrable could be recited, if the facts stated were not more than sufficient to form an idea of the indescribable misery caused by the few light-minded swindlers to so many thousands of their fellow-men, and of the formidable responsibility thereby heaped on their heads.[18]

The settlement of Fredericksburg, consisting of about one hundred and twenty men, women and children, mentioned in Knapp's description of the tribulations of the colonists, was established by Von Meuseback, on May 8, 1846. Other settlers who came in, and who survived the ordeals of pioneering, established homes in the general vicinity of these two towns. In the course of a decade other settlements were made between the Fisher grant and San Antonio and treaties concluded with the Indians, but the project of establishing the major colony on the Fisher site never materialized.

About the same time the *Verein* was sponsoring the German immigration movement, a French colonial project was also launched. It was headed by Count Henri de Castro, a native-born Frenchman of Portuguese descent. Up until 1840 Castro was a French Consul at Providence, Rhode Island, after which time he came to Texas to seek his fortunes. President Houston gave him a grant of 38,400 acres of land, situated on the Medina River west of San Antonio on the frontier. He was later appointed as a consular agent to Paris, France, and while serving the young republic in this capacity conceived the idea of sponsoring a French colony for his Texas grant. He recruited the major number of his colonists from the French inhabitants of Alsace, but he also accepted Germans from the Rhenish and Bavarian Palatinate, Baden, and Wurtemberg, and emigrants from Switzerland. In August, 1844, 485 families and 457 single men, transported by twenty-seven ships, arrived at Galveston, bound for western Texas. A short time later, a colony was established on the Medina. In spite of initial hardships and Indian attacks, the little colony prospered. A wooden dam was constructed across the river and a grist mill was set up, mustang grapes which grew in abundance along the Medina were used to make wine, and farms were established about the town,

18. Knapp's lecture is given in the *New York Tribune*, January 20, 1855.

which was called Castroville. The empresario also established west of Castroville the small settlements of Qhihi, Vanderburg, and D'Hanis. Travelers who later visited Alsatian Castroville were surprised to learn to what extent a French environment had been recreated in this part of the New World; the steep-roofed buildings, the quaint manners and customs of the inhabitants, and the unique industries—all gave evidence of Alsatian influence.

German immigrants did not enter the northern part of the southern plains area to any great extent until after the passing of the federal homestead act in 1862. Indeed, the major work of introducing European colonists to the plains of Kansas was carried out by the immigration department of the Atchison, Topeka and Santa Fe railway company. In order to dispose of its land grants, the immigration department of the railroad sought to attract industrious German homeseekers. In the summer of 1873, C. B. Schmidt, who directed the work of the department, chanced to meet Cornelius Jansen, a representative of Mennonite homeseekers. Jansen informed Schmidt that there were thousands of Germans who would migrate to the Kansas plains if the proper inducements were offered. Acting on information from this source, Schmidt made a trip to Europe, two years later, in the interest of his organization. He visited the thousands of Germans who had settled along the Black Sea and the Sea of Azov in southern Russia, distributed literature among them, and talked to their principal leaders. He created such a stir among them as to arouse the hostility of the Russian government, but before he could be driven from the country, his work was done. In 1875, more than nineteen hundred immigrants from this area arrived in western Kansas. They brought with them more than $2,225,000 in gold with which they purchased 60,000 acres of land in Marion, McPherson, Harvey, and Reno counties. Schmidt worked industriously at his task for a period of eight years, and as a result of his efforts 15,000 colonists were brought from Russia, Germany, and Austria. Although Schmidt's labors ended in 1883, colonists continued to arrive for the remainder of the century, and by 1905, more than 60,000 had occupied the prairie lands of western Kansas.[19]

During the last decade of the nineteenth century small colonial

19. C. B. Schmidt, "Reminiscences of Foreign Immigration Work for Kansas," in *Kansas State Historical Collections*, IX (1905-1906), 487, *et sqq.*

bands migrated from the first regions occupied in western Texas and Kansas and sprinkled the entire southern plains area with their settlements. Travelers at the close of the century found here and there German oases in the great sea of Anglo-American homesteaders. Their quaint culture was fused with that of the people among whom they lived, although they have maintained some of their traditions, manners, and customs down to the present time.

The Germans who migrated to the southern plains were a heterogeneous group. A visitor to New Braunfels in the early fifties lists the following tradesmen: carpenters and builders, wagon makers, blacksmiths, gun and locksmiths, coppersmiths, tinsmiths, machinists, saddlers, shoemakers, turners, tailors, button and fringe makers, tanners, butchers, and bakers. According to J. de Cordova in 1858, men who had passed the day in mauling rails or driving oxen presided at the piano in the evening, and executed in a superior manner not only the ordinary music of their country but the choicest morceaux of the Italian Opera. "Sundays and festival-days are more thoroughly days of rest and recreation here than in any other portion of the State; although the churches, of which they have two Protestant and one Catholic, are not overcrowded, the casinos and beer-saloons are well attended; but, strange to say, the appearance of a drunken man in the streets of this town would be a novelty."[20]

The thrift of the German immigrant is well known. Often the Teuton farmer cultivated only ten of fifteen acres of land, but he usually lived in a neatly built house, everything about which bespoke wide-awake progressiveness and frugality. A. H. Granger, in 1878, lists Comal County, of which New Braunfels was the principal town, as one of the finest counties in western Texas, and states that its population was increasing. Its population was 5,600; its assessed valuation of real and personal property was $1,230,940; and it was graced with six churches and nineteen schools.[21] There is little doubt that Teutonic thrift, resourcefulness, and progressiveness, as praised by early observers and as found in every town and on every farm of these people, went a long way to tone up and to make more colorful the culture of the Anglo-Americans in the same region.

20. *Texas: Her Resources and Her Public Men*, p. 249.
21. *Southwestern Texas Guide*, p. 62.

The high type of culture found among the German colonists from the earliest days of immigration until the southern plains was fairly well populated was often in striking contrast to that existing in neighboring Anglo-American settlements. Ferdinand Jacob Lindheimer, editor of the *Neu Braunfelser Zeitung*, and Karl Daniel Adolf Douai, editor of the *San Antonio Zeitung*, were two journalists as able as any in Texas during that time. Carl G. Iwonski, portrait painter, Richard Petri, whose favorite themes were biblical pictures and Indians, and Herman Lungkwitz, a landscape painter, were artists who had received training in Europe and did noteworthy work while in Texas.[22]

A distinguishing characteristic of the German immigrant both in Texas and in Kansas was the readiness to organize clubs (*Vereine*). At a club meeting the spirit of good fellowship and cheer prevailed. Literary societies, dramatic clubs, and singing societies were uniformly sponsored to promote the cultural development of each community. Usually the German immigrant strongly favored singing societies, and a short time after the settlement of New Braunfels, C. F. Blum, Dr. Adolf Douai, and others sponsored such an organization, called the *Germania*. It was so successful that other similar societies were organized throughout the area of German settlements, and from time to time each held its *saengerfest*. Indeed as early as 1853 a state song festival (*Staats-Saengerfest*) was held at New Braunfels, and in subsequent years other similar conventions were held.[23]

22. Biesele, *The History of the German Settlements in Texas, 1831-1861*, chaps. x and xi. This book is a well-balanced account of German colonization, and is indispensable to a study of the Teuton immigrant in Texas.

23. Formal invitations to important citizens were not uncommon. See invitation to attend a *Saengerbund* sent to Jacob Kuechler on August 24, 1870, MS, in Kuechler Letters, I, 1804-1872, Archives, Library, University of Texas.

17

AN EVENTFUL HORSE-RACE

I

THE period from 1803 to 1854 was one of remarkable development of states and territories west of the Mississippi River. In order to protect better the interests of settlers in the New Orleans area, on March 26, 1804, all of the Louisiana Territory south of the thirty-third parallel was set off as the Territory of Orleans; and the region north of this line, which was attached to the Indiana Territory for administrative purposes, was known as the District of Louisiana. The influx of immigrants, however, from states east of the Mississippi River so transformed the area that other territorial adjustments became necessary. In April, 1812, Orleans was admitted to the Union as the state of Louisiana, and soon thereafter the region north of the thirty-third parallel became the Missouri Territory. By 1818 the inhabitants in and west of St. Louis were clamoring for statehood, and within a period of three years this demand had been met by the creation of the state of Missouri. While this movement was in process of consummation, Congress created the Territory of Arkansas on March 2, 1819, which included the present state of Arkansas and all of Oklahoma south of the parallel of thirty-six degrees and thirty minutes. As a result of these evolutionary changes, within a period of less than fifty years a tier of states and territories had been carved from the region west of the Mississippi, stretching from the Gulf of Mexico on the south to the Canadian boundary on the north.

Concomitant with this movement the region occupied by the Five Civilized Tribes, known as the Indian Territory, was given its approximate boundaries. The Red River bounded it on the south, as far west as the one hundredth meridian. The eastern line was fixed by the Enabling Act which gave Missouri statehood (March 6, 1820), by an agreement between the federal government and the Choctaws (1825) and by a treaty (1828) which established the eastern boundary of the Cherokees as a line running from the southwest corner of Missouri to the northeast corner of the Choctaw reservation. The northern boundary of Oklahoma as far west as the one hundredth meridian was defined by the Kansas-Nebraska Act of 1854 and a subsequent agreement of 1872. From the south fork of the Red River, the one hundredth meridian was the western boundary between Texas and the Indian Territory as far north as the line thirty-six degrees and thirty minutes. From the intersection of these two lines to the Kansas line, and reaching westward to the one hundred and third meridian, was a strip of land one-half degree wide which the United States acquired from Texas in 1850. From this time up until 1890, this area was not under the jurisdiction of any state or territory; the few settlers who occupied it provided for their own courts and government. By the Organic Act of 1890, however, it was made a part of the Territory of Oklahoma and was subsequently known as the Panhandle.

Meanwhile the federal government had been confronted with the problem of moving Eastern Indians to new homes west of the Mississippi. Georgia abandoned her claims to western lands in 1802, on condition that the federal government relinquish Indian title to lands within the state as soon as it could be done. When federal authorities were slow in carrying out this agreement, the people of Georgia demanded immediate Indian removals. Settlers had pressed down on the Indian frontier, and all lands within the state were sorely needed to meet the demands of immigrants.

The federal government had not been wholly remiss in its promises. At the time Georgia agreed to relinquish her claims on western lands, the Creeks and Cherokees held 25,000,000 acres. After a period of twenty years these claims had been reduced to a little more than 10,000,000 acres. As early as 1803, President Thomas Jefferson seems to have had in mind the removal of Eastern Indians to the Louisiana Territory; and an act of March 26, 1804, which provided for the government of the newly acquired region, authorized him to make such proposals. President Jefferson suggested removal to the Chickasaws in 1805 and to the Choctaws three years later. In May, 1808, Cherokee leaders who were visiting in Washington requested the President to permit a part of their tribe to seek new homes west of the Mississippi. Jefferson, of course, was willing to grant this request but at that time he was able to offer them no definite area for occupation. In November of the same year, however, a treaty was concluded with the Osages whereby nearly all of the present state of Missouri and that part of Arkansas north of the Arkansas River was given to the federal government. This agreement prepared the way for removals of the Five Civilized Tribes.[1]

A part of the Cherokees, later known as the Western Cherokees, were the first to leave their old homes. They were given lands lying on the White and Arkansas rivers, in what is now the state of Arkansas. White settlers, however, soon crowded into the same region, and again the Indians moved—this time, to the northeastern part of what is now Oklahoma. By the summer of 1825, the United States had acquired all of the present state of Oklahoma from the Quapaws and Osages. Then, finally, in August, 1835, to forestall any trouble between the plains tribes and the newcomers, federal commissioners brought together representatives of the Cherokees, Creeks, Choctaws, Osages, Senecas, and Quapaws, and headmen of the Comanches and Wichitas, at "Camp Holmes on the eastern border of the Grand Prairie, near the Canadian River, in the Muscogee nation."[2] At this powwow the prairie Indians agreed to accept the Eastern tribes as friends, and the "Great Prairie west of the Cross Timbers" was provided as a common hunting ground. Two years later, the Kiowa and Kiowa-Apache tribes were brought into the same agreement.

From the time the Western Cherokees were first established on the Arkansas River until 1844, when little more than half the Seminoles had migrated, the removals of the Five Civilized Tribes from their Southern homes were gradually effected. On October 18, 1820, the Choctaws were given a tract of land between the Red River and the Canadian in what is now the state of Oklahoma. By treaties made with the Creeks and Seminoles, in 1832 and 1833, reservations were assigned these tribes between the lands of the Cherokees and Choctaws. The Chickasaws were the last to be assigned a new home in the Indian Territory. In January, 1837, they came to an agreement with the Choctaws at Doaksville, the

1. The most scholarly account yet written on removal of the Five Civilized Tribes to Oklahoma is Grant Foreman's *Indian Removal*.
2. Charles J. Kappler (ed.), *Indian Affairs, Laws and Treaties*, II, 435-36.

Choctaw capital, whereby they were received as a part of the Choctaw nation, although they were given a reservation west of the
Choctaws and were allowed to manage their own finances. Still later
their separation was made complete.

Keeping pace with the general movements of restricting the
hunting grounds of plains tribes and removals of Eastern tribes,
in 1832 Congress created a Bureau of Indian Affairs in the War
Department. Two years later the Indian Intercourse Act was
passed, which guaranteed these reservations against encroach-
ments of white people, except licensed traders; and federal agents
and troops stationed at frontier forts were assigned the task of
enforcing the new policy.

II

The attitude of the Oklahoma Indians toward the Union during
the period of the Civil War brought drastic changes to their reserves, when once the struggle had come to an end. In 1861 President Jefferson Davis of the Confederacy sent Albert Pike to the
Indian Territory to form alliances with tribes living there. The
Confederate commissioner found some of the tribes divided in their
sympathies. John Ross, Principal Chief of the Cherokees, could see
no advantage to be derived by the Cherokees if they should support either side; he believed that his people were little concerned
with the issues at stake. Yet, there were other leaders of his tribe
who were willing to go with the South. The Creeks and Seminoles,
too, were divided, although a majority in each tribe was pro-
Southern. These minorities stubbornly opposed Southern overtures,
but their efforts were for naught. Pike was successful in his mission.
He not only came to agreements with the Five Civilized Tribes,
but he also signed treaties with plains bands residing in the vicinity
of the Washita River.

From 1861 to 1865 the Indian Territory was in a state of turmoil
and confusion. Civil strife between tribal factions complicated the
main struggle between the North and South. The Territory served
as a buffer between the free state of Kansas and the pro-slave state
of Texas, and Indian lands were overrun by both armies. In one
instance, Northern sympathizers fled across the Kansas boundary
to seek protection of a federal army stationed there; and in another,

Southern adherents, placed the Canadian River between them and their Northern foes. During this period, therefore, the reservations were sadly devastated. Horses and cattle were stolen or requisitioned by the armies; fields were allowed to grow up in weeds and grass; many homes were burned and abandoned; and on every hand were evidences of desolation and neglect.

When the war came to a close the discouraged tribesmen faced an uncertain future. They were told that their support of the Confederacy had forfeited federal recognition of treaty rights, and that they must send commissioners to Fort Smith where federal agents would instruct them what they must now do. When they came, they were told that they must give up their slaves and allow them certain tribal rights, they must allow railways to be built across their reservations, and they must permit friendly Indians to be settled on their unoccupied lands. Finally, they were instructed to send commissioners to Washington for the purpose of drawing up treaties with the Indian Commissioner covering all these things.[3]

By these treaties the five tribes were forced to abandon more than half their holdings. The western boundary of the Cherokees was now the ninety-sixth meridian, that of the Creeks and Seminoles was approximately ninety-six degrees and thirty minutes, and that of the Chickasaws the ninety-eighth meridian. The federal government then began the task of locating plains tribes on these vacated lands. The Osages were given a substantial reserve between the Cherokee country and the Arkansas River; the Comanches, Kiowas, and Kiowa-Apaches were assigned to a large area between the Chickasaws and the North Fork of the Red River; and the Cheyennes and Arapahoes were located on still a larger reserve between the Kiowa-Comanche country and the Cherokee Outlet. These three reservations alone contained more than 7,500,000 acres. Fringing the western boundaries of the Eastern tribes were small reservations which were set apart for such bands as the Sac and Fox, Iowas, Kickapoos, Pottawatomies, and Shawnees. In fact, by 1879, there were twenty-two separate reservations distributed among eight agencies in the Indian Territory, on which were settled almost 75,000 Indians.

After all these tribal allotments had been created out of the lands once under the control of the Eastern Indians, there still

3. *Ibid.*, 910-15; 918-37; and 942-50.

remained the Public Land Strip (also known as the Panhandle), the Cherokee Outlet, and a small heart-shaped area in the center of the Territory called the "Oklahoma Lands"—in all, more than 11,500,000 acres of unassigned land. Moreover, much of the area under the control of the Indians was undeveloped. Projecting westward from unoccupied lands in New Mexico, therefore, the Indian Territory was an undeveloped peninsula, separating the populous plains of Kansas from the occupied lands of Texas.

III

During the first two decades after the Civil War the range cattle industry grew to such large proportions that it is estimated that more than six million cattle were driven over northern trails to Missouri and Kansas markets. A majority of these drives were made over the Chisholm and Western trails, across the area surrendered by the Eastern tribes in 1866. As the ranchers crossed and recrossed this region, they observed that its grasslands were ideal for ranching purposes, and they often stopped beside the way to graze their cattle. Later, they sought grazing licenses and leases from the Secretary of the Interior, but without success. Then they occupied the country in spite of these refusals, and when they were expelled by the military, they soon returned.

Gaining the consent of a greater part of the Cheyennes and Arapahoes, in 1883 John D. Miles, their agent, leased more than 3,000,000 acres to cattlemen at a rental of $62,000,000. The ranchers then sought the endorsement of Secretary H. M. Teller of the Interior Department, who refused to honor the leases but who promised "to see that parties having no agreement are not allowed to interfere with those who have." Irreconcilables among the Indians, however, became so threatening toward the "graziers" that in the summer of 1885 General Phil Sheridan brought troops into the country and forced the cattlemen to leave. Meanwhile, ranchers entered the Cherokee Outlet and established their ranges, and agents of the Cherokees after 1879 collected from them an annual tax of forty cents a head for all cattle grazed. Then, in order to protect their interests better, stockmen having ranges in this region met at Caldwell, Kansas, in 1883, organized the Cherokee Strip Live Stock Association, and secured a five year lease on the region at a rental of $100,000 a year. Thus, moving from the south, the west, and the north, ranchers so encroached on the western part of the Territory that by 1885 a large part of it was occupied by their ranches.

To thousands of homeseekers who had sought homesteads and found none, this situation was intolerable. They believed that the government was conspiring with the Indians and cattlemen to rob them of their rights. Here, lying idle, in the possession of indolent redskins, were millions of acres of as fine arable lands as could be found in the West; and still farther west were millions more occupied by the cattlemen to which homeseekers had a just claim under the Homestead Act of 1862. Propagandists pictured the region as a veritable paradise—beautiful forests, towering mountains, sparkling streams, and vast mineral deposits. Thousands of malcontents—adventurers, eager homeseekers, ne'er-do-wells, and vagabonds—were attracted by these reports and moved toward the "forbidden land." Under the direction of ambitious leaders they established temporary camps "at 'Rock Falls' on the Chickaskia River, 'Stafford' or 'Pearl City' on the Bois d'Arc, and at other places along the Arkansas River," or near such towns as Arkansas City, Caldwell, Elk City, Wichita, Emporia, and Bluff City. Similar camps were also pitched at strategic points along the Red River, and immigrants were quite willing to encounter occasional quicksands and floodwaters in this treacherous stream in order to establish homes north of it.

By 1889 the homesteading movement in Kansas and Texas had largely brought about the occupation of all tillable land. Still, all highways leading from Missouri, Arkansas, Louisiana, and other states toward the plains of Kansas and Texas were crowded with immigrant wagons, each carrying the family and household effects of a homeseeker; and when the newcomers could not find the expected "land of milk and honey" in either of these states they turned their eyes longingly toward Oklahoma. Their demands for the opening of the Oklahoma lands for settlement were vigorously proclaimed by the press of the Southwest. On March 27, 1874, the Little Rock *Daily Republican* stated that "the spirit of manifest destiny," and the "squatter element" in the West had long since regarded the "Indian Nation" as a Utopia. "The entire Southwest demands," asserted the writer, "that the war dance of the redskins shall not be practiced over the grave of venturesome and advancing civilization. In other words, the pressing need is that the 'Nation' shall be organized as a territory, and free alike to all citizens of the United States, without special favors or legislation to any." The Dallas daily *Herald*, on November 14 of the same year, thus added its support to the movement:

> Already the waves of immigration are surging up against the southern border of that territory. Soon a *crevasse*, so to speak, will take place from Kansas and the great West, and thousands of immigrants will pour into the territory over any technical obstacles the government may set up. It will be like the rush to California when it does commence, and commence it must soon, for the press is daily making known the mineral wealth, the soil, the lovely mountains, valleys and plains of the Indian Territory, and the American people, full of pioneer blood as they are, will overrun it, and make it blossom with the fruits of industry.

To what extent railway organizations which had lines across the Territory were propaganda agencies sponsoring the boomer movement will probably never be known, but it is certain that they disseminated among the incoming homeseekers thousands of circulars, immigrant guide books, and maps. Clever lobbyists were also maintained in Washington to keep before the attention of congressmen the demands of the boomers; other agents worked through the press.

Judge T. C. Sears was employed by the Missouri, Kansas and Texas as a lobbyist in Washington. Shortly after Congress had met in a called session, on March 19, 1879, he returned to Sedalia, Missouri, and issued a statement to the effect that his principal business in the national capital had been "to look after the organization of new committees on Indian Affairs and Territories, both in the House and Senate."[4] He then sought to arouse homeseekers to go into the forbidden land and occupy it even though Congress should enact no law opening the country to homesteaders.

Elias C. Boudinot, the son of a famous Cherokee chieftain, was another propagandist for the settlement of the unassigned lands. It is not known definitely that he was in the service of a

4. Joseph B. Thoburn, and Muriel H. Wright, *Oklahoma, A History of the State and Its People*, II, 510.

railroad at the time of his connection with this movement, but federal officials in the Indian country at that time believed that he was. According to Roy Gittinger, "Boudinot was and had been in communication with attorneys for the Missouri, Kansas and Texas railroad, although it is not necessary to assume that he was in their pay."[5] But when Judge Sears made a statement, after his return to Missouri, that while in Washington he had been associated with Colonel Boudinot, many Western people believed that he was so employed. Still another incident had strengthened this belief. On February 17, 1879, an article signed by Boudinot had appeared in the *Chicago Times* in which he referred to a large amount of unassigned land in Oklahoma which was available for homesteads. A month later he wrote to Augustus Albert that the United States had "an absolute and unembarrassed title to every acre of these 14,000,000 acres, unless it be to the 1,054,544 acres now occupied by the Sac and Fox, and Pottowatomi Indians," and that the unassigned portion was "an integral part of the public domain."[6] Those who knew Boudinot could not understand how he could carry on a prolific correspondence with those interested in Oklahoma, and how he could supply them with maps and literature on the country, unless he was furnished with money and materials by some railway organization.

Within a few months after Boudinot and Sears had made these statements three colonial ventures were organized. The first of these was at Kansas City, Missouri, under the leadership of Colonel C. C. Carpenter; a second was set up at Topeka by J. R. Boyd; a third was to move from Texas across the Red River, near Caddo, Indian Territory.[7] But no one of these organizations was successful; the appearance of federal troops in the vicinity of their camps so overawed the boomers that the movements soon disintegrated. That some of the agitators were men of ill-repute is seen in a statement made by John McNeil, an inspector in the Indian service. He wrote to E. A. Hayt, Commissioner of Indian Affairs, on May 4, 1879, that when he arrived at Coffeyville, Kansas, to

5. Roy Gittinger, *The Formation of the State of Oklahoma*, p. 100. This source is carefully documented, conservative, and well balanced.

6. E. E. Dale and J. L. Rader, *Readings in Oklahoma History*, 442-44.

7. Thoburn and Wright, *op. cit.*, p. 511; and Joseph B. Thoburn and Isaac M. Holcomb, *A History of Oklahoma*, p. 149.

investigate a boomer movement, he found it fairly in a state of dissolution. He said of Carpenter, its leader:

> The fact that a fellow like C. C. Carpenter is allowed to put himself at the head of the enterprise must operate against it in Missouri and Kansas where he is known.... He was the first man I met on my arrival. He is the same bragging, lying nuisance that I knew him seventeen years ago, when he infested Fremont's quarters. He will not put his head in danger by entering the Territory. It is a pity that the law could not hold him as a conspirator against the public peace. I gave him a few words of caution about getting honest men in trouble; but a pair of handcuffs would be the only convincing argument with him.[8]

In 1880 there appeared among the boomers a leader who was not to be so easily discouraged. The new organizer, David L. Payne, was a man of commanding personality and aggressive leadership. As a soldier in the federal army during the Civil War, and as a captain of state troops on the Indian frontier in Kansas, he had acquired a knowledge of men and frontier conditions which better fitted him for his new task. Then, as a member of the Kansas legislature for two terms, and as an assistant doorkeeper of the House of Representatives at Washington, until 1879, he had gained an intimate perspective of politics which helped him in his work. After years of wandering from one frontier community to another, where he came in contact with thousands of homeseekers he came to be a champion of the homesteader.

Payne's leadership of the boomer movement extends from 1880 to 1884. In his efforts to serve the boomers he was uncompromising and not easily discouraged. In April, 1880, he led a small colony across the Kansas line to the North Canadian River, but he and his followers were promptly escorted back to Kansas by federal troops under the command of Captain T. B. Robinson. Three months later he appeared with a second body of homeseekers, and again was expelled. This time Payne was cited to appear in November before the federal court at Fort Smith, but he was soon released. A third expedition was organized, but the watchfulness of the military prevented its crossing the Kansas line.

Having failed to gain entry by way of the Kansas approach,

8. Dale and Rader, *op. cit.*, 445-46.

Payne next tried a movement from the Texas side. In the fall of 1881 he crossed the Red River at the head of a small party and camped on Cache Creek, but the vigilant troops again expelled him.

The boomer leader believed that the soldiers deprived the home-seekers of their natural rights when they denied them entry. Like Carpenter, he could not understand why cattlemen were allowed to lease the grass-carpeted prairies of this region, while the boomers were expelled. After his colony on the Canadian had been broken up by the troops, he wrote a letter to Robert T. Lincoln, Secretary of War, reviewing at some length the whole affair. He thus complained of his treatment:

> But in any event, was it not a remarkable discrimination to drive us out and to permit (and to this easily proven fact I call your attention) hundreds of other white men to remain unmolested on the same lands, herding cattle, fencing in immense tracts of the best pastures—some thirty miles square, obstructing travel and inter-state commerce, cutting off mail routes and roads with strong barbed wire fences? While we only wished 160 acres each, and were willing not only to leave room for but to construct a roadway around every square mile; to develop and build up the country; to populate it with an energetic productive people.[9]

Payne seemed also aggrieved because the courts failed to give him a hearing, stating that on his knees he had begged a judge to try his case. In 1881 he brought suit in the United States District Court at Topeka against General John Pope who had command of the troops which had thwarted his efforts, but repeated postponements defeated his purposes. Again in 1883 he sought an injunction from the same court restraining the military from molesting the boomers, but again delays prevented a hearing. He also visited Washington in 1881 and sought a ruling from Secretary Teller, but he was unable to gain any satisfaction.

With these two avenues of hope closed to him he then redoubled his efforts among his followers. The boomers were organized as the Payne's Oklahoma Colony with Payne as president, J. M. Steele, treasurer, and W. H. Osborn, secretary. A membership fee of two

9. Payne's letter is found in the Payne collection, Oklahoma Historical Library, Oklahoma City.

dollars—which was later increased to six—was charged. This entitled each one "to the benefits and protection of said colony and an equal voice in all matters pertaining to the formation of its local government." Members were protected in their claims to homesteads against all comers. "In other words," writes Professor Gittinger, "the colony was to become a vigilance committee to protect the rights of its members in an extra-legal, not to say illegal way."[10]

Other similar organizations arose from which it was reported that Payne collected dues. In fact, Colonel Edward Hatch estimated that Payne collected $100,000 between 1880 and 1884.[11] Payne was generous, however, and if he thus profited he must have spent it largely in the cause of the boomers for he is said to have died a poor man.

When the organized movements began to appear the cattlemen holding leases in Oklahoma became alarmed. They saw in the rising tide of boomers a serious threat to their holdings. To ward it off, therefore, they distributed a liberal patronage among the newspapers located in towns along the southern boundary of Kansas. It is not known to what extent this influenced the press, but it is not without significance that soon thereafter the editorial attitude toward the boomers became decidedly hostile. Friends of the leader were quick to see what had occurred, for on April 24, 1882, one of them wrote him: "McCarter and Burnette, Edtrs of the *Wonder* say if Capt Payne will give us a few lots we will move our press there at once and so the[y] will. They say any information you want published they will publish, free of charge."[12] This invitation was not accepted, however. On January 12, 1883, Payne set up his own press at Caldwell, and called it the *Oklahoma War Chief*. Its office was changed from place to place as the varying fortunes of the movement dictated, but the publication was generally regarded as the official organ of the boomers until August 12, 1886, when it was suspended.

10. Gittinger, *op. cit.*, p. 111.
11. Filled-in applications on file in the Payne collection show that there were agencies to sell memberships to the Payne Colony located in the following towns: Franklin and Pulaski, Arkansas; Clinton, Ohio; Kingman, Butler, Harper, Leavenworth, Marion, Grand River, Greenwood, and Sumner, Kansas. It is also probable that many other similar agencies were established elsewhere.
12. B. E. Lowes to Captain D. L. Payne, April 24, 1882, MS, Payne collection, Oklahoma Historical Library, Oklahoma City.

Payne's most determined efforts to enter the forbidden land were made in 1884. Along the Kansas-Oklahoma boundary homesteaders were in high spirits. Covered wagons with the usual legends of "On to Oklahoma," "To the Promised Land," "Oklahoma or Bust," painted on their sides thronged the streets of Caldwell, Wichita, Hunnewell, and other towns. By spring five or six hundred colonists had assembled at Hunnewell, and in May a party of fifty succeeded in getting as far south as the Cimarron, only to be expelled by a detachment of cavalry. In June, another invasion was launched, and settlements were planted at Rock Falls and on the Bois d'Arc. Payne and some of his followers were again arrested, but they were soon released. In the movements of this year the boomers were becoming truculent and disposed to resist the military; it was reported that they were "armed to the teeth" and that Payne had preached a policy of violence in the event they were challenged by the troops. Payne's days, however, were numbered; on November 27, 1884, while dining with some friends at Wellington, he died suddenly.

W. L. Couch, who now came to the leadership of the boomers, was to head the last major expeditions into the forbidden land. By December 8 he had crossed the Kansas line with a large following. A short time later he established a camp on Stillwater Creek, estimated to contain more than three hundred and fifty men, and a few women and children. A small detachment of troops put in an appearance and demanded that the boomers leave the country, but Couch told the officer in charge that he and his men had come expecting a fight. On this point there was little room for argument, for the appearance of two hundred men armed with rifles and shotguns was proof enough for the statement made by their leader.

Although the troops left them for a short time because of this show of force, they soon returned reenforced, and for several hours it seemed that trouble of a serious nature must follow. In January, orders were sent from Washington to expel the boomers, even at the cost of blood. But Colonel Hatch made this extreme measure unnecessary by stationing a strong force north of the boomer camps on the Cimarron and Stillwater. This prevented additional boomer recruits coming from Kansas, and it also cut off supplies for those already in the country. The invaders then became restless, and began singly and in parties of twos and threes to move back toward

Kansas. At this juncture Colonel Hatch notified Couch that unless he and the remainder of his party left the territory within two days he would give orders to his soldiers to fire on their camps. Seeing that tenure was now impossible, the boomers reluctantly withdrew. A short time later Couch and twelve other leaders were arrested on a charge of treason against the United States and placed in jail at Wichita, but when Colonel Hatch and other witnesses failed to appear before the court they were released. In November, Couch and his followers again entered the forbidden land, but once more they were escorted out of the territory by the military.

IV

From 1885 until victory finally came to the boomer cause in 1889, the controversy was transferred to Washington. The boomers now joined forces with the railroads having land grants in the Indian Territory, and sought to prevail upon Congress to open the country to settlement. Opposed to them were the cattlemen, Indians, and "squawmen." The cattlemen had much to gain by opposing the movement for the opening of the Indian country. In a debate in the House on June 3, 1886, Representative Struble of Iowa cited a table prepared by the Secretary of the Interior, showing that thirty-two leases held by the ranchers comprised an area of 12,018,234 acres. Of this large grazing region about half, or 6,000,-000 acres, were in the Cherokee Outlet, leased to the Cherokee Strip Live Stock Association; 3,832,120 acres in the Cheyenne and Arapaho reservation; 388,000 acres in the Osage country; and the remainder (1,806,114 acres) on the lands granted to the Kiowas, Comanches, and Wichitas, the Sac and Fox, the Poncas, the Otoes and Missouris, the Pawnees, and Ottawas. It was estimated that almost 2,000,000 acres of these leases were located in Oklahoma proper. Some of them were dated in 1883, some in 1884, and others in 1885; and they were to run from two to ten years at rentals ranging from two to fifty cents an acre.

It is not necessary in a chapter of this scope to follow the varying fortunes of the boomer movement in Congress; it is enough to say that by persistent lobbying and by employing powerful friends the agitators were successful. On February 8, 1887, a long stride toward success was taken when the President approved the Dawes Act which provided for the allotment of land to the Indians in severalty, and which authorized the President to negotiate with the tribe for any surplus land after the allotment program had been completed. Then two years later the Creeks signed an agreement with William F. Vilas, Secretary of the Interior, whereby for a consideration of $2,280,000 they released all claims they had on the unassigned lands of Oklahoma. The final barrier to success was swept away when on March 2, 1889, President Cleveland signed an Indian appropriation bill which carried a rider providing for the payment of $1,902,000 to the Seminoles for claims which they had on the unassigned lands, and for the opening of this region for settlement.

In accordance with section eight of this law, President Harrison issued a proclamation on March 23, 1889, throwing open the Oklahoma Lands for settlement "at and after the hour of twelve o'clock, noon, on the twenty-second day of April."[13] According to a map issued by a boomer organization prior to the opening, the area thus made available for settlement consisted of 1,887,800 acres, or an area about three-fifths as large as the state of Connecticut. It was bounded on the south by the Chickasaw reservation, on the West by the Cheyenne and Arapaho lands, on the north by the Cherokee Outlet, and on the east by the small holdings of the Pottawatomies and Shawnees, Iowas, Kickapoos, and Sac and Fox.

During the period from March 23 until April 22 all the roads through southern Kansas leading toward the unassigned lands were thronged with homesteaders and their families in wagons, hacks, and buggies, and with horseback riders. Towns like Caldwell, Hunnewell, and Wichita were crowded with jostling, good-natured strangers. But the greatest concentration point was Arkansas City; a wildly excited throng of men, women, and children milled about the streets, filled the hotels to overflowing, and occupied with their tents much of the available space within the city limits. In the average crowd were found many classes: gamblers, swindlers, adventurers, ne'er-do-wells, ambitious homeseekers, honorable business men, politicians, bankers, ministers, physicians, and teachers— all ready to enter the new country. In describing the heterogeneous concourse at Arkansas City, Marion T. Rock says that the "scenes

13. Dale and Rader, *op. cit.*, p. 469.

in and about the depot on Sunday night [before the opening on the next day] reminded one of the vast, surging crowds at the Philadelphia railway station during the Centennial of 1876."[14] Indeed, by twelve o'clock on the following day fifteen trains, with passengers occupying every available place both inside and outside the cars, had pulled out from the station with the southern line of the Cherokee Outlet as their destination.

It is doubtful that President Harrison intended to open the Oklahoma lands by "a run." His proclamation had provided that the region was to be opened "to settlers under the homestead laws only." Since there were less than twelve thousand tracts of one hundred and sixty acres each, and since there were upward of one hundred thousand homesteaders ready to enter, a rush could not be avoided. This was unfortunate. Thousands of landless families who were desirous of entering the new country could not compete successfully with those in better circumstances. The animals which pulled their rickety or cumbersome vehicles were poor and feeble. The opening, therefore, was to inaugurate a race which promised victory to him who was well mounted and could first reach a desired claim. In order to meet this unusual situation many a driver unhitched his fleetest horse from a buggy or wagon, and mounted it for the race. "The most eventful horse-race in history," said one; and indeed it was!

The morning of the eventful day dawned bright and clear. For many miles along the northern boundary of the land to be opened thousands of homesteaders were camped, and hundreds of others were coming in hourly. Soldiers patrolled the southern side of the line to keep back any overly ambitious contestant, yet a majority of those who were present accepted such restrictions without complaint, and a spirit of good cheer and friendly banter seemed to prevail. Still, as the morning wore away, the waiting people became restless, and long before the time came to start they were arranging themselves in line along the boundary.

A signal officer, with a flag in one hand and a bugle in the other, took a position where all could see him. Promptly at twelve he sounded the note which sent thousands in a mad headlong dash towards the south; and other officers stationed at intervals along the boundary relayed the signal down the line. The din and confusion

14. Marion T. Rock, *Illustrated History of Oklahoma*, p. 21.

which followed is indescribable. Many horses hitched to vehicles became frightened with the sudden noise and clamor and broke away in runs, overturning vehicles and spilling their contents on the prairies; a choking cloud of dust enveloped the racers making it difficult for one to see another and thereby imperiling the lives of heedless contestants; the speeding trains disgorged their shouting and exulting passengers, who were sent sprawling on the ground or who struck the earth running; and horseback riders, leaning low over their laboring mounts, were strung out across the prairies or they raced side by side, and their loud oaths, laughter, and shouts accentuated the thundering hubbub.

Along the southern boundary of the land to be opened the confusion was almost as great. Thousands of contestants had congregated at Purcell and at other points on the southern bank of the Canadian River. This silt-filled stream was an effective barrier which made the work of patrolling soldiers easy. Several days before the opening, desirable crossings were located, and before the start was made long lines of horseback riders followed by vehicles were arranged before them. Opposite Purcell, on the north bank of the river, a short time before the signal was to be given Lieutenant Adair of the Fifth Cavalry, mounted on a white horse, took his station on a hill where all could see him. The atmosphere seemed to be charged with excitement and tenseness as the watchers saw him lift a bugle to his lips; and it is reported that even before the notes of the instrument were heard along the south bank, reckless horsemen were plunging into the turgid waters of the stream, making for the opposite bank, and that vehicles, in some cases loaded with families and household effects, were following closely behind them. Some of the vehicles mired in the quicksands, but the drivers unhitched their teams, mounted their favorite horses and continued the race. Within an hour the prairies on the northern side of the river were covered with excited homeseekers, some pegging down stakes on their claims, some engaged in heated controversies over priority rights, and some speeding on to other sites.

Perhaps the most amazing developments came with the creation of towns and cities. Within two hours after the crossing of the Canadian, a townsite company was busily engaged in surveying the municipality of Lexington, a little better than a mile distant from Purcell. It is estimated that fifteen thousand souls spent the first night in Guthrie, and ten thousand in Oklahoma City. Indeed upward of one hundred thousand settlers had entered Oklahoma by the end of the first day. Before townsites could be properly surveyed at Oklahoma City and Guthrie, homesteaders had established claims to lots, some of which had to be abandoned when it was found that they were athwart streets and alleys. Turbulent scenes were common; sometimes two or more homesteaders would claim the same lot, precipitating quarrels, fights, and litigation. Lumberyards were quickly set up and the work of constructing buildings began; but until this was done drygoods stores, groceries, hardware establishments, banks, and real estate agencies were conducted under canvas awnings or in tents. Under these circumstances sanitation was impossible since refuse, such as boxes, scraps of lumber, paper, and garbage, littered the ground; and in rainy weather the streets were so miry as to make the passage of vehicles difficult. Thousands became so discouraged because of these conditions, or because they were unsuccessful in establishing claims, that they moved from place to place or back to their old homes in Kansas, Arkansas, or Texas.

V

He who came into the territory before he was entitled to do so under the terms of the President's proclamation was called a "sooner." There is little doubt that hundreds had thus attempted to establish their claims. Hours before the entrance signals had been given, both along the northern and southern boundaries, on the sites that were to become Guthrie and Oklahoma City hundreds of "sooners" were busily engaged in locating claims and making preliminary arrangements for business enterprises. An organization of irate citizens of Oklahoma City, protesting claims and actions of purported "sooners" issued a pamphlet whose title page read: *Oklahoma. Information for Congress. Townsite Frauds. Don't Legalize Town Acts, nor give them any force: Copies of Ordinances, Judgements and Records.* Then follows a severe arraignment of the opposition, citing instances of fraud, their banding together to cheat rightful claimants of their just claims, and political wirepulling. On November 16, 1890, the Guthrie *State Capital* carried the following item on this controversy:

Apr 89

Sunday 21
About the Same as
yesterday nothing
new the North Fork
is too high to ford

Monday 2 2.
In camp till toward
noon then drove up to
the trail to take part in
Harrisons Hoss, race as the
Boomers call it at twelve
sharp they started those
horse back a head light
rigs next then heavy wagons
last some with oxen
following in the rear
Drove up the river and
found good claims all
taken then went across
to the deep fork and
along it all the best were
taken camped on sec 21
Tp. 13 R. 2 W. I m.

A page from the diary of an "eighty-niner"

AN EVENTFUL HORSE-RACE

Oklahoma City, November 15.—The greatest excitement prevails here over the anti-sooner decision of the United States land office. It is a well-known fact that the best claims adjoining the city are now held by men who entered the territory in violation of the President's proclamation. They have spent thousands of dollars in obtaining testimony in order to get the claims, but the register and receiver of the land office decided today that none can hold claims. The decision has created greater excitement than has been seen here before. Hundreds have perjured themselves and are being arrested and jailed as fast as possible.

At Guthrie the controversy was quite as heated, and charges and counter charges leaves the historian the difficult task of separating the true from the false. It is quite probable, however, that the claims of those who had abided by the President's proclamation, because of undue suspicion and anger, were distorted.

In the rural areas of Oklahoma evidences of "sooner" activities are just as manifest. At the time of the opening, the western and eastern borders were not so well guarded as the other two boundaries mentioned; consequently, many prior entries were effected. This also led to ill-feeling, strife, and court procedure; but it was also difficult here to determine who had abided by the terms of the proclamation and who had not, particularly if a "sooner" were disposed to press his claims.

Before establishing a right to a 160-acre tract or town lot, a claimant had to fill in the following form:

PRELIMINARY AFFIDAVIT

Land Office,............,
(Date)........, 18........

I, ..., of............., applying to enter (or file for) a homestead, do solemnly swear that I did not enter upon and occupy any portion of the lands described in the President's proclamation dated March 23, 1889, prior to 12 o'clock, noon, of April 22, 1889.

Sworn to and subscribed before me this.... day of......, 188.....

............, ...

Note..... This affidavit must be made before the register or receiver of the proper district land office, or before some officer authorized to administer oaths and using a seal in the Indian Territory.

Application No..........   Land Office at............,

...., 188...

I,...... ....., of...... ......, do hereby enter, under section 2289, Revised Statutes of the United States, the...... of section......., in township ...... of range ......, containing ...... acres.

My post-address is........

....

Land Office at............,

...., 188.....

I, ..., register of the land office, do hereby certify that the above application is for surveyed lands of the claim which the applicant is legally entitled to enter under section 2289, Revised Statutes of the United States, and that there is no prior valid adverse right to the same.

....,

Register[15]

Those who swore falsely in making out their affidavits were liable to prosecution, yet it is probable that many did so rather than lose their claims. General James B. Weaver, candidate for the presidency on the Greenback ticket in 1880, is reported to have advised those who inquired of him that it would not be a violation of the President's proclamation if they should go into the country and stake out their claims, providing they did not settle on them until after the run was made. There were many who were reported to have entered before April 22 under this theory. There were others who evidently knew that their entry was in violation of the terms of the opening, but they were willing to take all chances in order to establish their claims.

The editor of the Dallas daily *Herald* little knew how actually his statement would be fulfilled when he said that a *crevasse* would soon be made by the waves of immigration beating against the barriers of Oklahoma. "The eventful horse-race," which occurred

15. W. B. Matthews, *Oklahoma*, p. 59.

with the opening of the land, brushed aside the barrier and paved the way for the occupation of the last Great Plains frontier. One reserved area after the other was quickly thrown open to settlement, and by 1907 the Indian Territory and Territory of Oklahoma had been joined to form the state of Oklahoma. The opening of the Cherokee Outlet was on a larger scale than the Oklahoma lands, but it was not so significant a factor in southern plains culture as the first.

The passing of the Oklahoma frontier occurred in a transitional period; the coming of railroads, towns, and thousands of settlers soon brought about the development of a complex civilization. On this point Governor Abraham J. Seay, in his report to the Secretary of the Interior, in 1892, said:

> The social and industrial progress of our people is apparent, even to a casual observer. The marks and monuments of industry meet the traveler on every hand, in town and country, and the attainments already realized are the surprise of strangers within our gates. Better farms, implements, stock, houses, and barns are the rule, not the exception, among the agricultural population. In city and village the varied branches of business, the shop, mills, and factories, though yet in their infancy, give proof of faith in the future development of our Territory, as well as an attempt to utilize her present resources. The increasing number of attractive and comfortable homes in these towns evince that a portion of the capital brought or acquired here is being used not for greed or gain, but for culture and comfort.
>
> The newspapers, the schools, the boards of trade, the societies of Masons, Odd Fellows, Knights of Pythias, Knights of Honor, United Workmen, Legion of Honor, Grand Army, Ladies' Circle, Blue and Gray, Daughters of Rebecca, Eastern Star, Chautauqua, Ladies' Columbian Society, and the churches, with many other instrumentalities of good, are building up a social fabric out of a heterogeneous population that speaks well for our present, and augurs well for our future. While there are wrongs to be righted or eradicated, and the remedies may not be forthcoming as speedily as all good citizens could wish, yet we unhesitatingly attest the creditable social status of Oklahoma to-day.[16]

16. *Report of the Governor of Oklahoma to the Secretary of the Interior*, 1892, p. 11.

In a period of less than twenty years the wild Indians had been tamed and placed on restricted holdings; the buffalo had been destroyed; the far flung ranges of virgin grass lands had given way to neatly cultivated farms; dugouts and sod houses had been replaced by well-built frame structures; and the cow pony was now trained to follow the furrow. In short, thousands of home-building Anglo-Americans had brought in a new cultural pattern.

18

FRONTIER SCHOOLS

I

A TRAVELER who crossed the semi-arid land of western Kansas, western Texas, and eastern New Mexico a short time before the Civil War characterized the country as the "inhospitable plains." He observed that many of its trees, bushes, and plants were armed with thorns; poisonous reptiles and insects were found everywhere; and beasts of prey and hostile bands of Indians made prairie travel unsafe. Even the elements seemed to be arrayed against him; droughts, hot winds, sandstorms, blizzards, hailstorms, and tornadoes made his final occupation of the country doubtful. Later, when he returned to the southern plains as an immigrant, he found that his original impressions must be modified. Even where timber was not available for building purposes he could find shelter in a dugout, a *jacal*, a sod, or an adobe house; and he could use barbed wire to inclose his property. Although acreage production was not so great as it was in well-watered areas, he learned that his unit of cultivation could be larger. And after several decades of experimentation he discovered that certain varieties of seed were better to plant in an arid country than others, and that his procedure in cultivating the soil—known as dry farming—must be different. In the course of time, therefore, he became a plainsman, adapted to the conditions of his land, and trained to meet its peculiar problems.

The cultural growth of the country was concomitant with and affected by these initial experiences, and found expression in the language, home life, and vocational routine of the homesteader. Moreover, since his social contacts were few, and since his educational and religious opportunities were limited, his cultural development was strikingly regional in character. In previous chapters it has been explained to what extent the settler was restricted in his religious and social life. In order to give a more exact appraisal of his culture, therefore, it is now necessary to study his educational life.

In every Anglo-American community of any great size in the Transmississippi West there were always a few men and women who were apostles of education. As a rule they had migrated from older settlements where schools and churches were recognized as requisites for a well-ordered society. Having accepted this point of view, they were interested in transplanting it in the communities to which they came.

When Stephen F. Austin established his colony in Texas in 1821, he was confronted with a grave problem. In this remote Spanish province educational opportunities were few, and the Mexican settlers already there were allowing their children to grow up in ignorance. To the Anglo-American immigrant, who believed that a successful democracy must be based on an educated citizenship, this situation was intolerable; he therefore demanded of the Spanish government that it be corrected. Before anything could be done however, Mexico had gained her independence and Texas was joined with Coahuila to form a northern state of the new nation. But when delegates met at Saltillo in 1827 and drew up a constitution for the state, the desires of the colonists thus found expression:

> In all the towns of the State, there shall be established a competent number of common schools, (*primeras letras*) in which there shall be taught reading, writing, and cyphering; the catecism of the christian religion; a short and simple explanation of this Constitution, and the general one of the Republic; the rights and duties of man in society and that which can most conduce to the better education of youth.

> In those places in which it may be necessary, and where circumstances permit, there shall be institutions of learning, more suitable for disseminating in the State, public instruction in the useful arts and sciences, and in these shall be fully explained the aforesaid Constitutions.

> The method of instruction shall be uniform throughout the State, and to facilitate this end, the Congress shall form a general plan for public instruction, and shall regulate by means of statutes and laws, whatever appertains to this most important object.[1]

1. *Twenty-first Biennial Report, State Superintendent of Public Instruction, State of Texas, September 1, 1916 to August 31, 1918*, p. 16.

Although these constitutional expressions were high-sounding enough to meet the demands of the Anglo-American delegates, they remained as empty promises. The legislatures of the state did nothing to create a common school system. There is little doubt that this neglect sorely offended the colonists, for when they declared their independence from Mexico on March 2, 1836, they complained: "It [the Mexican Nation] has failed to establish any public system of education, although possessed of almost boundless resources, (the public domain,) and although it is an axiom in political science, that unless a people are educated and enlightened, it is idle to expect the continuance of civil liberty, or the capacity for self-government." Fifteen days later they drew up a constitution, of which Section 5 reads: "It shall be the duty of Congress, as soon as circumstances will permit, to provide by law a general system of education."

The Texans were successful in their revolution, but not until 1839 could they take the first step leading toward the creation of an educational system. At this time the congress of the young republic set aside three leagues (13,284 acres) of land in each county for the support of an academy and fifty leagues as an endowment for two colleges or universities. The next year another league in each county was set apart, from which the proceeds were to be used for schools. Generous grants of land and appropriations were also made by the legislature after Texas became a state of the American Union, and by continued support of this body a thorough-going system of schools was finally evolved.

In Kansas, Colorado, and New Mexico the situation was about the same; a majority of the newcomers were desirous of building school and church houses even though in so doing sometimes they must use their own time and resources. Superintendent Peter McVicar of Kansas observed in his report of 1868: "I find the people are very anxious to have schools. . . . . They have come to make Kansas their home, here to live and die, here to educate their children, and help in laying the foundations of society; to erect school houses and sanctuaries, and bequeath to succeeding generations the blessings bequeathed to themselves by generations preceding."

Before the period of state sponsorship of education, independent community programs were launched. A transient or local teacher would rent a residence or public hall for a school building, and would then solicit students. He would usually promise to hold a session for a certain length of time—two, three, or four months—in the season when it was most convenient for all; his tuition charge was two or three dollars a month; and he was generally willing to instruct a child in whatever kind of book was brought. The demands of the patrons were not exacting, however. If a teacher could train a child in "readin', writin', and 'rithmetic," little else was asked. Subscription schools of the southern plains were frequently held in dugouts and sod houses. Indeed, the late Dr. J. W. Hunt is authority for the statement that the first schoolhouse on the plains of Texas (at Estacado) "was a dugout with dirt roof and dirt floor."[2]

II

In many instances children who attended the first schools were uncouth, superstitious, and wild. Some had few social advantages except from members of their own families and occasional contacts with their nearest neighbors; and often their parents were as ignorant as they. Not infrequently children cared little for propriety and discipline and had little fear of an angry schoolmaster, even though he might be armed with a hickory or willow switch of formidable proportions. Disturbances both on the schoolgrounds and in the classroom were common. Boys would frequently engage in fisticuffs, and occasionally in affrays of a more serious nature in which one of the principals would receive a knife wound. Such instances of violence caused more than one ambitious teacher to reflect seriously on the choice of profession which he or she had made.

In this critical period it was perhaps fortunate that the average settler was willing for his child to be disciplined when the teacher thought it was necessary; "Spare the rod and spoil the child" contained a philosophy to which he subscribed. If the teacher were able to maintain strict order and discipline in his schoolroom, therefore, he could go far toward meeting the expectations of his patrons. In view of this prevailing opinion it is not surprising that

2. Roger A. Burgess, "Pioneer Quaker Farmers of the South Plains," in *Panhandle Plains Historical Review*, 1928, p. 122.

corporal punishment was frequently—and sometimes quite severely—administered. Indeed, a familiar accessory in many a schoolroom of the southern plains was a bundle of nicely trimmed switches leaning conspicuously in one corner of the room. When timber was not available from which to secure switches, a rope, a board, or a rawhide thong was used as a "persuader."

Experiences of border schoolteachers were often trying to an extreme degree. A young lady on the Texas frontier was slain when she chose to defend the children in her schoolroom against the attack of Indians; another in Kansas was forced to submit to the indignity of having her school broken up and her pupils driven to their homes in fright by Indians who were supposed to be friendly; and still another joined her boys and girls in fighting a prairie fire for an entire morning in order to save the school building. Experiences encountered in the ordinary routine of the day were frequently trying enough. A young woman who came to the wilds of Texas during the early fifties wrote:

Safely arrived in Texas. After a week's rest I entered upon my daily duties. Ye who ever lived in cities, and been accustomed to the comfortable, and often luxurious houses devoted to education would smile, perchance laugh outright, at the rough log cabin where I teach. It is pleasantly located in a grove of oak-trees, whose shade would be agreeable, were it not infested by legions of gnats, whose bite for venom and violence would do credit to large insects. It has one door, and a window without sash or glass, but there is no lack of ventilation, the spaces between the logs admitting the pure air in larger quantities than desired. With a brave heart I crossed the threshold and rang a little bell as a signal for the school to assemble. They came with a whoop and halloo, twenty-five in number. "Is it books, mem?" they shouted. "It is the school hour," I replied, and bade them be seated which they reluctantly did, crowding close to the new teacher, some of the boldest girls fingering my dress, and asking the price of my "calicur." Others plucked the artificial flowers from my bonnet, and arranged them into boquets for themselves.

Just as I had succeeded in establishing some degree of order, down dropped a dozen or two of wasps from a nest in the upper part of the roof, which sent the children and myself out of the house for safety. The wasps not finding anyone to molest, soon flew away, and we returned to our places. . . . . I had just commenced a lecture upon the duties of scholars, when I saw all eyes again directed to the roof. On glancing upward, what was my consternation at beholding an enormously long snake, coiling and uncoiling himself with the utmost sang-froid, and gazing with a twinkle in the corner of his eye on the scene below as if much amused at the fear we manifested.[3]

The Southwest's reputation for lawlessness during this early period offered little attraction to a schoolteacher. There were some, however, who were willing to seek fortune and adventure in this region in spite of its turbulence. Among this group was George S. Denison of Vermont who established a subscription school in San Antonio, Texas, in 1854. That conditions were disturbed is seen from statements made in a letter to his mother, Mrs. E. S. Denison, on July 7, 1855. For example, he describes a filibustering expedition which was being organized in the town for an invasion of Mexico; in the next paragraph he states that "two men had a fight with pistols in the streets this (Sunday) morning, about ten o'clock and one was killed. He concludes: "The Indians are very bad here now. Of late there have been several fights within twenty miles of town, and they come down within seven or eight miles and carry off horses or kill them. I saw a company of young fellows, 'armed to the teeth,' start out of town to pursue and attack them, but as they have not returned it is not known what has been the result."[4]

Notwithstanding these difficulties Denison seemed to succeed. Although he received from each pupil on the average but four dollars a month in tuition, and had to pay ten dollars a month for a schoolroom, still in January, 1855, he was thus able to write his mother: "I shall be able to pay my expenses, and perhaps in the course of time make enough money to come home with." The fact that he was able to maintain a school in which he had enrolled children from some of the best homes of the town was an evidence of his ability. In June he wrote of having made a short excursion to the San Antonio River in company with one of his students, Lewis Maverick, of whom he says: "He has been in my school ever since I came to San Antonio and I have fitted him for college. He

3. "Keeping School in Texas," in *Putnam's Monthly Magazine*, II (July to December, 1853), 151.
4. Denison letters, MSS, Division of Manuscripts, Library of Congress.

left this place last Sunday for Burlington, where he intends to become a student."

It is unnecessary to add that the average schoolmaster of the frontier was not so well trained as Professor Denison. Perhaps this was true for two reasons: first, the primary need of children was training in reading, writing, and ciphering, and a knowledge of these subjects could be had without any long period of preparation on the part of a teacher; second, the average settler was little interested in having his children taught grammar, composition, algebra, and history for more than once he referred to these subjects as "new-fangled ideas of education," and demanded that his child be taught those things which he himself had studied while in school. Concerning this group of reactionaries Superintendent H. D. McCarty of Kansas, in 1872, observed:

"Old things have passed away! Behold! I make all things new," is an edict promulgated by the Great Eternal. But notwithstanding this high authority for progress, for change, for improvement, and reform, some there are who yet "Can't see it," and who rigidly persist in traveling the "old ways," of following with puritanical exactness in the footsteps of the fathers. More especially has this been the case in the administration of our educational affairs; the "old ways" have been, and still are, too clearly cherished too blindly followed, too reluctantly given up by many whose high privileges it is to push forward the educational car.

The time-honored structure, the "old log school house," with its mud-smeared ceilings, its slab-slats and surroundings to match, is in the notion of some "good enough" yet. This same class of people are, also, partial to "ye pedagogue of long ago," such for example as

"The school marms who governed with absolute sway,
Who taught us our reading, writing, and spelling,
And whaled us like blazes about every day."
Or, if the teacher be of male persuasion,
"A man severe he was and stern to view."[5]

Opposition to school reforms was not confined to illiterate settlers; occasionally a teacher joined his voice in protest. He did not like the new program which called for supervision of county schools, allowing only those to teach who held a first, second, or third grade

5. *Annual Report of the Superintendent of Education of the State of Kansas*, 1872.

certificate, and of substituting an organized course of study for the old "hit and miss" methods. In carrying out his duties as superintendent of Lyon County, A. D. Chambers sent out report forms to his teachers. When they had been filled in and returned, he found that some of the questions had been answered facetiously. In his annual report to the State Superintendent in 1875, he listed the following replies: "The man who got up this form is a fool or a snob" [He evidently did not know that it came from the State Superintendent]; "Yes sir, the district owns the books. Bought 'em you bet"; "Our school is graded 67 grades from A, B, C, to Algebra"; "You must explain what tuition means"; and "You must get somebody else to answer these questions."[6]

The "old fogy" problem was encountered not only in Kansas, but also in Colorado, New Mexico, and Texas. Reactionaries could see little need in having normals, and teachers' institutes, and in requiring teachers to pass examinations before they were given certificates. Perhaps this feeling was due in part to the indifference of examining boards and superintendents. A Texas "Cross Timbers" superintendent is reported to have granted an applicant a certificate because of his ability to spell "Surcingle." Throughout the entire plains country those coming up for examination frequently complained that questions submitted for second and third grade certificates in one county would be as difficult as those submitted to applicants for a first grade certificate in an adjacent county. Some of these complained that their superintendents were little more than "political figure-heads," entirely ignorant of the needs of their schools and the qualifications which a teacher should have; and occasionally there were heard charges of "gross incompetence," "caprice," and "favoritism."

That many teachers knew little more than their students is a fact well established by contemporary records. Not infrequently they worked long hours during the night to keep one or two lessons ahead of their students, and yet were unable to parse simple sentences, solve problems in arithmetic in which fractions were involved, or read understandingly from ordinary prose. State Superintendent O. N. Hollingsworth of Texas was so impressed with the necessity of raising the standards of teaching that in his

6. *The Fifteenth Annual Report of the Superintendent of Public Instruction, Year Ending, December 31, 1875,* p. 79.

report to the Governor in 1874 he dwelt at some length on this deplorable state of affairs. He cautioned county superintendents to exercise the "utmost discretion, prudence and wisdom in the examination and granting of certificates to teachers"; and in attempting to analyze general conditions, said:

How many parents, after having spared no pains to secure to their son or daughter the advantages of a liberal education, even curtailing home comforts and home pleasures, to gratify the fond desire, have sadly realized, after years of expense and anxiety, in maintaining their child at school, that but little or no progress has been made beyond the mere fact of cramming the mind with the prescribed rules and dates and facts given in the text book; that self-control, self-reliance, the exercise of individual thought, will, the study of human nature, of men and things, have all been neglected, and the child treated more as a machine, as a vessel that had to be crammed with a heterogeneous mass of divinity in the power and susceptibility of the mind.

This grievous defect in our system of education, both public and private, grows out of the ruinous disposition to employ cheap labor, in this the most important duty entrusted by the God of nature and nations to man and State.

We seek not for a cheap smith, doctor, attorney or mechanic; we ask for the best and most experienced, because we have learned, although it may cost us the most at the time, in the end it is the cheapest. But that highest interest entrusted to our care, upon which society and State rest for their foundation and hope, ambition and immortality, rely for their inspiration, is committed without a serious thought of the great results involved to any one whom chance or fortune may prompt to apply; and with proper endorsement, any broken down doctor, lawyer, preacher, or penniless though ambitious youth, who, for want of experience and proper endorsement, cannot get a clerkship, resorts to a school; or worse than all, any reckless, unknown adventurer, without home or kindred, or social tie; or any one with even an ordinary common school education, who has made a signal failure in everything else, and, as a dernier resort sits quietly down in the teacher's chair and complacently says: "At last I have found a place to rest."[7]

7. *Fourth Annual Report of the Superintendent of Public Instruction of the State of Texas for the Scholastic Year Ending August, 1874*, p. 32.

Perhaps Superintendent Hollingsworth was too severe in his indictments for there were many worthy teachers during this early period; and perhaps, too, he would have been more tolerant had he thoroughly understood actual conditions in frontier communities. Not only were many schools conducted in sod houses, dugouts , and adobes which were poorly lighted and ventilated, but few of them had adequate equipment. Through the long hours of the day, children sat on long rough benches, boxes, nail kegs, earthen seats, and the floors of these structures. Few of the schoolhouses had blackboards, charts, and other kinds of equipments, for trustees were either too miserly in their expenditures, or they classified such equipment as "new fangled things" and refused to buy them.

III

The routine work of the schoolmaster was both educational and social, and required tact and skill. There came trooping into his schoolroom each morning children who represented a cross-section of frontier society; some were filthy in attire, others wore garments made clean by much washing, and the clothing of others indicated comfortable circumstances in home life. Some were foul-smelling, their bodies and heads were covered with vermin, and unable to give their undivided attention to their studies because of skin diseases. Sometimes the teacher had the embarrassing task of training a tousled-headed boy to use a handkerchief—when he had one—rather than the sleeve of his coat in rendering first aid to his nose; or in calling his attention to the many days' accumulation of dirt on his hands and feet. When parents were quite sensitive to corrections of this kind, the schoomaster found this problem quite difficult to solve, if, indeed, he ever solved it.

The school day would generally begin at eight or nine o'clock in the morning and end at four o'clock in the afternoon, with an hour's intermission at noon and a fifteen minute recess in both the forenoon and afternoon periods. All during "books" (period for study) a teacher's time would be spent in "giving out words" to pupils from the "Blue-back" speller, in "hearing" reading exercises from McGuffey's Readers, helping a backward child to understand the intricacies of fractions—if he understood them himself—or a problem in percentage. Generally, the teacher stressed ciphering, parsing sentences, correct spelling, and important dates in history; specifically, he sought to divide his time in such a way as to conduct fifteen or twenty classes, to administer correction or corporal punishment whenever it was necessary, and to care for the educational and social needs of those who did not fit into class groups.

Occasionally a schoolmaster would meet with outside interference from community "bullies" who would visit the school during class hours and cause disturbance by laughing and talking, or by encouraging a refractory boy to be disobedient. Or the bully would come to the schoolhouse after class hours and overturn benches, scarify the blackboard or write thereon uncomplimentary statements about the teacher, steal the bell, maps, or charts, and other things.

There were also handicaps of the unintentional kind. Patrons generally used the schoolhouse for all purposes; religious services, public lectures, concerts, and literary society functions would often leave the schoolmaster—who was both teacher and janitor—a discouraging task to perform before he could "take up books" the next day. Even as late as 1912 the State Superintendent of New Mexico thus reported to the Governor: "The dilapidated school rooms, which were primarily built for dancing purposes, have been remodeled to a great extent, new furniture has been installed, and now have the appearance of sure-enough school rooms. On account of the destruction of school property and of interference with the school, dancing has been prohibited in all the schools." He then listed 1007 buildings in use, of which 788 were owned by the districts, 219 were rented, and 357 were of adobe construction. As to their condition, he stated that 124 were excellent, 353 good, 169 fair, and 164 poor.

Because of such discouraging circumstances it is not surprising that teaching was of poor quality. When patrons had to be convinced that it was to their own interest to send their boys and girls to school, when structures in which school children were housed were sometimes little better than barns in which farmers kept their cows and horses, when trustees showed little interest in grading the school or buying equipment for it, and when patrons in general evidenced little sympathy for the movement to train better prospective teachers, county and state superintendents had proof enough that standards were low.

Yet under these distressful circumstances the " 'Fesser" (Professor), or "Schoolmarm" (Schoolmistress), was generally regarded as an outstanding social, and often religious, leader of the community. He not only presided over his schoolroom, but he was generally the spokesman of community assemblies, social, industrial, or educational. He often waited on the sick, sat up with a corpse, helped to organize the community literary society, presided at occasional concerts, advised his patrons concerning legal matters and the planting of crops, visited on week-ends, and sometimes throughout the week, from one pupil's home to another, eating and complimenting the food placed before him by his hostess whether it was good or bad, and occasionally sleeping at night with three or four small children. Because of these many activities, the settlers came to regard the schoolmaster as the guiding genius of social life. He generally provided programs for the literary society and the annual concert, subjects for community debates, and he conducted in person various kinds of functions.

As a rule once or twice a month, on Friday afternoon, a spelling match or literary society would be held at the schoolhouse for the benefit of parents and friends of the students. If the schoolmaster announced a spelling match he would appoint two captains who would "choose up," that is, choose contestants from their classmates—and occasionally from obliging visitors. Those chosen would then stand in two rows along the opposite sides of the building, with the teacher and guests occupying the intervening space. From a spelling book the teacher would select a group of words which he believed to be within the range of all the contestants, and in a stentorian voice commence the contest. He would pronounce the syllables of each word carefully, and the head of the first line would promptly spell the word, pronouncing each syllable as he spelled it. If it were spelled correctly, the next word would be given the captain of the next line; and so, alternating from side to side, the teacher would gradually move down the room, submitting a word to each contestant until he had given them to all, when he would begin his procedure over again. Those who misspelled words took their seats, and the contest went on, the line becoming shorter and shorter until all contestants of one side were eliminated. In close contests where one remained on each side the teacher would sometimes present a hundred or more words before the winner was declared. The victor was generally regarded with much respect by both the teacher and visitors, even to the extent of matching him in a contest with a neighboring community champion.

A literary society function required considerable preparation on the part of those appearing on the program. A timid performer would "say his piece" before an older brother or sister again and again, weeks in advance, until he memorized it, or two or more would practice their dialogue until each knew his lines. Recitations of eight or ten poems, one or two essays, one or more dialogues, and two or three songs, usually made up a program. An occasion of this kind seldom required elaborate stage setting for the selections were simple and required little acting: "Mary had a little lamb" and "The boy stood on the burning deck," were recited many times by bashful boys and girls; and "Resolved that fire is more destructive than water" was the subject of many a heated debate.

A "concert" to the southern plains settlers was a literary society function on a grander scale and with certain variations; indeed, it was the grand finale of the school year. Weeks before the occasion was to be held the "schoolmarm" or " 'Fesser" would be occupied in training students who were to accept roles, even returning to the schoolhouse after school hours for rehearsals. Outsiders would also be called in to take part in the functions, such as the play and negro minstrel. As the time would draw near, rehearsal periods were more frequent and protracted, until each could play his or her part if occasionally prompted by someone standing behind the side curtain.

The stage setting was generally simple. If the trustees and patrons could afford to contribute enough money to buy lumber with which to build the stage, there were others who were willing to construct it. If this could not be done, an outdoor stage was prepared at one end of the schoolhouse, the walls, doors, and windows, serving as the rear part of the stage. Inexpensive curtains were made of cloth or, when cloth was not available, wagonsheets were often used. Parents were called upon to furnish lamps, lanterns, and torches to provide light for the occasion; and children usually brought flowers, ferns, and vines with which to decorate the stage.

The program would generally consist of introductory remarks by the schoolmaster, tableaux, a three-act play, music by a string band during the intermissions, and sometimes a negro minstrel. The event was regarded with so much favor that often long before night people riding horseback, in wagons, buggies, and hacks would begin to arrive, for it was considered an intercommunity affair, to be attended by visitors from many miles about. The program would start about eight o'clock in the evening and last until after eleven. Those who came, however, found no fault with the lengthy program for such an event was held only once a year. Those taking part in the performance vied with each other in making the occasion enjoyable to all, while members of the audience would stare in wide-eyed wonder at the transformations produced by the gaudy costumes of the participants. They were usually loud in their praises of the various features of the performance, even though an actor had his back turned to the audience for the greater part of the time he was saying his lines, and even though another would forget his lines and have to be prompted again and again by an anxious relative or friend. It mattered little to them if the prompter's voice "was a mite too loud," and they could hear only half that was said so long as they could "git the general drift" of the play.

IV

The foundation work accomplished by frontier teachers was to reveal itself in the rapid cultural advances made by the southern plains during the last quarter of the nineteenth century; what had been border communities came to be large towns, villages, and rural areas with educational and religious institutions much like those found in Eastern states. Teacher training was much improved, text books were standardized, splendidly built schoolhouses replaced the dugouts and sod structures, and the educational *esprit de corps* of the citizens was much improved.

This transformation was most complete in Kansas. In 1860, its population was only 107,206, with 37,423 boys and girls of school age, of which only 2,310 were enrolled; in 1879 the population had increased to 849,978, with 283,326 children of school age, of which 188,884 were enrolled in school. "Of the influx since 1870 probably a fifth has been of foreign birth; Mennonites and their co-religionists from Russia, Germans, Scandinavians, French, Italians, English, Scotch, Welsh and Irish; and with these have come also large numbers from all the Atlantic States, Canadians, Mexicans, and of late negroes, making their exodus from the Southern States to Kansas, as pre-eminently the land of freedom." This heterogeneous immigration tended to enrich the culture of the state, and stimulated the growth of towns. Largely since the days of the Civil War, this development was so marked that by 1880 there were thirty-nine towns in the state boasting of populations ranging from 1,031 to 16,550. In 1880 the state had 2,200,000 acres of unsold school lands, and the amount raised and expended for common schools in the state in 1878 was $1,261,459.14, of which $980,435.07 was paid as wages to teachers (the male teachers receiving an average salary of $32.99 a month, and the female teachers $26.04). The aggregate membership of the nine leading religious denominations was 135,713, and their church properties were valued at $2,037,508.[8]

A similar change was taking place in Colorado. The *Rocky Mountain News* (Denver, Colorado), of February 23, 1870, contained a report of the first state teachers' institute, which was held at Boulder. At this meeting the teachers passed resolutions calling upon the directors of public schools to supply schoolhouses with globes, maps, charts, and blackboards, and directing the attention of the public to the necessity of using uniform textbooks.

Since Texas had been under the influence of a "carpet-bag" regime from 1865 to 1875, the quickening influences of culture were not so apparent as in the other two states, yet there is abundant proof that considerable progress had been made. On July 20, 1877, the Dallas Daily *Herald* carried the following article:

> There is a district to the west and south of Dallas comprising the counties of Hamilton, Comanche, Brown, Coleman, Erath, Shackleford, Eastland, and perhaps a dozen others, equally good, which for all the purposes of settlement cannot be excelled on the continent of America, and the germ of the population already planted there is sound in all its parts. The ruling people, they who give tone and character to the settlements, are the better classes from all the states who have sent out their sons to make a foothold in the new land of promise.
>
> . . . . The blessed gospel attended by her handmaiden the common school marches on in the van of our ever-extending line of frontier settlement. The border homes of Texas are instinct

8. L. P. Brockett, *Our Western Empire*, 884-85.

with all the progress of the age, and as they grow older even the graces of ultra civilization are found thickly scattered among them. The settler from the East who had made up his mind to rough it for the remainder of his life, among the boors of the ranche, is agreeably surprised to find intelligence and culture, instead of vulgarity and ignorance; piety and purity instead of profanity and immorality.

There is little doubt that many Eastern people of this time regarded Southwestern people as being "boors." Indeed, long after the end of the period of Indian depredations and outlaw disturbance, the area was regarded as unsafe for white occupation. Some Easterners, however, timidly came to the area to serve as missionaries, others as schoolteachers, and still others as newspaper and magazine correspondents. The press agents were sent out to make "correct observations" on the true status of the country and to report the same for the benefit of the reading public. For example, the publishers of *Scribner's Magazine* sponsored such a tour in 1873-74, sending to the Southwest and to the South an able observer, Edward King, and as an illustrator, J. Wellis Champney; and even as late as the fall of 1892, the *St. Louis Globe-Democrat* sent one of its best correspondents, Walter B. Stevens, to Texas "with instructions to go where he pleased, stay as long as he pleased and write about everything he saw."[9] The "observations" made by some of those who came to the frontier were perhaps written to please the reading public, for they were superficial and rhetorical. In a few instances, however, they were comprehensive and conservative and therefore constitute a valuable source of information on the development of the country, its institutions, and its culture.

The point of view that Texas as late as March 26, 1874, was still regarded as "wild and wooly" is reflected in an article in the *Jackson Whig and Tribune*, quoted by the Dallas *Herald*, under the caption "Too Refined for Texas Society":

A few days ago a wagon, drawn by a yoke of long-horn Texas cattle halted on Lafayette Street. The wagon contained a good-looking woman, seven children and considerable plunder. A man,

9. For discussion of the two tours see Edward King's *The Southern States of North America*, "Publishers' Preface"; and Walter B. Stevens, *Through Texas: A Series of Interesting and Instructive Letters*, "Introduction."

a small boy, and a dog that had run to tail were the adjuncts. The party were from Texas and were returning to their old home in Decatur County. An alderman of the city, who had passed many years of his life in the Lone Star State, approached the wagon. He said to the woman, "From Texas, I presume?" "Yes sir." "Didn't you like the climate?" "Oh yes." "Did you have good health out there?" "Yes." "How about the crops?" "Oh, we made splendid crops." "Well, then, Mam, what on earth is your objection to Texas?" "Why sir," she replied, "I couldn't stand the society in that rough country;" and then she turned to the small boy, her son, and cried, "Sam, drive that dam dog outen the dinner pot; don't you see he's got his nasty snout in the vittles?"

In this connection the important consideration is not that the incident occurred or did not occur, although it was probably in part a fabrication, but that it reveals a decided tendency in older settled areas of the nation to regard lightly the claims of the people of Texas to culture.

Statistical data of this period help to throw some light on educational conditions of Texas. In 1860 the total population of the state was 604,215, of which 233, 417 were of school age, with less than fifty per cent enrolled in schools. The report of the Superintendent of Education for 1878 listed 324,181 boys and girls of school age, of whom 133,568 were enrolled. At this time 4,330 teachers were employed, the average pay for whom was, males, forty-two dollars, females, thirty-three dollars. Religious conditions, too, showed decided improvement over an earlier time. In 1875 there were 839,250 adherents of all the denominations, 2,050 church organizations, 1,307 ministers, and 1,764 church edifices valued at $1,979,-600.

The previously quoted article in the Dallas *Herald* for July 20, 1877, relative to frontier counties of Texas, gave conditions existing in a tier of counties running north and south. In 1890 the Passenger Department of the Union Pacific Railroad issued an immigrant guide book entitled *The Resources and Attractions of the Panhandle of Texas*, giving educational statistics based on developments in nineteen frontier counties, running from east to west along the right-of-way of the Denver and Rio Grande. Since all but five of these counties were beyond the frontier line of settlements in 1875, the figures given indicate the rapidity by which civilization advanced westward. The total school population of the nineteen counties was given at 24,134, and other statistics as follows: schoolhouses 251, teachers 481, total number of pupils enrolled 22,212, average attendance 9,467, and the average length of school term 90.7 days.

The last half of the nineteenth century witnessed a marvelous change in the southern plains country. Indian villages gave way to prosperous towns and cities, and dim warpaths and cow trails were broken up by the turning plow and barbed wire fences. The buoyant spirit of optimism which possessed the new inhabitants was well expressed in town and home building. Dugouts and sod-houses were rapidly replaced by splendidly constructed buildings of frame, brick, and stone. Municipal organizations advertised the merits of paved streets, electric lights, water works, and commodious public structures; and larger towns and cities boasted of institutions of higher learning in which the boys and girls of the land could be trained in liberal arts and sciences. Indeed, the frontier was no more; and with its passing, the folkways of the region came to the threshold of a new era.

BIBLIOGRAPHY

Materials used as a basis for this study are varied. Several kinds of manuscripts, federal and state documents, newspapers, magazines, publications of learned societies, published diaries and journals, and out-of-print books, the most of which were contemporary with the frontier period, were examined for information dealing with the southern plains incident to its topography, climate, flora and fauna, land problems, transportation, and the varied experiences of its early settlers. These materials fall within certain general classifications and are so listed.

A. MANUSCRIPTS

Since the southern plains during the era studied was primarily an Indian frontier many of the sources relied on concerned the relations of the settlers with the native tribes. But in them are also found many facts pertaining to border life. For example, in letters, in journals of reconnaissances and expeditions, in diaries, and in reports are not only descriptions of topography, climate, roads and trails, but also allusions to such subjects as freighting, stagecoaching, and general frontier experiences. The Central Superintendency papers of the Bureau of Indian Affairs are the most complete of the Indian collections; the Kiowa-Comanche and the Darlington Agency (Cheyenne-Arapaho) files, in the Oklahoma Historical Library, and the Indian papers of the University of Texas Library are also important.

Closely associated with and similar to the Indian papers are the frontier army materials of the Old Records Division, Adjutant General's Office, War Department, Washington, D. C. Those relied on more generally of this class were in the "Old Files Section," consisting of official correspondence, letters from border people in respect to Indian raids, to the ransom of captives, to border conditions, and to reports of various kinds, all filed in large wooden letter boxes.

Other smaller collections are related more intimately to frontier life. The letters of George Denison, a New England school teacher who lived in San Antonio, Texas, during the period, 1854-62, are found in the Division of Manuscripts, Library of Congress. They throw much light on outlawry, Spanish-American customs, and the religious and social life of the Anglo-Americans in western Texas. The John Charles Beales papers of the Texas State Library, Austin, lend corroboration to the Sarah Ann Horn narrative as well as important facts relating to the Rio Grande colony. The "Texas Archives," in the Office of the American Secretary of State, Washington, contain transcripts of letters from Daniel Webster, President Anson Jones, and others on Texas Indian relations, and experiences of captives. In the archives of the University of Texas Library are five important collections: the Obadiah M. Knapp papers, 1865-68; the Gunter-Munson letter press, 1873-75; the Jacob Kuechler letter cases (I, 1804-72; II, 1873-76; and III, 1877-1907), written in Spanish, German, and English; the J. M. Daugherty papers, 1872-92; and the D. H. Snyder papers, written during the eighties. These manuscripts relate largely to climatic conditions, topography, surveys, land claims, Indian raids, stagecoaching, and border life in general, in Texas, New Mexico, and Kansas.

The Oklahoma Historical Library, at Oklahoma City, has manuscript records related to immigration, society, and "the runs" to the Oklahoma lands during the Indian territory period, the Cherokee Strip livestock problem, and to the immigration movements in Texas and Kansas. Of these, the David L. Payne papers are the most important. The diary of L. G. Carroll (an Oklahoma eighty-niner) gives interesting sidelights on the first run. Also the "Record Book of Beaver, Neutral Strip, Indian Territory," reveals important and novel details of the self-governing activities instituted by the squatters of that "no man's land."

Many other manuscripts, not found in large and well-known depositories, were also helpful. The minutes of the "Northwest Texas Cattle Raisers' Association" (now in possession of the Southwestern Cattle Raisers' Association, at Fort Worth, Texas); the "Deed Records," Vol. 26, of Jones County, Texas, and the "Minutes of the Forty-third Judicial District," Vol. 378, Jack County, Texas, are records of this kind. Some records were loaned the author such as the minute books of the Crystal Falls, Texas, Baptist Church, during the frontier period, the penciled memoirs of Mrs. Melissa J. Evarts, and the C. F. Doan reminiscences, and are too numerous to list in detail.

BIBLIOGRAPHY

B. GOVERNMENT PUBLICATIONS

1. Federal

Annual reports of the Secretary of War, 1865-90.

Annual reports of the Secretary of the Interior, 1850-90.

Ninth Annual Report of the United States Geological and Geographical Survey of the territories embracing Colorado and parts of adjacent territories: being a report of the exploration for the year 1875 (Washington, 1876).

Reports of Explorations and Surveys to ascertain the most practicable route for a railroad from the Mississippi River to the Pacific Ocean, 1853-54 (Washington, 1855-60). 13 vols.

House Executive Documents: Twenty-ninth Congress, second session, No. 76, Vol. IV; Thirty-third Congress, second session, No. 91, Part III; Thirty-ninth Congress, first session, No. 1; Fortieth Congress, second session, No. 277, Vol. XVII, Part 2; Forty-second Congress, third session, No. 62, Vol. VII; Forty-third Congress, second session, No. 1, Vol. I, Part 2.

House Miscellaneous Documents: Forty-first Congress, second session, Nos. 137, 139, and 142; Forty-first Congress, third session, No. 99, Vol. II.

Senate Executive Documents: Special session, March, 1853, No. 3; Fortieth Congress, second session, No. 60, Vol. II; Forty-sixth Congress, second session, No. 10, Vol. I; Forty-sixth Congress, first session, No. 20, Vol. I; Forty-seventh Congress, first session, No. 111, Vol. V; Forty-eighth Congress, second session, Nos. 16 and 17, Vol. I; Fifty-first Congress, first session, No. 72, Vol. IX.

Senate Miscellaneous Documents: Forty-second Congress, third session, No. 64, Vol. I; Forty-third Congress, second session, No. 60, Vol. I.

Senate Report: Thirtieth Congress, first session, No. 171 (52 pp.).

2. State

The state documents used were the annual reports of the adjutant generals, secretaries of state, and superintendents of public instruction, of Kansas, New Mexico, and Texas, during the period 1870-1910 (incomplete). Also, the annual reports of the Texas and New Mexico superintendents of immigration were examined for points of entry, classes and nationalities of settlers, and areas settled.

C. NEWSPAPERS

Bulletin (Leavenworth, Kansas), July 20, 1867 to April 1, 1871.
5 vols.

Daily Express (San Antonio, Texas), January 3, 1867 to December
31, 1874. 8 vols.

Daily New Mexican (Santa Fe, New Mexico), April 25, 1870 to
December 29, 1877. 6 vols.

Daily Republican (Austin, Texas). February 6, to December 31,
1868.

Daily Republican (Little Rock, Arkansas), May 24, 1867 to December 6, 1877. 7 vols.

Herald (Dallas, Texas), March 26, 1874 to December 22, 1877.

Kansas State Record (Topeka, Kansas), July 1, 1874 to April 28,
1875. 1 vol.

News (Denison, Texas), April 17, 1873 to June 4, 1876.

Rocky Mountain News (Denver, Colorado), February 19, 1868 to
December 27, 1871. 3 vols.

Semi-Weekly Review (Albuquerque, New Mexico), January 21,
1868 to December 11, 1869. 2 vols.

Tri-Weekly News (Galveston, Texas), May 31, 1869 to December
31, 1873. 4 vols.

Weekly New Era (Fort Smith, Arkansas), January 20, 1869 to
November 20, 1884. 6 vols.

D. PUBLISHED DIARIES, JOURNALS, AND LETTERS

Abel, Annie H. (ed.), *The Official Correspondence of James S. Calhoun While Indian Agent at Santa Fe and Superintendent of
Indian Affairs in New Mexico* (Washington, 1915).

Anonymous, "Winter Experiences and Observations," in *Six
Months in Kansas* (Boston, 1856).

Battey, Thomas C., *The Life and Adventures of a Quaker Among
the Indians* (Boston, 1875).

Biddle, Ellen McGowan, *Reminiscences of a Soldier's Wife* (Los
Angeles, 1927).

Biggers, Don H., *Shackleford County Sketches* (no place, 1908).

Drum, Stella M. (ed.), *Down the Santa Fe Trail and into New
Mexico. The Diary of Susan Shelby Magoffin, 1846-1847* (New
Haven, 1926).

Dunkle, Rev. W. F., "A Choctaw Indian's Diary," in *Chronicles
of Oklahoma*, IV (1926), No. 1, 61-69.

BIBLIOGRAPHY

Galloway, T. B., "Private Letters of a Government Official in the Southwest," in *Journal of American History*, III (1909), No. 4.

Glisan, R., *Journal of Army Life* (San Francisco, 1874).

Kendall, George W., *Narrative of the Texan Santa Fe Expedition* (New York, 1844), I.

"Letters from the Indian Missions in Kansas," in *Kansas State Historical Collections*, XVI (1923-25), 227-71.

Möllhausen, Baldwin, *Diary of a Journey from the Mississippi to the Coast of the Pacific. . . .* (London, 1858), I.

"The Records of an Early Texas Baptist Church," in the *Southwestern Historical Quarterly*, XI (1907-8), and XII (1908-9).

E. PERIODICALS

Andrews, E. N., "A Buffalo Hunt by Rail," in *Kansas Magazine*, III (May, 1873), No. 5, 450-58.

"A Ride on the Texas Frontier," in *Overland Monthly*, July, 1868. Examined as a separate (All periodicals listed here without volume, number, date, and pages given were found as separates).

"A Stage Ride to Colorado," in *Harper's Magazine*, XXXVIII (1869), 792-95.

"Adventure in Texas," in *Leisure Hour*, XII (London, 1863), 5 *passim*.

Ames, Mrs. L. D., "The Missouri Play Party," in *Journal of American Folk-Lore*, July-September, 1911, 295-318.

Berryman, Jerome C., "A Circuit Rider's Frontier Experiences," in *Kansas State Historical Collections*, XVI (1923-25), 177-226.

Bieber, Ralph P., "Some Aspects of the Santa Fe Trade, 1848-1880," in *Missouri Historical Review*, XVIII, No. 2.

Biesele, Rudolph L., "The First German Settlement in Texas," in *Southwestern Historical Quarterly*, XXXIV (April, 1931), 334-39.

——, "German Settlers and the Indians in Texas, 1844-1860," *ibid.*, XXXI (1927-28), 116-29.

Bingham, Anne E., "Sixteen Years on a Kansas Farm," in *Kansas State Historical Collections*, XV (1919-22), 501-23.

Bookwalter, John W., "The Farmer's Isolation and the Remedy," in *The Forum*, XII (September, 1891-February, 1892), 54-55.

Botkin, B. A., "The Oklahoma Literary Society," in *Folk-Say, a Regional Miscellany*, 1930, 266-71.

Bradford, L. C., "Among the Cowboys," in *Lippincott's Magazine*, June, 1881.

Buck, Solon J., "Settlement of Oklahoma," in *Transactions* of the Wisconsin Academy of Science, Arts, and Letters, XV, 325-80.

Burgess, Roger A., "Pioneer Quaker Farmers of the South Plains," in *Panhandle Plains Historical Review*, 1928, 117-23.

Clift, George D., "The Kansas Settler," in *The Kansas Magazine*, III (February, 1873), No. 2, 152-56.

Davis, T. R., "A Summer on the Plains," in *Harper's Magazine*, February, 1868, 292-307.

————,"A Winter on the Plains," *ibid.*, June, 1869, 22-34.

Dobie, Bertha McKee, "Tales and Rhymes of a Texas Household," in *Texas and Southwestern Lore*, VI (Austin, 1927), 23-30.

"Education in Kansas," in the *Kansas Magazine*, I (April, 1872), No. 4, 381-82.

Folsom, Rev. W. F., "Phil. D. Brewer," in *Chronicles of Oklahoma*, IV (1926), No. 1, 55-61.

Geiser, Samuel Wood, "Ferdinand von Roemer and his Travels in Texas," in *Southwest Review*, XVII (July, 1932), 421-60.

Harby, T. C., "Texan Types and Contrasts," in *Harper's Magazine*, July, 1890, 229-46.

Harger, C. M., "Cattle Trails of the Prairies," in *Scribner's Magazine*, June, 1892.

Hayes, A. A., Jr., "The Cattle Ranches of Colorado," in *Harper's Magazine*, November, 1879, 877-95.

Hayes, Edward C., "Effects of Geographic Conditions on Social Realities," in *American Journal of Sociology*, XIX, 813-40.

Hobart, T. D., "Some of the Characters and Customs of Old Mobeetie," in *Panhandle-Plains Historical Review*, II (1929), 123-29.

Hogue, E., "Spanish-American Folk-Songs," in *Journal of American Folk-Lore*, July-September, 1911, 323-31.

Holden, W. C., "Immigration and Settlement in West Texas," in *West Texas Historical Association Year Book*, V (June, 1929), 66-86.

Hoyt, A. W., "Over the Plains to Colorado," in *Harper's Magazine*, June, 1867, 1-21.

Hutchinson, Clinton C., "The Plains," in *Kansas Magazine*, I (March, 1872), No. 3, 224-32.

Ingalls, John G., "Blue Grass," *ibid.*, II (September, 1872), No. 3, 270-77.

Jenness, Theodora R., "The Indian Territory," in *Atlantic Monthly*, LXIII, 444-52.

"Keeping School in Texas," in *Putnam's Monthly Magazine*, II (August, 1853).

BIBLIOGRAPHY

Kelly, H. B., "No Man's Land," in *Kansas State Historical Collections*, IV, 324-31.

Kleberg, Rosa, "Early Experiences in Texas," in *Texas State Historical Quarterly*, I (1897-98), 297-302; and II (1898-99), 170-73.

Lake, Mary Daggett, "Pioneer Christmas Customs of Tarrant County," in *Publications* of the Texas Folk-Lore Society, V (Austin, 1926), 107-12.

Leonard, M. H., "Southwestern Kansas Seen with Eastern Eyes," in the *Atlantic Monthly*, LVI (1885), 101-8.

Lesley, Lewis B., "The Purchase and Importation of Camels by the United States Government, 1855-1857," in *Southwestern Historical Quarterly*, XXXIII (July, 1929), No. 1, 18-33.

Lewis, Mrs. James E., Jr., "A Romance Century," in *Kansas State Historical Collections*, X (1907-8), 43-50.

"Life in Texas," in *The Spectator* (London), July-December, 1884, No. 2.

Loeb, H. W., "One Hundred Years of Medicine in Missouri," in *Missouri Historical Review*, XIV, 74-81.

McKinnon, Bess, "The Toll Road over Raton Pass," in *New Mexico Historical Review*, II (1927).

Mooney, James, "Calendar History of the Kiowa," in Seventeenth Annual Report of the Bureau of American Ethnology (1895-96), Part 1.

Morgan, J. K., "The New Kansas," in *Carter's Monthly*, XII (June, 1897), 155-73.

W. B. Morrison, "The Choctaw Mission of the American Board of Commissioners for Foreign Missions," in *Chronicles of Oklahoma*, IV (1926), No. 2, 166-83.

"On the Texas Prairies," in *Overland Monthly*, January, June, 1869.

Owens, William A., "The Play Party in Texas," in *Southwest Review*, XVIII (1933), 169-78.

Peabody, Charles, "A Reconnaissance Trip in Western Texas," in *American Anthropologist*, April, May, June, 1909, 202-16.

Platt, Mrs. E. G., "Some Experiences as a Teacher Among the Pawnees," in *Kansas State Historical Collections*, XIV (1915-18), 784-94.

Raber, Charles, "Personal Recollections of Life on the Plains from 1860 to 1868," *ibid.*, XVI (1923-25), 316-40.

Reynolds, Charles, "What I saw in Colorado," in *Kansas Magazine*, II (November, 1872), No. 5, 389-94.

Richardson, R. N., "Some Details of the Southern Overland Mail," in *Southwestern Historical Quarterly*, XXIX (July, 1925), No. 1, 1-18.

Rister, C. C., "Outlaws and Vigilantes of the Southern Plains," in *Mississippi Valley Historical Review*, XIX (March, 1933).

———, "Significance of the Jacksboro Indian Affair," in *Southwestern Historical Quarterly*, XXIX, No. 3.

———, "Harmful Practices of Indian Traders," in *New Mexico Historical Review*, VI (July, 1931), No. 3.

Robinson, Edgar E., "Recent Manifestations of Sectionalism," in *American Journal of Sociology*, XIX, 446-67.

Roosevelt, Theodore, "In Cowboy Land," in *Century Magazine*, June, 1893, 276-84.

Rollins, A. W., "Ladies' Day at the Ranch," in *Harper's Magazine*, June, 1885, 3-17.

Sheffy, L. F., "The Experimental Stage of Settlement in the Panhandle of Texas," in *Panhandle Plains Historical Review*, III (1930), 79-103.

Smalley, E. V., "The Isolation of Life on Prairie Farms," in *Atlantic Monthly*, LXXII (1893), 378-82.

Spearman, F. H., "The Great American Desert," in *Harper's Magazine*, July, 1888, 232-45.

Steele, James W., "Among the New Mexicans," in *Kansas Magazine*, I (February, 1872), No. 2, 105-12; "Sons of the Border," *ibid.*, II (July, 1872), No. 1, 33-38; "The Harvest Time of the Pueblos," *ibid.*, II (August, 1872), No. 2, 177-83; "Women Under Difficulties," *ibid.*, II (September, 1872), No. 3, 224-29; and "La Señorita," *ibid.*, II (November, 1872), No. 5, 458-62.

Street, William D., "The Victory of the Plow," in *Kansas State Historical Collections*, IX (1905-6), 33-44.

Swanson, Nina, "The Development of Public Protection of Children in Kansas," *ibid.*, XV (1919-22), 249-78.

"The Reminiscences of Mrs. Dilue Harris," in *Southwestern Historical Quarterly*, IV (1900-1), 214-22.

"The Story of Oklahoma," in *The Nation*, XLVIII (1889), 279-80.

Turner, Thomas F., "Prairie Dog Lawyers," in *Panhandle Plains Historical Review*, II (1929).

Urquhart, Hugh John, "An Adventure at a Buffalo Hunt," in *Tait's Edinburgh Magazine*, New Series, XVIII (January-December, 1851), 623-29.

Wardell, Morris L., "Early Protestant Missions Among the Osages," in *Chronicles of Oklahoma*, II (September, 1924), No. 3, 285-97.

Webb, W. P., "George W. Arrington," in *Panhandle Plains Historical Review*, VIII (1935).

BIBLIOGRAPHY

White, Mrs. S. B., "My First Days in Kansas," in *Kansas State Historical Collections*, XI (1909-10), 550-60.

Wicks, Hamilton S., "The Opening of Oklahoma," in *Cosmopolitan*, VII, 460-70.

Williams, A. M., "The Giants of the Plains," in *Lippincott's Magazine*, October, 1883, 362-71.

Williams, R. L., "The Judicial History of Oklahoma," in *Report* of the Oklahoma State Bar Association, V (n.p., 1911).

Wilmer, John. "The German Colony in Texas," in *Tait's Edinburgh Magazine*, New Series, XV (March, 1848), 219-24.

Wright, R. M., "Frontier Life in Southwestern Kansas," in *Journal of American History*, October to December, 1922, 333-45.

Yatt, L., "Cowboy Life," in *Outing Magazine*, December, 1891, 181-263.

Young, Della I., "The Singin Schule," in *Folk-Say, A Regional Miscellany*, 1929, 86-94.

———, "The Pioneer Dance," *ibid.*, 1930, 253-65.

F. MISCELLANEOUS

Adams, Andy, *The Log of a Cowboy* (New York, 1903).

———, *The Outlet* (New York, 1905).

———, *Cattle Brands* (New York, 1906).

———, *Red Anthony, Cowman* (New York, 1907).

———, *The Ranch on the Beaver* (New York, 1927).

Ainsworth, W. F. (ed.), *All Round the World*. . . . . (London, and Glasgow, 1877).

Aldridge, Reginald, *Ranch Notes in Kansas, Colorado, the Indian Territory and Northern Texas* (London, 1884).

Allen, Rev. William. *Five Years in the West; or, How An Inexperienced Young Man Finds His Occupation*. . . . . (Nashville, 1890).

Anderson, J. W., *From the Plains to the Pulpit* (Goose Creek, 1907).

Anonymous, *On the Frontier, or Scenes in the West* (Boston, 1864).

Atkeson, Mary M., *The Woman on the Farm* (New York and London, 1924).

Baker, Rev. William M., *The Life and Labors of the Rev. Daniel Baker* (Philadelphia, 1858).

Baldwin, Alice Blackwood, *Memoirs of the Late Frank D. Baldwin, Major General* (Los Angeles, 1929).

Bancroft, H. H., *History of Arizona and New Mexico* (*Works*, XVII, San Francisco, 1889).

———, *History of the North Mexican States and Texas* (*Works*, II).

Beadle, J. H., *The Undeveloped West* (Philadelphia, 1873).

———, *Western Wilds and the Men Who Redeem Them* (San Francisco, 1880).

Benton, Frank, *Cowboy Life on the Sidetrack* (Denver, 1903).

Biesele, Rudolph L., *History of the German Settlements in Texas, 1831-1861* (Austin, 1930).

Bird, Isabelle L., *A Lady's Life in the Rocky Mountains* (New York, 1879).

Brady, Cyrus T., *Recollections of a Missionary in the Great West* (New York, 1900).

Branch, E. Douglas, *Westward: The Romance of the American Frontier* (New York, 1930).

———, *The Hunting of the Buffalo* (New York, and London, 1929).

Bristol, Rev. Sherlock, *The Pioneer Preacher* (Chicago, New York and Toronto, 1887 and 1898).

Brown, Rev. John (ed.), *Twenty-five Years a Parson in the Wild West* (Fall River, 1896).

Campion, J. S., *On the Frontier* (London, 1878).

Carroll, J. M. (edited by J. B. Cranfill), *A History of Texas Baptists* (Dallas, 1923).

Kit Carson's Fight with Comanche and Kiowa Indians, No. 12, New Mexico Historical Society (Santa Fe, 1911).

Carter, Captain R. G., *The Old Sergeant's Story* (New York, 1926).

———, *On the Border with Mackenzie, or Winning West Texas from the Comanches* (Washington, 1935).

Carvalho, S. H., *Incidents of Travel and Adventure in the Far West* . . . . (New York, 1857).

Catlin, George, *North American Indians* (Edinburgh, 1926), II.

Chittenden, W. L., *Ranch Verses* (New York, 1925).

Clay, J., *My Life on the Range* (Chicago, 1924).

Coan, Charles F., *A History of New Mexico* (Chicago, and New York, 1925). 3 vols.

Conard, Howard L., *"Uncle Dick" Wooton* (Chicago, 1890).

Connelley, William E., *Standard History of Kansas and Kansans* (Chicago, 1918).

———, *Doniphan's Expedition* (Kansas City, 1907).

———, *Wild Bill and His Era* (New York, 1933).

Cook, J. H., *Fifty Years on the Old Frontier* (New Haven, 1923).

Cook, John R., *The Border and the Buffalo* (Topeka, 1907).

Cordova, J. de, *Texas; Her Resources and Her Public Men* (Philadelphia, 1858).

BIBLIOGRAPHY

Crane, Charles J., *Experiences of a Colonel of Infantry* (New York, 1923).

Cranfill's Chronicle. A Story of Life in Texas (New York, 1916).

Custer, Elizabeth B., *Tenting on the Plains, or General Custer in Kansas and Texas* (New York, 1893).

Dale, Edward E., *The Range Cattle Industry* (Norman, 1930).

———, and Jesse L. Rader, *Readings in Oklahoma History* (New York, 1930).

Daniels, H. F., and Taylor, N. A., *The Coming Empire* (New York, 1877).

De Shields, J. T., *Border Wars of Texas* (Tioga, 1912).

Dixon, William Hepworth, *New America* (London, 1867).

Dobie, J. Frank, *A Vaquero of the Brush Country* (Dallas, 1929).

Dodge, Richard Irving, *Hunting Grounds of the Great West* (London, 1877).

———, *The Plains of the Great West*, ... (New York, 1877).

———, *Our Wild Indians* (Hartford, 1882).

Duffus, R. L., *The Santa Fe Trail* (London, 1930).

Dunbar, Seymour, *History of Travel in America* (Indianapolis, 1915), IV.

Ebbutt, Percy G., *Emigrant Life in Kansas* (London, 1886).

Eby, Frederick, *The Development of Education in Texas* (New York, 1925).

———, *Education in Texas; Source Materials* (Austin, 1925).

Edwords, Clarence E., *Camp-fires of a Naturalist* (New York, 1893).

Eickhoff, Anton, *In der neuen Heimath* (New York, 1884).

Eisele, W. R., *The Real Wild Bill Hickock* (Denver, 1931).

Farnham, Eliza H., *Life in Prairie Land* (New York, 1852).

Fisher, Rev. H. D., *The Gun and Gospel. Early Kansas and Chaplain Fisher* (Chicago, 1896).

Foreman, Grant, *Indian Removal* (Norman, 1932).

———, *A Traveler in the Indian Territory* (Cedar Rapids, 1930).

———, *Advancing the Frontier* (Norman, 1933).

Freeman, G. D., *Midnight and Noonday, or the Incidental History of Southern Kansas and the Indian Territory* (Caldwell, 1892).

French, H. W., *Some Recollections of a Western Ranchman* (New York, n.d.).

Fulton, Maurice G., *Pat F. Garrett's Authentic Life of Billy the Kid* (New York, 1927).

Galveston, Harrisburg, and San Antonio Railroad's Immigration Guide to Western Texas (n.p., n.d.).

Gittinger, Roy, *The Formation of the State of Oklahoma* (in University of California Publications in History, VI, Berkeley, California, 1917).

Gladstone, T. H., *The Englishman in Kansas* (New York, 1857).

Governors Messages, Coke to Ross, 1874-91 (Austin, 1916).

Greene, Rev. T. W. (ed.), *From the Stage Coach to the Pulpit, Being an Autobiographical Sketch, with Incidents and Anecdotes, of Elder H. K. Stimson, the Veteran Pioneer of Western New York, now of Kansas* (St. Louis, 1874).

Greenleaf, A. B., *Ten Years in Texas* (Selma, 1880).

Gregg, Josiah, *Commerce of the Prairies* (in Thwaites' *Early Western Travels,* 1748-1846, XIX, XX, Cleveland, 1905).

Grinnell, George B., *The Fighting Cheyennes* (New York, 1915).

———, *The Cheyenne Campfires* (New Haven, 1926).

Guide to El Paso, Texas. A Complete History of the City and Review of its Business (El Paso, n.d.).

Hafen, L. R., *The Overland Mail* (Cleveland, 1926).

Haley, J. Evetts, *The XIT Ranch of Texas and Early Days of the Llano Estacado* (Chicago, 1929).

Hardman, Francis, *Frontier Life; or, Tales of the South-western Border* (Philadelphia, n.d.).

Hartley, Cecil B., *Hunting Sports in the West* (Philadelphia, 1859).

Hastings, F. S., *A Ranchman's Recollections* (Chicago, 1921).

Hayes, A. A., *New Colorado and the Santa Fe Trail* (New York, 1880).

Henry, Stuart, *Conquering Our Great American Plains* (New York, 1930).

Hill, Luther B., *A History of Oklahoma* (Chicago and New York, 1909), I.

Holden, W. C., *Alkali Trails, or Social and Economic Movements of the Texas Frontier, 1846-1900* (Dallas, 1930).

———, *Rollie Burns* (Dallas, 1932).

House, E., *A Narrative of the Captivity of Mrs. Horn and her two Children with that of Mrs. Harris, by the Commanche Indians....* (St. Louis, 1839).

Houston, Mrs., *Texas and the Gulf of Mexico; or Yachting in the New World* (London, 1844), II.

Howe, Henry, *The Great West* (Cincinnati, 1851).

Howlett, Rev. W. J., *Life of the Right Rev. Joseph P. Machebeauf, D.D.* (Pueblo, 1908).

Hughes, John T., *Doniphan's Expedition; Containing an Account of the Conquest of New Mexico. . . . .* (Cincinnati, 1847).

Hughes, Thomas, *Gone to Texas* (London, 1884).

BIBLIOGRAPHY

Humphrey, Seth K., *Following the Prairie Frontier* (Minneapolis, 1931).

Inman, Col. Henry, *Buffalo Jones' Forty Years of Adventure* (London, 1889).

———, *The Old Santa Fe Trail* (Topeka, 1916).

Jackson, George, *Sixty Years in Texas* (Dallas, 1908).

James, George W., *New Mexico, the Land of Delight Makers* (Boston, 1920).

James, W., *Cowboys, North and South* (New York, 1924).

Jaques, Mary J., *Texan Ranch Life* (London, 1894).

Jenkins, Jeff, *The Northern Tier, or Life Among the Homestead Settlers* (Topeka, 1880).

Jennings, N. A., *A Texas Ranger* (Dallas, 1930).

Kappler, Charles J. (ed.), *Indian Affairs, Laws and Treaties* (Washington, 1903). 3 vols.

Keim, De B. Randolph, *Sheridan's Troopers on the Border: A Winter Campaign on the Plains* (Philadelphia, 1885).

Kendall, George W., *Narrative of the Texan Santa Fe Expedition* (London, 1848). 2 vols.

King, Edward, *The Great South* (Hartford, 1875).

Kingsbury, W. G., *Emigration. An Interesting Lecture on Texas and California* (London, 1883).

Koener, Gustav, *Das Deutsche Element in den Vereinigten Staaten von Nord-amerika, 1818-1848* (Cincinnati, 1880).

Kuykendall, Judge W. L., *Frontier Days* (n.p., 1917).

Lehmann, Herman, *Nine Years with the Indians* (Austin, 1927).

Lomax, J. A., *Cowboy Songs* (New York, 1929).

Lowe, Percival G., *Five Years a Dragoon* (Kansas City, 1906).

Lummis, Charles F., *A Tramp Across the Continent* (New York, 1902).

McBride, Thomas H., *In Cabins and Sod Houses* (Iowa City, 1928).

McConnell, H. H., *Five Years a Cavalryman* (Jacksboro, 1889).

McCormick, Fannie, *A Kansas Farm or the Promised Land* (New York, 1892).

McCoy, Joseph G., *Historic Sketches of the Cattle Trade of the West and Southwest* (Kansas City, 1874; reprinted, Washington, 1932).

Majors, Alexander, *Seventy Years on the Frontier* (Chicago, and New York, 1893).

Marcy, Randolph B., *The Prairie Traveler.* . . . . (London, 1863).

———, *Thirty Years of Army Life on the Border* (New York, 1866).

Matthews, William A., *Crossing the Plains* (San Francisco, 1915).

Matthews, William B., *Matthews' Guide for Settlers upon the Public Land* (Washington, 1889).

Meline, Colonel James F., *Two Thousand Miles on Horseback* (New York, 1867).

Mendenhall, E., *Western Texas* (n.p., 1860).

Meredith, Grace E., *Girl Captives of the Cheyennes* (Los Angeles, 1927).

Milburn, William Henry, *The Pioneer Preacher* (New York, 1860).

Miles, General Nelson A., *Personal Recollections* (Chicago, 1896).

Millard, F. S., *A Cowpuncher of the Pecos* (n.p., n.d.).

Nix, E. D., *Oklahombres* (St. Louis, 1929).

North, Thomas, *Five Years in Texas* (Cincinnati, 1871).

Oklahoma, Argument of Colonel E. C. Boudinot Before the Committee on Territories, January 29, 1878. The Committee Having Under Consideration H. R. Bill ——.

Olmsted, Frederick Law, *A Journey Through Texas; or A Saddle-Trip on the Southwestern Frontier* (New York, 1857).

Orpen, Mrs., *Memories of the Old Emigrant Days in Kansas, 1862-1865* (New York, and London, 1928).

Osgood, E. S., *The Day of the Cattleman* (Minneapolis, 1929).

Parish, Randall, *The Great Plains* (Chicago, 1907).

Paxson, F. L., *History of the American Frontier, 1763-1893* (Boston, 1924).

——, *The Last American Frontier* (New York, 1922).

Peters, Dewitt C., *Kit Carson's Life and Adventures. . . .* (Hartford, 1874).

——, *Pioneer Life and Frontier Adventures* (Boston, 1881).

Pierson, Rev. Hamilton W., *In the Brush; or, Old-Time Political and Religious Life in the Southwest* (New York, 1881).

Powell, Lyman P., *Historic Towns of the Western States* (New York, 1901).

Prentis, Noble L., *A History of Kansas* (Winfield, 1899).

Price, James P., *Seven Years of Prairie Life* (Hereford, England, 1891).

Proceedings of the Convention to Consider the Opening of the Indian Territory. Held at Kansas City, Missouri, February 8, 1888 (Council Bluffs, 1871).

Raht, C. G., *The Romance of the Davis Mountains and the Big Bend Country* (El Paso, 1919).

Raine, William M., *Famous Sheriffs and Western Outlaws* (New York, 1929).

Richardson, Albert D., *Beyond the Mississippi; From the Great River to the Great Ocean* (Hartford, 1867).

Richardson, R. N., *The Comanche Barrier to South Plains Settlement* (Glendale, 1933).

BIBLIOGRAPHY

————, and C. C. Rister, *The Greater Southwest* (Glendale, 1934).

Rister, C. C., *The Southwestern Frontier, 1865-1881* (Cleveland, 1928).

Rock, James L., and Smith, W. I., *Southern and Western Texas Guide for 1878* (St. Louis, 1878).

Rodenbough, Theodore F. (ed.), *From Everglade to Cañon with the Second Dragoons* (New York, 1875).

Root, Frank A., and Connelley, W. E., *The Overland Stage to California* (Topeka, 1901).

Routh, E. C., *The Story of Oklahoma Baptists* (Oklahoma City, 1932).

Royce, Sarah, *A Frontier Lady* (New Haven, 1932).

Rusling, James F., *The Great West and Pacific Coast* (New York, 1877).

Ruxton, George F. A., *Adventures in Mexico and the Rocky Mountains* (London, 1849).

————, *Life in the Far West* (New York, 1859).

Sabin, Edwin L., *Kit Carson Days* (Chicago, 1919).

Santleben, Auguste, *A Texas Pioneer—Early Staging and Overland Freighting* (New York, 1910).

Schoolcraft, Henry R., *Personal Memoirs of a Residence of Thirty Years with the Indian Tribes on the American Frontier. . . .* (Philadelphia, 1851).

Seely, H., *A Lone Star Bo-Peep* (New York, 1885).

Shaw, Rev. James, *Pioneer Life in Kansas* (Atchison, 1886).

Shepherd, W., *Prairie Experiences in Handling Cattle and Sheep* (London, 1884).

Sheridan, P. H., *Personal Memoirs* (New York, 1888). 2 vols.

Smith, R. F., *Universal Guide to the Country Along the Line of the Missouri, Kansas, and Texas Railway* (Council Bluffs, 1871).

Sowell, A. J., *Rangers and Pioneers of Texas* (San Antonio, 1884).

Spotts, David L., *Campaigning with Custer and the Nineteenth Kansas Volunteer Cavalry in the Washita Campaign, 1868-1869* (Los Angeles, 1928).

Stanley, Henry M., *My Early Travels and Adventures in America and Asia* (New York, 1905).

Stewart, Elinore Pruett, *Letters of a Woman Homesteader* (New York, 1914).

Sweet, Alex E., and Knox, J. Armoy, *On a Mexican Mustang Through Texas* (London, 1884).

Texas and Her Capitalists (New York, 1880).

Texas Pioneer Magazine, The American Sketch Book (Austin, 1880).

The Catholic Presbyterian. An International Journal—Ecclesiastical and Religious, I (January-June, 1879), 282-89.

The Farmers' and Immigrants' Complete Guide, or a Handbook with Copious Hints, Recipes, and Tables Designed for Farmer and Emigrant (Cincinnati, 1854).

The People's Illustrated Almanac; Texas Handbook and Immigrant Guide for 1880 (St. Louis, 1880).

The Resources and Attractions of the Texas Panhandle for the Home Seeker, Capitalist, and Tourist (Battle Creek, 1890).

The Southwestern Immigration Company (Austin, March 8, 1881).

The Texas Almanac for 1867 (Galveston, n.d.).

Thoburn, Joseph B., and Holcomb, Isaac M., *A History of Oklahoma* (San Francisco, 1908).

———, and Muriel H. Wright, *Oklahoma, A History of the State and Its People* (New York, 1929), II.

Thrall, H. S., *Texas—Pictorial History—Indian Wars* (St. Louis, 1880).

Townsend, H. C., *Plain Facts About Arkansas and Texas* (Chicago, 1883).

Triplett, Colonel Frank, *Conquering the Wilderness* (New York, and St. Louis, 1883).

Twitchell, Ralph E., *Leading Facts of New Mexican History* (Cedar Rapids, 1911), II.

Turner, Frederick J., *The Significance of Sections in American History* (New York, 1932).

Union Pacific; Texas. A Complete and Comprehensive Description of the Agriculture and Stock Raising Resources of the Texas Panhandle Country (St. Louis, 1891).

Van Tramp, John C., *Prairie and Rocky Mountains Adventures, or Life in the West* (St. Louis, 1860).

Viele, Mrs., *Following the Drum: A Glimpse of Frontier Life* (New York, 1858).

Webb, W. E., *Buffalo Land* (Philadelphia, 1873).

Webb, W. P., *The Texas Rangers: A Century of Border Defense* (Boston, 1935).

———, *The Great Plains* (New York, 1931).

West, Edward, *Homesteading; Two Prairie Seasons* (London, 1918).

Western Border Life; or What Fanny Hunter Saw and Heard in Kansas and Missouri (Philadelphia, 1863).

Wheeler, A. C., *The Iron Trail* (New York, 1876).

Wheeler, H. W., *Frontier Trail* (Los Angeles, 1923).

———, *Buffalo Days* (Indianapolis, 1926).

BIBLIOGRAPHY

Whittaker, Frederick W., *A Complete Life of General George A. Custer* (New York, 1876).

Wilder, Daniel A., *The Annals of Kansas* (Topeka, 1875).

Williams, R. H., *With the Border Ruffians. Memories of the Far West 1852-1868* (London, 1907).

Wilson, Rufus R., *Out of the West* (New York, 1933).

Wright, R. M., *Dodge City, The Cowboy Capital* (n.p., n.d.).

INDEX

INDEX

INDEX

Ernst, Frederick: 214
Evans, Gov. John: 102

F

FANDANGO, Spanish: in New Mexico, 210-11
Fargo, G.: 53
Farmer, plains: hard life of, 157-58
Federal Indian policy: shortcomings of, 97
Ficklin, Ben: 55
Fisher, Henry F.: 215
Fitzpatrick, Thomas: 98
Flint, Edward R.: 52
Food: Spanish, 209
Fontain, A. J.: 24
Forsythe, Thomas: 5
Fort Concho: 16-17
Fort Davis: 83, 178
Fort Dodge: 92
Fort Duncan: 54
Fort Griffin: 10, 126, 196
Fort Kearney: 50
Fort Laramie: xiii, 97
Fort Mason: 163
Fort McPherson: 3 n.
Fort Phantom Hill: 163-64
Fort Riley: 135
Fort Sill: 93
Fort Smith: 227
Fort Worth, Texas: 33; early society of, 193
Franklin, Missouri: 34
Frans, J. M.: 178
Freighting: 32 ff.; over Santa Fe Trail, 33;
    in western Kansas, 38
Fremont, John C.: 7
Frontier Battalion: Texas, 205
Frontier justice: 189 ff.

G

GAIL, Borden County, Texas: 150-51
Galveston, Texas: 22
Germania, Texas: organization of, 222
Germans: Kansas settlements of, 25;
    southern plains colonies of, 214-20;
    culture of, 221 ff.
German sisters: Cheyenne captivity of, 113
    ff.; Julia and Adelaide, rescue of, 114-15;
    Catherine and Sophia, rescue of, 115;
    General N. A. Miles provides for, 116
Gobble, Bart: 200
Goodnight, Colonel Charles: 120
Grasshoppers: plains scourges of, 151-54
Gray Beard; Cheyenne Chief, 114-15
Great Plains: described as desert, xii
Greenleaf, A. B.: 84-85
Greer, Mrs. Doctor: 117
Gregg, Josiah: 33, 104, 148
Grinnell, George B.: 61

Gros Ventres: at Ft. Laramie, 97
Guthrie, Oklahoma: 146, 147-48, 240, 241

H

HAMILTON County, Texas: Indian raid in,
    118
Hamlin, Texas: 65
Harrison, Mrs. Emily Haines: 62-63, 117
Harrison, President Benjamin: 228
Hasson, Alexander B.: 163-64
Hatch, Colonel Edward: 234
Hayt, E. A.: 231
Heroines, border: lives of, 104 ff.
Hickok, "Wild Bill": 126
Hockaday and Liggett Express Company:
    50
Holladay, Ben: stage coach operations of,
    50-51; inspects stage line, 52; early con-
    tracts, 52
Hollingsworth, O. N.: 252-53
Homes, border: accommodations in, 56, 58
    ff.; adobe, 60-62; dugout, 65-66; interests
    of, 70 ff.; Indian perils of, 89; pleasures
    of, 85
Homeseekers: southern plains, 27
Honey, Miss Rosella S.: 117-18
Horn, Mrs. Sarah Ann: 106-9
Hospitality, border: 81 ff.; 209 ff.
Hoyt, Dr. Henry F.: 167-68
Howard, Miss Amanda: 119
Hubbard, Governor: 26
Hunnewell, Kansas: 235
Hunt, Dr. J. W.: 248
Hunter, buffalo: 10, 11, 17-18

I

INDEPENDENCE, Missouri: 34
Indian Bureau: creation of, 226
Indian Intercourse Act: passage of, 226
Indian Territory: boundaries of, 223-24;
    civil war in, 226-27; number of Indians
    in (1879), 227; end of, 243
Indians: hostility, causes of, 93-95; Texas
    watch chloroform experiment, 163; on
    southern plains, xiii, raid Kansas border,
    92
Iowa Indians: Oklahoma reservation of, 227

J

JOHNSON's Station: 55

K

KANSAS: southern plains part, xi; wild
    horses of, 13; increase in population of,
    29; German colonization of, 25; freighting

[285]

INDEX

INDEX

Wet Mountain Valley, Colorado: German colony in, 26

"White Steed of the Prairies": reputed prowess of, 16

Whiting, Albe B.: address of, 105

Whitney, Miss Ann: 118

Wichitas: range of, xiv; at peace councils, 93, 225

Wichita, Kansas: 229, 235

Wild horses: southern plains, 12-16; Nolan catches, 13; Catlin describes, 13; Chadwick kills, 13-14; methods of catching, 14-15; antecedents of, 15-16

James Wilkinson: 12

Women: border, hard lot of, 157-58

Wright, R. M.: 194

Wynkoop, Major E. W.: attempts to protect Cheyennes, 99

X

XIT Ranch, Texas, 122

Y

Young, Ewing, 104

SOUTHERN PLAINSMEN by CARL COKE RISTER, is composed on the Monotype in Caslon 337, popularly known as Caslon Old Face and is a faithful recutting of one of the world's most famous type faces. The text is set in ten point with two point leading. The famous Caslon type had its origin in 1722. Two years earlier William Bowyer, the elder, observed a signature which William Caslon appended to a font of Arabic type. The freshness and solidity of the letter compelled Bowyer's admiration and he encouraged Caslon to complete the alphabet. Accordingly, in 1722, Caslon Roman was born. The letters were modelled from Dutch types but they had a variety of design and a delicacy of line which few Dutch types possessed. The letters analyzed separately are at times awkward and apparently unwieldy but in mass their effect is pleasing. They reflect the Anglo-Saxon temperament—sturdy honesty, ingenious practicality— and are particularly fitted for the printing of "common-sense" material. Caslon and modified forms of it were popular during the greater part of the eighteenth century when they fell into disfavor. Caslon was revived again in 1844 by Pickering and Whittingham at the Chiswick Press. In 1859 the Johnson Type Foundry of Philadelphia brought to this country strikes of the Caslon punches, and the type was used sporadically for a few years. It was not until 1915 that a good version of Caslon became popularly used in America. In that year the Lanston Monotype Machine Company produced the "337 Cas- lon," which generally follows the tradi- tional Caslon design. The long as- cenders and descenders are faithfully produced, espe- cially in the ten point as used in this volume

THE PRINTED PAGE IS   EVERYMAN'S UNIVERSITY

UNIVERSITY OF OKLAHOMA PRESS : NORMAN